Culture, Environment, and Conservation in the Appalachian South

Culture, Environment, and Conservation in the Appalachian South

EDITED BY

Benita J. Howell

UNIVERSITY OF ILLINOIS PRESS
URBANA AND CHICAGO

Manufactured in the United States of America
1 2 3 4 5 C P 5 4 3 2 1

This book is printed on acid-free paper.

Library of Congress Cataloging-in-Publication Data
Culture, environment, and conservation in the Appalachian South /
edited by Benita J. Howell.
p. cm.
Includes bibliographical references and index.
ISBN 0-252-02705-1 (cl.)
ISBN 0-252-07022-4 (pbk.)
1. Appalachian Region, Southern—Cultural policy.
2. Environmental policy—Social aspects—Appalachian Region, Southern.
3. Historic preservation—Appalachian Region, Southern.
4. Landscape protection—Appalachian Region, Southern.
5. Appalachian Region, Southern—Environmental conditions.
6. Human ecology—Appalachian Region, Southern.
7. Community development—Appalachian Region, Southern.
8. Land settlement—Appalachian Region, Southern—History.
I. Howell, Benita J.
F217.A65C85 2002
363.6'9'0974—dc21 2001003340

CONTENTS

PREFACE

This volume explores historic and contemporary relationships between culture and environment in southern Appalachia. It is an outgrowth of my conviction, shared with many colleagues in anthropology and allied disciplines, that to overlook culture when addressing natural resource issues hampers efforts to fashion sound policy or to find effective solutions to persistent environmental problems.

Various professional experiences shaped this conviction and this book. While conducting contract research on Cumberland Plateau folklife in the late 1970s, I found that the most critical cultural conservation issues lay somewhere between the turf of social impact assessment and cultural resource preservation, in terrain claimed by neither. During the 1980s, I lent some support from the sidelines as applied ethnography gained institutional standing in the National Park Service. In 1988–89, as federal resource management agencies began to embrace ecosystem management, I represented cultural anthropology on a multidisciplinary panel of academics and federal agency scientists who assessed and recommended new priorities for research and resource management in the National Park Service. I have participated in national and international meetings in which conservation of culture and natural resources were treated as interrelated dimensions of environmental planning. These gatherings offered the exhilaration of viewing culture as central to environmental studies, congruent with key conceptual models and methods of ecological anthropology. In the bureaucratic world of federal and state agencies, however, culture generally is relegated to the realm of historic preservation, cutting off many opportunities for cultural perspectives to enrich environmental studies.

The framework and organization of environmental assessment and planning for the Southern Appalachian Biosphere Reserve is an example of bureaucratic division of labor that inhibits integrative multidisciplinary collaboration. Since 1988, the Southern Appalachian Man and Biosphere (SAMAB) consortium of federal and state agencies, academic institutions, and communities has jointly conducted research and initiated planning to protect the biosphere reserve in the Great Smoky Mountains and its surrounding regional zone of cooperation. Cultural resources are a concern of SAMAB, but a marginal concern not well articulated with the primary environmental sciences agenda.

In administering a research fellowship program funded by the Canon Corporation and in various other contexts, the National Park Service uses the categories *natural, social,* and *cultural sciences.* For readers who have grown accustomed to thinking of science and cultural studies in opposition to one another, the label *cultural science* may present difficulties; however, this terminology suggests that all research attempting to expand the store of reliable knowledge pertinent to agency concerns is welcome. The antiscience stance of extreme postmodernism deterred dialogue with environmental scientists about culture, so the rapprochement between scientific and humanistic work now emerging within anthropology is a welcome development.

In that spirit of mutual respect between disciplines, this book seeks to encourage more comprehensive and culturally grounded thinking about human culture in the southern Appalachian biosphere by presenting case studies that highlight various cultural dimensions of regional environmental history and cultural perspectives on conservation and development issues. The authors write as citizen activists, professional cultural specialists, planners, and scholars in the fields of prehistoric and historic archaeology, cultural geography and landscape architecture, history and ethnography, and folklore and folklife studies.

• • •

In addition to the contributors, many of whom have been supportive colleagues for many years, I would like to thank others who have influenced this work indirectly, especially Muriel Crespi, George Gummerman, Setha Low, Ruthanne Mitchell, Katy Moran, Tony Paredes, Rich Stoffle, John van Willigen, Erve Zube, and the late John Peterson. Thanks to Claire Jantz, who made time in a busy graduate school schedule to prepare the regional map especially for this volume. I appreciate Tanya Faberson's meticulous editorial assistance with the first version of the manuscript. At the University of Illinois Press, Judy McCulloh's unwavering encouragement of the project and technical assistance from Theresa L. Sears, Carol Peschke, and Cope Cumpston were invaluable. I am especially grateful to reviewers Gordon McKinney and Robert Gipe for detailed comments and thoughtful insights that helped me rework and strengthen the book's introduction. As always, my husband, Tom, has my deepest gratitude for his constant encouragement and support of my work.

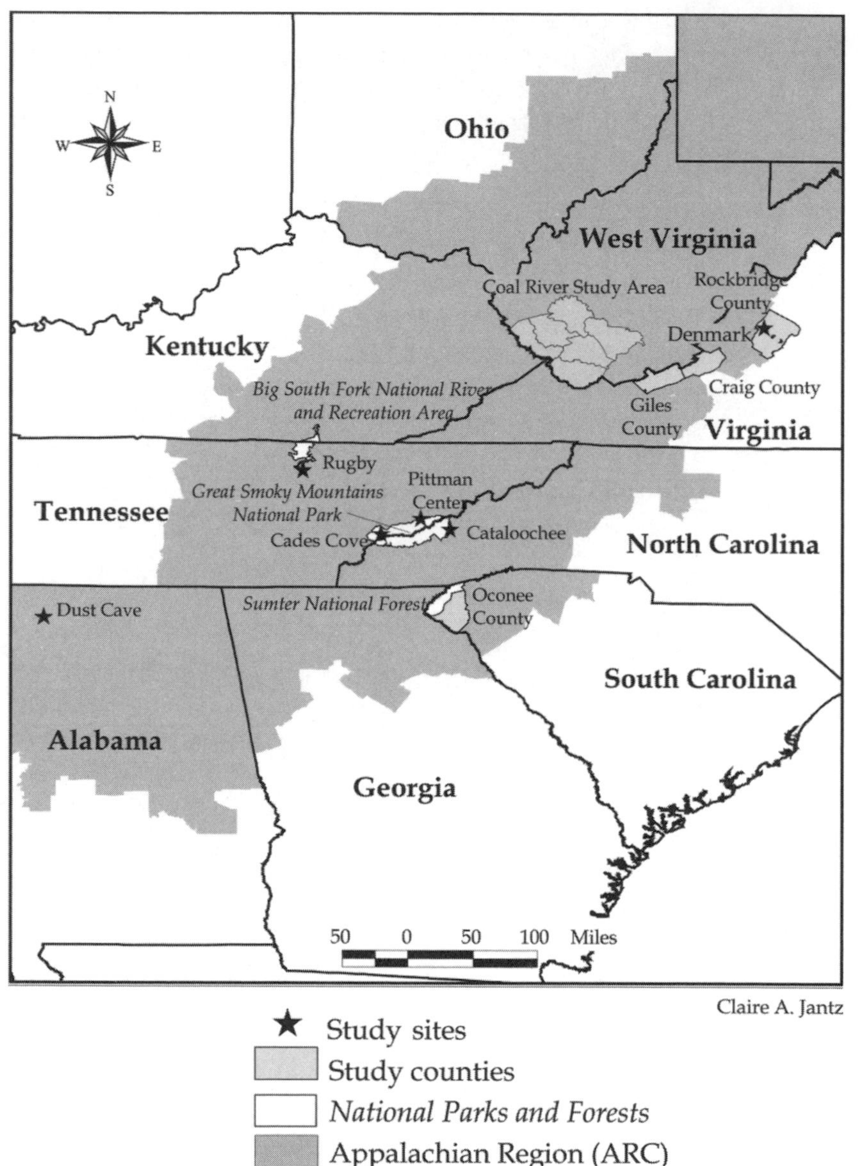
N
S
W
E
Ohio
West Virginia
Kentucky
Coal River Study Area
Rockbridge County
Denmark
Craig County
Giles County
Virginia
Big South Fork National River and Recreation Area
Rugby
Great Smoky Mountains National Park
Pittman Center
Cades Cove
Cataloochee
Tennessee
North Carolina
Dust Cave
Sumter National Forest
Oconee County
South Carolina
Alabama
Georgia
50 0 50 100 Miles
Claire A. Jantz
Study sites
Study counties
National Parks and Forests
Appalachian Region (ARC)

Culture, Environment,

and Conservation in

the Appalachian South

1 Appalachian Culture and Environmental Planning: Expanding the Role of the Cultural Sciences

BENITA J. HOWELL

What does Appalachian culture have to do with the environment? For someone familiar with regional history and public policy, the associations that first come to mind might be worn-out, eroded farmland; clear-cut or burned-over forest; the desolation of strip-mined land; and polluted, garbage-choked streams prone to flash flooding. If Appalachian culture is implicated in all these environmental problems, why should environmental scientists, resource managers, and planners treat it with anything other than disdain? Aren't defective cultural attitudes and practices an impediment for environmentalists who want to steer the region away from abuse of resources toward a sustainable future? This book challenges environmental scientists, resource managers, and planners working in southern Appalachia to rethink these assumptions about culture, environment, and Appalachian people and to interact more effectively with cultural scientists whose work is pertinent to regional environmental studies.

Whether one is interested in interspecies relationships and energy flows through a local ecosystem or in evolutionary change over the course of human history, culture is crucially important in environmental studies (Kottak 1999). The human animal is part of the web of nature, even though we have dominated other species and continually reconstruct our world through the cultural means of language, society, and technology. Therefore, solving environmental problems requires cultural thinking, not simply technical management of natural resources.

In environmental planning, protection, and projects promoting conservation and sustainable development among contemporary indigenous peoples, the relevance of culture is now acknowledged (Machlis 1995:53–54; Machlis and Soukup 1997:161–62). This book advocates for Appalachia (and for the United States at large) the same kind of interdisciplinary collaboration between natural and cultural sciences that is now common practice internationally. Why is such advocacy necessary? Institutional barriers, particularly within federal agencies, tend to exclude culture from its rightful place in environmental science. But more importantly, Appalachia's environmental history, with its reading of Appalachian people as ignorant or willful despoilers, reinforces the inclination to keep culture at arm's length.

CULTURAL SCIENCES AND ENVIRONMENTAL STUDIES

The disciplines that federal and state agencies look to for managing cultural resources—prehistoric and historic archaeology, history and architectural history, landscape architecture and planning, cultural geography, and the applied ethnography used by cultural anthropologists and folklorists—are conveniently grouped under the rubric *cultural sciences.*[1] During the last quarter of the twentieth century, the relevance of the cultural sciences to environmental issues became increasingly evident in academic research and in international development circles.

Environmental science models generally assume that humans degrade natural environments through overuse of resources and intentional or unintended actions with adverse repercussions at all scales (Machlis and Forester 1994, 1996). In fact, humans have always manipulated their surroundings, and some anthropogenic effects have been more beneficial than destructive. These human actions represent sound, sustainable ethnoecology. For example, Posey (1985) and Balée (1994) have shown that indigenous peoples in Amazonia intentionally manipulated their habitat to create useful plant assemblages, thereby increasing rainforest biodiversity. With such examples in mind, international efforts to institute resource conservation increasingly attend to local cultural knowledge, attitudes, and practices (Ellen and Fukui 1996; McNeely 1995; Redford and Padoch 1992). Locally based, economically feasible sustainable development strategies offer the best alternative to exploitive development schemes promoted by national governments and international financial interests (Greaves 1994; Hyndman 1994).

Reviewing recent developments in ecological anthropology in the *American Anthropologist,* Biersack (1999:5) heralds "a new materialism that overrides the dichotomies and debates of the past—idealism v. materialism, for example, and nature v. culture." Biersack's pronouncement prefaces research reports on Malaysia, Madagascar, and the highlands of Papua New Guinea that exemplify increasing integration of cultural sciences and environmental studies within academe. On the other hand, among federal resource managers in the United States, little synthesis transcending the nature-culture dichotomy is apparent.

CULTURAL SCIENCES AND FEDERAL RESOURCE MANAGEMENT

Land management bureaucracies in the United States have long confined the cultural sciences to a narrow cultural resource preservation role. Environmental resource management as conceived, regulated, and practiced by federal and state agencies consequently overlooks opportunities for collaboration between the cultural and natural sciences that would integrate cultural factors into agency-sponsored ecological research. This is not to imply that federal agencies have neglected culture. On the contrary, the historic preservation programs and federal recognition accorded "intangible expressions of cultural diversity" present many opportunities to address a diverse array of cultural heritage conservation issues (Hufford 1994). Grassroots local history projects, ethnic and regional festivals and museums, and state encouragement of cultural tourism also reflect the burgeoning enterprise known as cultural heritage conservation. Since the 1980s, this expanded approach to culture has augmented preservation of material culture with ethnographic investigation and efforts to sustain and foster living cultural traditions. But as long as federal agencies focus chiefly on managing tangible "cultural resources" (i.e., architecture, archaeological sites, and artifacts), cultural knowledge and practice are too easily excluded from the broader environmental agenda.

In the late 1980s, the National Park Service began to reframe its research and resource management agenda in ecological terms. Various problems with the practice of designating park units either "natural" or "cultural" became apparent. The "natural park" designation implied that parks such as Yellowstone and Yosemite, created in response to John Muir's wilderness preservation movement, were somehow "untrammeled by man" because Native Americans were no longer visible there or because these "primitives" were thought, erroneously, to have had negligible impact on the natural environment. The illusion of pristine nature certainly could not be sustained in creating the Appalachian parks, where habitation and industrial activity were everywhere apparent. Nevertheless, the Park Service aimed to restore an illusion of wilderness[2] and protect nature from further human insults by removing residents and their activities from within park boundaries. Soon the Appalachian parks were being managed to protect the scenic value of rural cultural landscapes as well as natural resources. Selected material traces of Appalachian culture were curated, but ongoing ecological relationships between local residents and their environs were curtailed even as environmental impacts from visitation and development outside park boundaries accelerated.

Even though the National Park Service and other resource management agencies have embraced ecological thinking, the artificial nature-culture dichotomy still complicates Park Service management policy for "natural zones" within parks. For example, one guideline states: "Interference with natural processes . . . will be allowed only (1) when directed by Congress, (2) in some emergencies when human life and property are at stake, or (3) to restore native ecosystem functioning that has been disrupted by past or ongoing human activities" (NPS 1988:4.2). Ironically, the next statement suggests that certain past human activities were desirable and cannot be replaced by natural processes alone. "Ecological processes altered in the past by human activities may need to be abetted to maintain the closest approximation to the natural ecosystem where a *truly natural system* is no longer attainable. Prescribed burning is an example" (NPS 1988:4.2; italics added). What exactly is a "truly natural ecosystem" dependent on past human activities such as livestock grazing or regular burning of underbrush for its creation and continued human intervention for its maintenance?

Since the 1980s, the Park Service has begun to sponsor new kinds of research with potential to transcend the untenable nature-culture dichotomy. One is the resource ethnography that highlights indigenous knowledge of resources, their cultural significance, historic patterns of resource use, and sustainability of traditional management practices (Crespi 1987). These studies focus attention squarely on humans within, not apart from, ecosystems. The second is the comprehensive landscape study, which calls for tracing the record of human-land interactions through broadly interdisciplinary environmental history (Miller 1987).

CULTURE AND ENVIRONMENT IN SOUTHERN APPALACHIA

Unlike most anthologies in environmental anthropology (e.g., Moran 1990; Turner 1990; Crumley 1994; Descola and Pálsson 1996), this volume focuses on the single region of southern Appalachia. Following John C. Campbell's delineation of the region in his classic *The Southern Highlander and His Homeland* (1969 [1921]), we include in southern Appalachia the mountainous area from north Alabama to West Virginia. Each chapter concerns a particular locality and varying time periods, but their common regional frame of reference offers an opportunity for the reader to perceive and reflect on patterns and trends that have characterized human-environment interaction from prehistory through the 1990s. The chapters in this volume illustrate prehistoric, historic, and contemporary interrelations of human societies and cultures with the physical and biotic elements of the southern Appalachian environment, showing the impact of beliefs and values as well as the imprint of human activities.

As in any human environment, dynamic interplay between nature and culture has been central to the experiences whereby Appalachian people have transformed physical space and resources into place and lifeways. But beyond this, southern Appalachia's very emergence as a distinctive region in the minds of other Americans depended on manipulation of nature and culture as symbolic constructs (Batteau 1990). As a resource extraction periphery of industrial America, later the site of extensive public lands and federal intervention, southern Appalachia is especially fertile ground for exploring the historical roots and cultural ramifications of persistent environmental problems. The discourse on Appalachian environmental history illustrates the crucial importance of cultural beliefs and values, reflected as much in outsiders' attitudes about Appalachian people as in their own practices. Scientists, bureaucrats, developers, and reformers have defined and responded to environmental issues in disparate ways that reflect their own assumptions and agendas.

The regional history that emerged from Appalachian studies scholarship in the 1970s and early 1980s was a story of resource exploitation and degradation during industrialization, sometimes checked by federal government intervention, itself a new form of colonial domination imposed from outside the region. After the Civil War, "Philadelphia lawyers" and local land agents retained by absentee timber and coal corporations used the complications of imperfect land titles, partial truths, or outright deceit to acquire title to land and mineral rights from mountain farmers. Did industrialization end a Jeffersonian era during which yeoman farm families lived in relative harmony with their surroundings while producing a sufficiency for themselves and earning enough cash for taxes and a few imported necessities from free-range livestock herding, root and herb collecting, winter trapping, and timber cutting? This was Eller's (1982) interpretation. Or, as Shifflett (1991) contended, were marginal farmers rapidly reaching the limits of survival by the 1880s, so that the opportunity to sell out and take up "public work" was a welcome rescue from poverty and starvation? In other words, did the environmental abuse that has plagued southern Appalachia in the twentieth century originate with the "exploit and get out" capitalist mentality of nineteenth-century industrialists, or had Appalachian people been bad environmental stewards all along?

Revisionist regional history of the 1990s complicates these questions but also suggests some answers by pointing up the complexities of social class relations and political economy that characterized Appalachia from earliest Euro-American exploration and settlement (Pudup et al. 1995). Dunaway (1996) scrutinized land ownership patterns in the colonial era and concludes that land speculation and absentee ownership predated industrialization by at least a century. As Salstrom (1994) has shown, Appalachian development differed subregionally. The Great Valley of Virginia and Tennessee ("Older Appalachia") experienced greater internal economic development than western North Carolina, while the last settled subregion, the Cumberland and Allegheny Plateau coal fields, experienced the most dependent development and remained poorest into the twentieth century. Hsiung (1997) counters conventional wisdom about Appalachian isolation with evidence of eighteenth-century commercial relations and political activity linking upper east Tennessee to global commodity chains and extralocal public affairs. More importantly, he documents class differences: "two worlds" increasingly at odds with one another as elites struggled to maintain external connections while poor people became more isolated and marginalized during the nineteenth century.

Resource-rich areas such as the salt district of Clay County, Kentucky, experienced home-grown industrialization together with dramatic distinctions in wealth, control of resources, and political power well before the Civil War (Billings and Blee 2000). Local elites, who were connected to Bluegrass society and state politics, exerted political economic control that undermined civil society and led to a reign of violence in Clay County. Ironically, outsiders, in their shocked fascination with supposedly atavistic feuding, attributed it to poor, uncivilized hillbillies and argued for relocating them or reforming them through modernization and "the civilizing railroad" (Billings and Blee 2000:314).

When railroads financed by northern capital finally penetrated the southern mountains beginning in the 1870s and continuing into the 1920s, they brought a host of observers and commentators whose impressions, filtered through their own backgrounds and agendas, became persistent regional stereotypes. Despite a steady stream of revisionist history and "back talk" from scholars in Appalachian studies (Billings et al. 1999), these well-worn stereotypes continue to inform popular thinking, not least the assumptions that professionals often bring to their work in the region. In this respect, scientists, federal bureaucrats, and environmentalists follow in the footsteps of the missionaries and social workers who accompanied industrialists into the region after the Civil War.

Certainly the most knowledgeable and sympathetic observer of southern

Appalachia in the early twentieth century was John C. Campbell, who reported on observations he made as head of the Southern Highland Division of the Russell Sage Foundation. Campbell (1969 [1921]:288) commented that the forest was "desecrated and ruined in many sections by the operations of logging companies." He forthrightly stated that "the axe of the woodman, forest fire, commercial short-sightedness, and greed have conspired to do their worst" (Campbell 1969 [1921]:231). Campbell also reported, "The mountaineer himself is doing much to lessen the value of these forests" by cutting valuable trees for firewood, whether the waste was caused by absence of transportation or perhaps "some antagonism toward trees in general" (Campbell 1969 [1921]:232). He described "one mountain home visited (in which) the meal was being cooked over glowing coals of black walnut. In the yard were many logs of the same wood ready to be cut into fireplace lengths. The owner of the house was amply able to buy a cook-stove, but his wife preferred the old-fashioned ways. In reply to a protest against the burning of such valuable wood, she replied that it was 'a right smart of trouble to haul timber down the branch,' and that there were 'several walnut trees' (a goodly number) about there, and moreover, they 'didn't need the money nohow'" (Campbell 1969 [1921]:232).

Campbell also described how farmers burned trees and brush to open corn fields, grew corn until all fertility was mined from the soil, then cleared still more forest to repeat the process (Campbell 1969 [1921]:232, 252–53). He perceived that population increase had pushed farmers to clear and crop progressively steeper hillsides, where erosion soon took its toll. Campbell was writing soon after the U.S. Forest Service was charged with controlling flooding and managing water for power generation as well as conserving timber for wise rather than wasteful use. The Forest Service had been authorized to purchase more than 1.3 million acres in Virginia, North Carolina, Tennessee, Georgia, West Virginia, Alabama, and South Carolina by 1919, and Kentucky had just granted the federal government the right to acquire acreage for national forests (Campbell 1969 [1921]:233). Campbell summarized various federal reports and echoed expert opinion that federal intervention in resource management was desirable to curtail the thoughtless waste of mountain people as well as the greed of timber corporations.

By the 1920s, proponents of eastern national parks were gaining support for their campaign from urban boosters, wealthy industrialists, and schoolchildren alike. During the 1930s, the most scenic areas of southern Appalachia were protected from further resource extraction but opened to the public through establishment of Great Smoky Mountains National Park, Shenandoah National Park, the Blue Ridge Parkway, and Skyline Drive. Whereas the Forest Service purchased acreage from willing sellers, land for the national parks was acquired through the states exercising eminent domain, then donating land to the federal government. In retrospect, if scientists and bureaucrats blamed mountain people for environmental abuse and even their champion John Campbell concurred, then little wonder that park proponents had few qualms about displacing residents from the parks.

The pace of federal intervention increased during the Great Depression. The Civilian Conservation Corps, in addition to carrying out park construction, planted seedlings on cut-over forest land, while the Tennessee Valley Authority (TVA) embarked on bigger water power and flood control projects than John Campbell could have imagined (McDonald and Muldowny 1982; Whisnant 1994). County agricultural extension agents and the Soil Conservation Service, acting in concert with TVA (Selznick 1949), intervened to reforest marginal pasture and crop acreage and to prevent erosion and improve farmers' yield from land they judged arable. Criticism of mountain farming had become common in outsiders' observations long before, however, when nineteenth-century travelers interpreted backwoods "deadenings" as visible signs of laziness and bad farming.

Such were the observations of J. G. Häcker, who visited Morgan County, Tennessee in 1848 on behalf of prospective German immigrants. He reported, "The American farmer of the region has modest needs and, therefore, only works when he cannot avoid it. He is always faithful to the principle of earning his living with the least possible effort. He therefore avoids everything that requires extended work. Stock raising, which requires no work at all here, is his principal source of income; agriculture is only incidental to produce bread for himself and his family and, perhaps, also to grow enough corn so that he can keep his stock from getting too hungry in the winter" (Häcker 1970 [1849]:60).

Despite urging his compatriots not to fall into the Americans' slovenly ways, Häcker advised German immigrants to begin with the same livestock and corn farming system as the Americans and to undertake improvements only gradually because labor was scarce and expensive (Häcker 1970 [1849]:66–67). In other words, the American farming practices that Häcker observed were suited to the frontier situation of abundant land and sparse population (Otto and Anderson 1982; Jordan and Kaups 1989). But they had persisted after increasing population density made them maladaptive.

The dismantling of New Deal programs signaled only a temporary halt to federal intervention. While the National Park Service slowed the pace of park construction, TVA dam building continued unabated during World War II to furnish electric power to support the war effort. Into the 1960s and 1970s, both TVA and the U.S. Army Corps of Engineers proposed additional projects for hydroelectric power, flood control, and recreation (Wheeler and McDonald

1986). In every case, the rural people threatened with displacement through eminent domain protested these plans (e.g., Howell 1990).

Coal strip mining was the source of Appalachia's most visible and highly publicized environmental degradation. First there were small "truck mines" made possible by highway building during the 1920s and 1930s, then the huge stripping operations of recent decades destroyed timber, water resources, and whole mountaintops. Along with creating War on Poverty programs and the Appalachian Regional Commission, Congress provided funds to purchase and restore land and watersheds damaged by timber cutting and mining. The Land and Water Conservation Act of 1965 specified that most available land acquisition funds would be spent in the East, thereby addressing Appalachia's environmental problems while developing recreation areas within a day's drive from the eastern seaboard's large metropolitan population (Howell 1998). Environmental scientists and resource managers supported the transfer of Appalachian lands to public ownership and bureaucratic management to reverse and prevent further environmental degradation.

ENVIRONMENTAL STEWARDSHIP AND RURAL APPALACHIANS: RETHINKING OLD ASSUMPTIONS

The rationale for successive interventions to salvage Appalachian resources and "rescue the land from its people" (Howell 1989) rested on, and in turn reinforced, stereotypic assumptions that cast "hillbillies" as the arch Euro-American despoilers of the environment. In this case, the symbolic opposite to the stereotypic "hillbilly" is not the usual civilized, middle-class urbanite but rather the American Indian as mythic "noble ecologist" (Krech 1999). This theme pervades popular writing in environmental philosophy (e.g., Snyder 1990; Martin 1992), but some scientists have embraced its assumptions as well. It is implicated in National Park Service policy concessions that permit continued use of traditional subsistence resources by Native Americans and seek cooperation with tribal experts to comanage those resources. On a more abstract level, the biophilia hypothesis proposes that love of fellow life forms is a primordial hunter-gatherer impulse that coevolved with and is integral to our humanity (Kellert and Wilson 1993). Similarly, Dasmann (1991) contrasts the unrestrained consumption of modern "biosphere people," who have degraded the environment on a global scale, with the ecological wisdom of locally anchored (i.e., tribal) "ecosystem people." Katcher and Wilkins (1993:173–74) caution that linking science too closely with the environmentalist political-moral agenda may discourage skeptical testing of assumptions such as these.

Rather than being villainous foils to the mythic ecological Indian, rural

Appalachian people, like real American Indians, have a mixed record of resource management that deserves thoughtful empirical investigation. Certainly, Appalachian people of all socioeconomic classes, newcomers and natives, outsiders and insiders, have exploited resources for utilitarian purposes; but poor rural people, the focus of most cultural opprobrium, have been comparatively marginal consumers in the global capitalist economy. In fact, comparison between Appalachian underdevelopment and underdevelopment elsewhere in the world suggests that political economic conditions probably pushed marginal farmers and rural industrial workers into environmental abuse. The family labor system encouraged by landlords and industrialists, coupled with possibilities for self-provisioning and income pooling to counter low wages, made large families an adaptive short-run strategy for the poor, even though high fertility had adverse long-term consequences for the land and people. In this respect, rural Appalachians did not tread lightly on the earth, but in certain other respects many of them have behaved and continue to behave as "ecosystem people." They often possess, hand down, and regularly use detailed, localized knowledge of their surroundings. They value self-sufficiency and resist capitalist values and consumerism to a remarkable degree. Many Appalachians of all social classes express a place attachment that encompasses historical and spiritual connections to family land, to ancestors who have occupied that land, and to the heirs who will follow.

Cultural scientists and environmental activists need to help the Appalachian people who have been excluded to participate rather than remain marginalized bystanders while federal agencies and natural scientists dominate the discourse on regional environmental issues and set an agenda for the twenty-first century. But this can happen only if these camps can interact based on reliable knowledge about culture rather than corrosive stereotypes or dubious generalizations.

This is a book of case studies illustrating many of the disciplinary perspectives and methods used by the cultural sciences. Its purpose is to promote understanding and appreciation for cultural dimensions of environmental issues and to encourage scientists, resource managers, planners, and environmental activists in southern Appalachia to reframe their thinking to incorporate cultural considerations. Each chapter deals with a specific locality, an area or place that is delimited by human activity and sufficiently circumscribed to be researched in detail.

The first section of the book explains and illustrates a few of the empirical methods that yield substantive information about human behavior and environmental impacts in the past. Renee Walker introduces the methodology of zooarchaeology and the process of reasoning from animal remains found in archaeological sites to a reconstruction of climate change and human adaptation during the transition into the Holocene. She joined a team of archaeological specialists to excavate and analyze data from Dust Cave, Alabama, which was inhabited repeatedly during the transition into the Holocene. By examining the remains of those occupations, archaeologists can reconstruct how humans modified their subsistence strategies in response to climate change.

Working as part of a National Park Service cultural landscape survey team, Claire Jantz evaluated and synthesized multidisciplinary literature to produce a summary of anthropogenic landscape change in Cades Cove during the past ten thousand years. In this case, conclusions about prehistoric humans are derived principally from paleoethnobotany, another specialized archaeological technique that uses a natural science (palynology) to address guiding questions about human behavior. Jantz also mined documentary sources for evidence of historic period landscape impacts.

Michael Gregory moves the time frame forward to reconstruct a picture of nineteenth-century development and twentieth-century decline in the Denmark community of Rockcastle County, Virginia. Detailed data from historical archaeology, written documents, and oral history combine to challenge the obvious reading of Denmark's landscape that a casual windshield survey might yield to the traveler, who probably would interpret the scant remains now visible to the untrained eye as evidence of rural isolation. In all these cases, cultural scientists are striving to generate reliable knowledge through painstaking triangulation of findings from multiple data sources. Hypotheses about what happened in the past must withstand scrutiny and repeated empirical testing against specific cases such as these. In addition to addressing different time periods with different methodologies, chapters in the first section of the book illustrate the quantitative pole of the cultural sciences' analytical spectrum.

Gregory's metaphor of walking through Denmark moves the reader toward qualitative methods because it describes ethnography and oral history as well as archaeological reconnaissance. In the second section, folk culture scholars Michael Ann Williams and Mary Hufford and cultural anthropologist Melinda Wagner explore various facets of sense of place, a complex phenomenon accessible to researchers only through qualitative ethnography. Like thorough historical research, ethnography takes time, but it also relies on communicative interaction between researcher and researched. If nonscientists find the first section of the book daunting, natural scientists may have difficulty recognizing the cultural science in ethnographic encounters. Sense of place is an intangible quality expressed through people's perceptions, thoughts, feelings, and values. As these chapters illustrate, cultural meaning—what anthropologists call the emic perspective on experience—is best captured from people's talk, whether it be everyday conversation and anecdote, personal histories, or more formal interviews conducted on the basis of mutual trust.

Writing about anti-environmentalism in the Great Smoky Mountains, Williams shows that resource managers and planners undermine their own projects when they ignore local perceptions and feelings because these "cultural intangibles" guide people's behavior. On a more positive note, Hufford offers vignettes of Coal River, West Virginia, lifeways and narratives that reveal local environmental knowledge, stewardship values, and conservationist activism. Finally Wagner, whose work in impact assessment has been most directly subject to scientific and bureaucratic challenge, presents a detailed discussion of replicable methodology through which recorded talk yields reliable knowledge about cultural themes and values. In qualitative as well as quantitative analysis, cultural scientists are aware that analytical frameworks, methods, and findings are provisional and always open to challenge and revision. In striving to report and interpret emic perspectives as clearly and fairly as possible, cultural scientists share with all scientists the goal of producing credible accounts based on appropriate evidence.

Whereas the first two sections of this book primarily illustrate perspectives and research tools used in various cultural science disciplines, chapters in the final section show how research findings can benefit resource management agencies, threatened communities, and communities organizing and planning to shape their own futures. Doris Link, David Brady, and Nancy Givens, members of the Clover Hollow and Plow Screw communities in southwest Virginia, describe how they conducted and used their own research on local history and land tenure to combat the unwanted intrusion of a power transmission line. By applying for rural historic district status, they have moved beyond fighting an immediate threat toward long-term preservation of their community and the heritage encoded in its distinctive cultural landscape. Gerald Schroedl's archaeological investigations at the lower Cherokee town of Chattooga in northwest South Carolina provided Sumter National Forest information needed to better manage the cultural resources that are its responsibility. Through the "Windows in Time" program, this project also trained citizen volunteers, especially K–12 teachers, enhancing their understanding of Cherokee cultural history and issues of cultural resource management on public lands. This project enriched environmental education by involving citizens first hand in resource management. The final chapters are case studies in community planning. Benita Howell and Susan Neff describe how good environmental design used in the original 1880 town plan for Rugby, Tennessee, provided a blueprint for successful preservation planning in 1980. In the last chapter, Annette Anderson describes and evaluates the FutureScapes planning process that equipped Pittman Center, Tennessee citizens to take account of local history, place attachment, and best practices in environmental design as they explored the concept of sustainable development and envisioned their future.

Many of the chapters in this book offer glimpses of a future for Appalachian land and people better than the past, but having argued against overgeneralization, we avoid the lure of proposing a comprehensive regional environmental agenda for the twenty-first century. Rather, following the field-based bent of our disciplines, we offer these examples so that readers will be persuaded to integrate cultural science perspectives in working out culturally grounded local solutions for local problems.

Notes

The second section, "Cultural Sciences and Federal Resource Management," draws on my previously published essay "Linking Cultural and Natural Conservation in National Park Service Policies and Programs" (Howell 1994).

1. Machlis includes anthropology among the social science disciplines relevant to ecosystem analysis in proposals to promote social science in international environmental research and park planning (Machlis and Forester 1994; Machlis and Soukup 1997). His "Usable Knowledge" (1996), a formal proposal for National Park Service social science, explicitly excludes anthropology, however, in deference to that agency's existing organization and management structures. Therefore, although *cultural sciences* is a convenient cover term for these disciplines, separation of cultural research from both social sciences and natural sciences continues to reinforce existing barriers that discourage broadly interdisciplinary ecological research (see also Ficker and Machlis 1998).

2. Cronon's (1996) critique of wilderness as environmentalist priority calls attention to the adverse consequences for policy that follow from "getting back to the wrong nature" (one that is a figment of literary and philosophical imagination).

References Cited

Balée, William L. 1994. *Footprints of the Forest: Ka'apor Ethnobotany: The Historical Ecology of Plant Utilization by an Amazonian People.* New York: Columbia University Press.

Batteau, Allen W. 1990. *The Invention of Appalachia.* Tucson: University of Arizona Press.

Biersack, Aletta. 1999. "Introduction: From the 'New Ecology' to the New Ecologies." *American Anthropologist* 101(1): 5–18.

Billings, Dwight B., and Kathleen Blee. 2000. *The Road to Poverty.* New York: Cambridge University Press.

Billings, Dwight, Gurney Norman, and Katherine Ledford, eds. 1999. *Confronting Appalachian Stereotypes: Back Talk from an American Region.* Lexington: University Press of Kentucky.

Campbell, John C. 1969 [1921]. *The Southern Highlander and His Homeland.* Lexington: University of Kentucky Press.

Crespi, Muriel. 1987. "The Ethnography of Alaska Resource Use." *CRM Bulletin* 10(1): 24–25.

Cronon, William. 1996. "The Trouble with Wilderness; or, Getting Back to the Wrong Nature." *Environmental History* 1(1): 7–28.

Crumley, Carole L., ed. 1994. *Historical Ecology: Cultural Knowledge and Changing Landscapes.* Santa Fe, N.Mex.: School of American Research Press.

Dasmann, Raymond F. 1991. "The Importance of Cultural and Biological Diversity." In *Biodiversity: Culture, Conservation, and Ecodevelopment.* Ed. M. L. Oldfield and J. B. Alcorn. 7–15. Boulder, Colo.: Westview Press.

Descola, Philippe, and Gísli Pálsson, eds. 1996. *Nature and Society. Anthropological Perspectives.* London: Routledge.

Dunaway, Wilma A. 1996. *The First American Frontier: Transition to Capitalism in Southern Appalachia, 1700–1860.* Chapel Hill: University of North Carolina Press.

Ellen, Roy F., and Katsuyoshi Fukui, eds. 1996. *Redefining Nature: Ecology, Culture, and Domestication.* Oxford, England: Berg.

Eller, Ronald D. 1982. *Miners, Millhands, and Mountaineers: Industrialization of the Appalachian South, 1880–1930.* Knoxville: University of Tennessee Press.

Ficker, Jared D., and Gary E. Machlis. 1998. "Progress Establishing Cooperative Ecosystem Studies Units." National Park Service Web site, November 1999. <www.aqd.nps.gov/pubs/yir/yir98/chapter03/chapter03pg5.html>.

Greaves, Tom, ed. 1994. *Intellectual Property Rights for Indigenous Peoples: A Source Book.* Oklahoma City: Society for Applied Anthropology.

Häcker, J. G. 1970 [1849]. "Report about and from America Given from First-Hand Observations in the Years 1848 and 1849 and Published for Emigrants." Trans. Richard O'Connell. Reprinted in *MVS Bulletin* 3:5–73.

Howell, Benita J. 1989. "The Anthropologist as Advocate for Local Interests in National Park Planning." In *International Perspectives on Cultural Parks: Proceedings of the First World Congress.* 275–80. Washington, D.C.: U.S. National Park Service, in association with the Colorado State Museum.

———. 1990. "Mediating Environmental Policy Conflicts in Appalachian Communities." In *Environment in Appalachia: Proceedings from the 1989 Conference on Appalachia.* 275–80. Lexington: Appalachian Center, University of Kentucky.

———. 1994. "Linking Cultural and Natural Conservation in National Park Service Policies and Programs." In *Conserving Culture: A New Discourse on Heritage.* Ed. M. Hufford. 122–37. Urbana: University of Illinois Press.

———. 1998. "National Recreation Areas in Appalachia: Citizen Participation in Planning and Management." In *Culture: The Missing Element in Conservation and Development.* Ed. R. J. Hoage and K. Moran. 51–64. Dubuque, Iowa: Kendall/Hunt Publishing.

Hsiung, David C. 1997. *Two Worlds in the Tennessee Mountains: Exploring the Origins of Appalachian Stereotypes.* Lexington: University Press of Kentucky.

Hufford, Mary, ed. 1994. *Conserving Culture: A New Discourse on Heritage.* Urbana: University of Illinois Press.

Hyndman, David. 1994. "Conservation through Self-Determination: Promoting the Interdependence of Cultural and Biological Diversity." *Human Organization* 53(3): 296–302.

Jordan, Terry, and Matti Kaups. 1989. *The American Backwoods Frontier: An Ethnic and Ecological Interpretation.* Baltimore: Johns Hopkins University Press.

Katcher, Aaron, and Gregory Wilkins. 1993. "Dialogue with Animals: Its Nature and Culture." In *The Biophilia Hypothesis.* Ed. S. R. Kellert and E. O. Wilson. 173–97. Washington, D.C.: Island Press.

Kellert, Stephen R., and Edward O. Wilson, eds. 1993. *The Biophilia Hypothesis.* Washington, D.C.: Island Press.

Kottak, Conrad P. 1999. "The New Ecological Anthropology." *American Anthropologist* 101(1): 23–35.

Krech, Shepard, III. 1999. *The Ecological Indian: Myth and History.* New York: W. W. Norton.

Machlis, Gary E. 1995. "Social Science and Protected Area Management: The Principles of Partnership." In *Expanding Partnerships in Conservation.* Ed. J. A. McNeely. 45–57. Washington, D.C.: Island Press.

———. 1996. "Usable Knowledge: A Plan for Furthering Social Science in the National Parks." National Park Service Web site, November 1999. <www.nps.gov/htdocs3;socialscience/waso/tsocscip.html>.

Machlis, Gary E., and Deborah J. Forester. 1994. "Social Factors as Driving Forces: Towards Interdisciplinary Models of Global Change." In *Biodiversity, Temperate Ecosystems, and Global Change.* Ed. T. J. B. Boyle and C. E. B. Boyle. 19–52. Berlin: Springer-Verlag.

———. 1996. "The Relationship between Socio-Economic Factors and the Loss of Biodiversity: First Efforts at Theoretical and Quantitative Models." In *Biodiversity in Managed Landscapes: Theory and Practice.* Ed. R. C. Szaro and D. W. Johnston. 121–46. New York: Oxford University Press.

Machlis, Gary, and Michael Soukup. 1997. "Usable Knowledge for National Park and Protected Area Management: A Social Science Perspective." In *National Parks and Protected Areas.* Ed. J. G. Nelson and R. Serafin. 161–73. Berlin: Springer-Verlag.

Martin, Calvin. 1992. *In the Spirit of the Earth: Rethinking History and Time.* Baltimore: Johns Hopkins University Press.

McDonald, Michael J., and John Muldowny. 1982. *TVA and the Dispossessed: The Resettlement of Population in the Norris Dam Area.* Knoxville: University of Tennessee Press.

McNeely, Jeffrey A., ed. 1995. *Expanding Partnerships in Conservation.* Washington, D.C.: Island Press.

Miller, Hugh C. 1987. "Preserving Landscapes: Rural Landscapes." *CRM Bulletin* 10(6): 1–4.

Moran, Emilio F., ed. 1990. *The Ecosystem Approach in Anthropology: From Concept to Practice.* Ann Arbor: University of Michigan Press.

National Park Service. 1988. "Management Policies." Washington, D.C.: USDI National Park Service, December 1988.

Otto, John S., and N. E. Anderson. 1982. "Slash-and-Burn Cultivation in the Highland South: A Problem in Comparative Agricultural History." *Comparative Studies in Society and History* 24:131–47.

Posey, Darrell. 1985 "Indigenous Management of Tropical Forest Ecosystems: The Case of the Kayapo Indians of the Brazilian Amazon." *Agroforestry Systems* 3:139–58.

Pudup, Mary Beth, Dwight Billings, and Altina Waller, eds. 1995. *Appalachia in the Mak-*

ing: The Mountain South in the Nineteenth Century. Chapel Hill: University of North Carolina Press.

Redford, Kent H., and Christine Padoch, eds. 1992. *Conservation of Neotropical Forests: Working from Traditional Use.* New York: Columbia University Press.

Salstrom, Paul. 1994. *Appalachia's Path to Dependency: Rethinking a Region's Economic History, 1730–1940.* Lexington: University Press of Kentucky.

Selznick, Philip. 1949. *TVA and the Grassroots: A Study in the Sociology of Formal Organization.* Berkeley: University of California Press.

Shifflett, Crandall. 1991. *Coal Towns: Life, Work, and Culture in Company Towns of Southern Appalachia, 1880–1960.* Knoxville: University of Tennessee Press.

Snyder, Gary. 1990. *The Practice of the Wild.* San Francisco: North Point Press.

Turner, B. L., II, ed. 1990. *The Earth as Transformed by Human Action: Global and Regional Changes in the Biosphere over the Past 300 Years.* New York: Cambridge University Press.

Wheeler, William Bruce, and Michael J. McDonald. 1986. *TVA and the Tellico Dam, 1936–1979: A Bureaucratic Crisis in Post-Industrial America.* Knoxville: University of Tennessee Press.

Whisnant, David E. 1994. *Modernizing the Mountaineer.* Rev. ed. Knoxville: University of Tennessee Press.

PART 1 Cultural History and Environmental Change

American anthropology from its inception in the nineteenth century sought to reconstruct the unwritten history of North America's peopling and comprehend the proliferation of distinctive lifeways in response to new environmental challenges and interchange among diverse Native American peoples. An integrative discipline encompassing biological anthropology, archaeology, sociocultural anthropology, and linguistics emerged to address this research program. In those early years, anthropology borrowed historical-geographic methods of comparison from various social sciences, especially cultural geography, comparative linguistics, European ethnology, and folklore studies.

When anthropologists began to focus attention on ecological studies after 1950, archaeological excavation and analysis techniques were becoming finer grained and more rigorous, permitting more empirically grounded reconstruction of prehistoric human activity. As archaeology directed its attention toward understanding processes of human adaptation to environmental opportunities and constraints, it became clear that prehistoric humans not only had responded to climate change and its effects on subsistence resources but also had caused measurable environmental change. Certain archaeological specialties are intimately linked to environmental sciences because of their ability to track and document humans as actors within ecosystems. These cultural sciences are building a reliable empirical body of knowledge that often challenges philosophical speculation about human interactions with the physical environment and with other species.

In this section, Renee Walker explains basic techniques of zooarchaeology used to retrieve, analyze, and interpret nonhuman faunal remains, mostly bone, found in archaeological sites. Her data come from Dust Cave in northern Alabama, an extraordinarily rich prehistoric site where large multidisciplinary research teams have worked over many field seasons. Because of its lengthy occupation through a critical period of climate change, Dust Cave offers an unparalleled opportunity to understand shifting subsistence strategies during the transition into the Holocene. Zooarchaeology is only one piece of a complex story at Dust Cave, and interpretation entails comparing data from this site with contemporaneous sites elsewhere in the region.

The earliest clues in Claire Jantz's reconstructed environmental history of Cades Cove, located on the Tennessee side of the Great Smoky Mountains National Park, come from pollen found preserved in pond bottoms and retrieved for identification and analysis by core sampling. Paleoethnobotanists apply techniques of palynology to fossilized pollen grains found in soil samples collected from archaeological sites and also analyze other retrieved plant parts. Their goal is to reconstruct prehistoric patterns of plant use, effects of human disturbance on plant communities, and the processes that led to mutual interdependence between humans and domesticated plants, such as *Zea maize*. The reconstructed botanical history of the Great Smoky Mountains clearly shows the cumulative and accelerating effects over millennia of human activities, both intentional modifications such as forest clearing and unintended impacts such as the introduction of "weedy" exotic plants along with livestock.

Jantz's work, extending the Cades Cove story backward in time from the comparatively well-documented period of Euro-American settlement, makes us aware that few places on Earth can be considered true wilderness, certainly not the restored "wilderness areas" of Appalachia's national parks and forests. Because change is ever present in dynamic ecosystems, landscape histories cannot in themselves resolve management dilemmas for national park locales such as Cades Cove, but landscape history does assemble essential baseline data from diverse sources to provide an appropriate starting point for formulating appropriate management options.

Michael Gregory, like Jantz, develops a landscape history of a specific locale, in this case the rural community of Denmark in Rockbridge County, Virginia. To understand the settlement and economic development of this area during the nineteenth century, Gregory deciphers traces of past activities on the landscape. He supplements clues gathered in the archaeologist's careful surface survey conducted on foot with other sources. These include informant interviews and a variety of archival sources such as estate inventories, land deeds, census data, store ledgers and other business records, personal letters, and a community column published in the *Rockbridge County News*. Denmark and its environs experienced rapid development of market opportunities and transportation networks during the antebellum period; the local economy rebounded after the Civil War with resumption of normal farming and expansion of two businesses: iron mining and the Rockbridge Alum Springs spa. As new technologies and competition with more distant markets undermined local farming and industry, Denmark's decline from the late nineteenth century onward left the erroneous impression that this had been a largely self-sufficient rural backwater community. Gregory's meticulous research clearly illustrates how multiple techniques from the cultural sciences can be used to test dubious assumptions about regional history that have become unquestioned tenets of conventional wisdom.

These sketches span most of the duration of human history in the region. Read together, they reveal how the forces of globalization gradually and then more rapidly increased the scope and scale of external impacts on local ecosystems and on culturally constituted localities such as Denmark, Virginia. As biosphere relationships have come to dominate local ecosystems, places such as Denmark have experienced centralization of political and economic power on the county, state, and national levels. Loss of population to areas with more job opportunities, erosion of local political and economic institutions, and loss of local identity (at least in the eyes of outsiders) have compounded the difficulties rural Appalachian communities face if they attempt to follow the environmentalist dictum to think globally and act locally. This theme, suggested in the chapters that follow, is elaborated in parts 2 and 3.

2 Early Holocene Ecological Adaptations in North Alabama

RENEE B. WALKER

The migration of humans into Alabama during the end of the Pleistocene was the beginning of an extensive and varied history. Because of the increasingly warmer climate, humans occupying the area at this time were subject to changes in environment, flora, and fauna. Traditional sources of food such as large Pleistocene mammals were becoming increasingly scarce. Therefore, hunter-gatherers adjusted their way of life to exploit new habitats and prey. The faunal remains from a cave in Alabama called Dust Cave, which was inhabited intermittently by hunter-gatherers between 10,500 and 5,200 years ago, reveal information about prey and habitat selection during a critical period of climate change between 12,500 and 8,000 years ago. This chapter describes methods that zooarchaeology has developed to analyze animal bone and their application at Dust Cave.

INTRODUCTION

Recent data from several sites and the reanalysis of data from other sites suggest that human occupation of the Americas may have occurred as early as 20,000 years ago and perhaps even earlier (Dillehay 2000:2). However, widespread colonization of North America probably transpired during the Late Paleoindian period between 12,000 and 10,000 years ago (Anderson 1990; Anderson and Sassaman 1996; Meltzer 1989). These Late Paleoindian people adapted to a variety of environments and fauna, with some emphasis on Pleistocene megafauna (Fladmark 1983). Pleistocene fauna associated with early humans in the New World include mammoth, mastodon, extinct bison, tapir, sloth, extinct horse, peccary, and giant tortoises (Mead and Meltzer 1984). These people were very well adapted to the environment and hunted their prey with tool kits containing large projectile points in addition to knives, scrapers, and other stone tools. However, at around 12,000–10,000 years ago a major climatic change occurred in which the environment became much warmer, initiating the Holocene period.

The beginning of the Holocene was marked by extinctions of the megafauna and shifts in forest type from boreal forest (spruce-fir) to oak-hickory–southern pine in southern Appalachia (Delcourt and Delcourt 1983; Mead and Meltzer 1984). Humans faced a lifestyle and subsistence crisis in that their common prey species were disappearing. Thus, the transition between the Late Pleistocene and Early Holocene is of particular interest in early Native American studies. How did people cope with the change in their environment? How did they adjust their lifestyle to new prey species? Were the changes generalized or specific to certain areas of the North American continent? Analysis of faunal remains holds some answers to these questions.

ZOOARCHAEOLOGICAL METHOD AND THEORY

Zooarchaeology is the study of animal bones from archaeological sites, but specific techniques used to interpret faunal assemblages are varied and complex. Quantification of faunal remains is an important issue because the specific technique used to count remains affects interpretation (Chaplin 1971; Grayson 1973, 1984; Hesse and Wapnish 1985; Klein and Cruz-Uribe 1984). In addition, taphonomic factors (postmortem modification by human or nonhuman agents) also affect interpretations of faunal assemblages (Lyman 1994). Finally, specific interpretations, such as seasonality, may vary with the factors used to assess them. Therefore, faunal analyses must specify the methods on which interpretations are based.

Quantification

Zooarchaeology arose as a way to infer subsistence patterns from archaeological sites. Its increasing significance in the past few decades has resulted in a proliferation of faunal reports and studies. Zooarchaeologists have developed a variety of techniques for quantifying and reporting their data, but one of the major criticisms of these efforts has been the lack of standardization (Grayson 1973, 1984). Proponents of standardization argue that similar techniques of quantification must be used to compare faunal assemblages. The pros and cons of common techniques used by faunal analysts are presented here.

The most widely used and reported technique for evaluating faunal remains is number of identified specimens (NISP). This most basic quantification measure counts the number of bone fragments at a site (Davis 1987). However, NISP is subject to a number of biases. First, NISP is affected by the degree of bone fragmentation at a site. Taphonomic factors such as butchering and carnivore gnawing affect the completeness of elements. Second, NISP is affected by varying degrees of bone preservation, weathering, abrasion, and fossilization. The advantages of this technique are that it is easily calculated and it is included in almost all faunal reports.

The estimation of minimum number of individuals (MNI) by White (1953) brought about another avenue for quantifying zooarchaeological data. MNI is calculated by taking the most abundant sided element of a species (for example, right forelimbs of white-tail deer) to represent the numbers of individuals. This in turn allows calculation of edible meat weight for species (White 1953). MNI was adopted by zooarchaeologists in the 1960s and widely presented in faunal reports. However, Grayson (1984) documented a degree of bias in MNI estimates. He discovered that the MNIs of small samples are overestimated, and the MNIs of large samples are underestimated. Grayson's (1984) critique generated debate in zooarchaeology over the merits of using MNI or NISP; however, MNI is valuable for estimating pounds of edible meat and is still widely used in zooarchaeological studies.

Taphonomy

Taphonomy was largely ignored in the reconstruction of subsistence and environments until recently, but it has become one of the most important areas in zooarchaeological research. Today, almost all zooarchaeological analyses involve at least some aspects of taphonomy (Lyman 1994). Archaeologists and zooarchaeologists alike have amassed considerable information on taphonomic processes affecting animal remains from archaeological sites (Behrensmeyer and Hill 1980; Bonnichsen and Sorg 1989; Gifford-Gonzalez 1989; Hudson 1993).

Taphonomic studies now distinguish between depositional and postdepositional processes (Bonnichsen and Sorg 1989; Gifford-Gonzalez 1989; Hudson 1993). Depositional processes are affected by a variety of human and nonhuman factors. Human factors include hunting practices, butchery, and transport; nonhuman factors include gnawing of carnivores and rodents on animal remains and raptor deposits of bones (Lyman 1985, 1987, 1988, 1994).

Human agents of taphonomic impact are a major focus of archaeological studies. Hunting practices and prey selection play a significant role in taphonomy because the technique and choice involved in acquiring meat affect what is later deposited at archaeological sites. For example, a large prey animal killed by bow and arrow at a far distance from the site may not necessarily be brought back entire to the site (Binford 1981). When large mammals are procured, such as a bison weighing 1,000 to 2,000 pounds, the carcass generally is butchered at the kill site and the meatier parts brought back to a residential site for consumption (Frison 1991). In contrast, a whole white-tail deer from the southeastern United States, weighing around 100–150 pounds (Burt and Grossenheider 1976), probably could be carried back to camp by one to two hunters.

Taphonomic studies by Binford (1978, 1980, 1981) and others (Guilday et al. 1962; Lyman 1987) have included cut marks, bone cracking for marrow, and the deposition of bone debris. In addition, different aspects of butchering such as skinning, defleshing, and disarticulating often leave specific signatures (Binford 1984). Bone burning also has been identified as a human impact on faunal remains. Bone can be burned by both direct and indirect causes. Direct causes include heating of meat during cooking and discard of bone debris in fires. Indirect burning of bone has been documented when bone is located as much as 15 centimeters below a fire (Bennett 1996). These factors must be considered when interpreting taphonomic effects of burning on faunal assemblages.

Animals are an important taphonomic factor at prehistoric sites. In North America, zooarchaeologists have studied the impact of dog gnawing on animal remains from archaeological sites (Morey and Klippel 1991; Snyder 1991). Dogs have been documented in burials from prehistoric Native American sites and were probably domesticated around 8,000 years ago (Morey 1992). Often dogs consume all but the densest portions of bone (i.e., a distal humerus), so their activity undoubtedly biases the archaeological record. Also, the bones of young animals (such as deer fawns) can be destroyed by carnivores so that they are not observable in excavations of an archaeological site (Snyder 1991). Rodents also gnaw on bones left behind by humans. The impact generally is less than that of carnivores, but rodents drag bones around to gnaw on them. Gnawing by rodents generally is characterized by long, parallel striations. These gnaw marks are easily recognizable as caused by rodents (Lyman 1994:196–97).

Raptors, such as owls, are also a factor in archaeological deposits of cave sites. Owls tend to roost in the same place over the course of the year, regurgitating the remains of meals and thereby producing accumulations of the small animals they have consumed (Klippel et al. 1987; Klippel and Parmalee 1982). Caves make excellent roosts for owls and are therefore prone to bone accumulations by these nonhuman agents. As in the case of Granite Quarry Cave, located in southeast Missouri, bone accumulations may be created largely by owls (Klippel et al. 1987:155). Therefore, the impact of owls on faunal assemblages must be considered when studying faunal remains, particularly from caves.

Seasonality

Hunters and gatherers procure specific resources at different times of the year, live in different places, and congregate and disperse during different seasons (Anderson and Hanson 1988; Binford 1981; Lyman 1994). Therefore, inferring site seasonality from the archaeological record has been a great concern for archaeologists (Davis 1983, 1987; Dunnell 1990; Lyman 1994; Monks 1981; Wing 1977). Knowing what faunal resources inhabit an area at certain times of the year is key to understanding seasonal movements of humans. Techniques that can be used in zooarchaeology to determine site seasonality include species presence/absence, bone growth, and mortality data (Davis 1987; Stiner 1990, 1991).

Species presence/absence can be quickly and easily applied to most faunal assemblages to interpret season of site occupation. The basic principle is that certain animals are present in an environment, or easily accessible, at certain seasons of the year and not present during other seasons (Davis 1987). One example is the presence/absence of migratory birds. By relating migratory bird remains found at archaeological sites to information on modern flyways, it is possible to determine season of site occupation. Despite the simplicity of this approach, there are several problems with this method. First, migratory waterfowl may not have been a part of prehistoric diet. Second, climatic conditions might interrupt the timing of seasonal migration patterns. Finally, the evidence of waterfowl may represent species-specific hunting during a particular season and not actual seasonal site occupation but does not preclude occupation during other seasons.

Another species presence/absence method is the identification of amphibian and reptile remains. The same principles are involved, but using amphibian and reptile remains is even more problematic than using migratory waterfowl. For example, the presence of turtle remains has been used to infer warm season occupation of a site. Turtles are not entirely absent from an area during the cold season, however; they burrow into the mud during the winter so that they are largely inaccessible (Conant and Collins 1991). The same applies to amphibian remains.

A useful but imprecise technique for interpreting seasonality is differential bone growth, such as antler growth (Davis 1987; Wemmer 1987). Cervids such as white-tail deer grow antlers at certain times of the year (Wemmer 1987). The presence of antler remains can be used to indicate fall occupation of a site. However, antlers can be picked up after male deer shed them in the late winter. In addition, bone tools such as antler tines may have been acquired at a fall occupation site but carried year-round as a valuable part of a tool kit.

Mortality data also have contributed to zooarchaeological interpretations of seasonality (Grigson and Payne 1982; Todd 1991). Often animals such as cervids and bovids have births at certain times of the year. If this birth season is known and the age at death can be estimated, then one can infer the season of site occupation (Davis 1983; Frison 1991; Lyman 1987; Todd 1991). Mortality data from white-tail deer (Beauchamp 1993; Konigsberg et al. 1997), elk (Klein et al. 1981; Klein and Cruz-Uribe 1983), and bison (Frison 1991; Todd 1991) have been used to interpret seasonality.

Several problems exist for this method as well. One problem is that the birth date of species can fluctuate according to climatic conditions. For example, white-tail deer in Maine birth primarily in early May, but birthing can range from April to June (Jacobson and Reiner 1989), so one must assume long seasons (such as three months for fall and three for winter). In addition, the techniques used to age the animals must be accurate. Despite these problems, mortality data offer a useful way to assess season of site occupation.

Summary

Zooarchaeological studies must specify the analytical techniques used. NISP and MNI are essential for site comparisons because most other faunal reports use this type of quantification. Taphonomic factors must also be investigated to document the effect of human and nonhuman agents on bone. Finally, a determination of seasonality from study of animal remains is useful to document hunter-gatherer mobility patterns. These techniques were applied to the faunal assemblage from Dust Cave, Alabama, to document taphonomic impacts, resource selection, habitat exploitation, and site seasonality.

LATE PLEISTOCENE AND EARLY HOLOCENE ENVIRONMENT OF THE SOUTHERN APPALACHIANS

Knowing the type of environment at the time of Dust Cave's habitation allows a better interpretation of human-land interactions and reconstruction of human behavior. Environment during the Late Pleistocene changed significantly. The climate became appreciably warmer, causing the Laurentide ice sheet to retreat northward. Changes also occurred in flora as much of the southeastern United States shifted from a southeastern evergreen forest at the end of the Pleistocene to a mixed deciduous forest in the Holocene. Studies by Delcourt and Delcourt (1979, 1981, 1983, 1985) of the eastern United States pollen record suggest that forests of around 25,000 years ago were primarily jack pine, spruce, and fir. Between 19,000 and 16,300 years ago the pollen record suggests full glacial conditions, with spruce and jack pine being primarily represented. Around 12,500 years ago, the spruce and jack pine forests were reduced and replaced by a variety of deciduous trees as the climate gradually warmed. Finally, at around 10,000 years ago, the forest contained abundant oaks, ash, ironwood, hickory, birch, walnut, elm, beech, sugar maple, basswood, and hemlock (Delcourt and Delcourt 1979).

Dust Cave is situated between two pollen study sites of Anderson Pond, Tennessee and Goshen Springs, Alabama (Delcourt and Delcourt 1983). Anderson Pond is situated at approximately 36 degrees north latitude, 85 degrees west longitude. At around 20,000 to 12,000 years ago the environment around Anderson Pond shifted from boreal forest (20,000 B.P.) to a short interlude as mixed conifer-northern hardwoods (12,000 B.P.), finally becoming cool-temperate deciduous forest at around 10,000 B.P. (Delcourt and Delcourt 1983). The pollen record for Goshen Springs, located at approximately 31 degrees latitude, is almost unchanging (Delcourt et al. 1980). The vegetational pattern from 20,000 years ago to the present is a warm-temperate southeastern evergreen forest (Delcourt and Delcourt 1983:269).

Dust Cave is located at approximately 34 degrees 46 minutes north latitude, 2 degrees south of Anderson Pond and three degrees north of Goshen Springs. The vegetation around Dust Cave between 10,000 and 8,000 years ago was primarily cool-temperate deciduous forest. At 8,000 years ago the vegetation around Dust Cave shifted to a warm-temperate deciduous forest. According to Delcourt et al. (1983), extreme rates of change in the physical environment trigger major biotic readjustments, including extinction, migration, and speciation.

Paleontological and archaeological animal remains have been very important sources of information about Late Pleistocene and Early Holocene environments. Many of these animal remains have been recovered from cave deposits because the conditions for preservation in caves are good. In the southeastern United States, extinct species and species not currently present in the area were recovered from Pleistocene deposits at Savage Cave, Clark's Cave, and Baker's Bluff Cave. Savage Cave, located in southwestern Kentucky, produced two extinct species: the flat-headed and the long-nosed peccary (Guilday and Parmalee 1979). Other species not present in the area today are the porcupine, red squirrel, and pocket gopher. In addition, prairie chicken remains suggest that a grassland habitat was located near the cave (Guilday and Parmalee 1979:10). Thus, the paleontological remains at Savage Cave suggest different climates and therefore different faunal species available during the Pleistocene and the Holocene.

Guilday et al. (1977) interpreted the site of Clark's Cave in the central mountainous area of Virginia as a possible owl roost. It contained a variety of paleontological remains providing information on the local environment. The presence of ptarmigan and least chipmunk indicates a colder climate during late glacial times. In addition, other species present at the site suggested a spruce and pine forest with nearby meadowlands. Baker's Bluff Cave, located in Tennessee, has faunal remains that represent a transition from a cool temperate climate to open woodland environment (Guilday et al. 1978). Most of the nonextinct mammals are now found in areas north or west of the site; others are located at higher elevations (Guilday et al. 1978). Six extinct or extirpated species were identified from the site, including jaguar, beautiful armadillo, giant beaver, fugitive deer, flat-headed peccary, and tapir. Thus, the faunal evidence from Baker's Bluff corresponds to environmental conditions found in other paleontological assemblages from Late Pleistocene contexts in the Southeast.

Archaeological research conducted at Stanfield-Worley Bluff Shelter, Smith Bottom Cave, and Russell Cave has documented that there were changes in faunal assemblages from the Pleistocene to the Holocene (DeJarnette et al. 1962; Parmalee 1962; Snyder and Parmalee 1991; Styles and Klippel 1996; Weigel et al. 1974). Stanfield-Worley Bluff Shelter is located in northwestern Alabama and was excavated in 1960 and 1961 (Parmalee 1962). Faunal remains from the lowest levels (the Dalton zone) of the site were associated with an Early Holocene environment. Mammals such as white-tail deer, squirrel, rabbit, fox, opossum, raccoon, chipmunk, wood rat, bobcat, porcupine, and skunk were recovered (Parmalee 1962). Birds included turkey, passenger pigeon, woodpecker, crow, barred owl, hawk, black vulture, and bobwhite. In addition, several turtle, fish, and snake species were identified. These remains are all common at archaeological sites occupied throughout the Holocene; however, the occurrence of porcupine at Stanfield-Worley Bluff Shelter suggests that the Early Holocene environment around the site was slightly cooler than at present (Hall and Kelson 1959:782).

Faunal remains from Smith Bottom Cave in the northwest corner of Alabama were investigated by Snyder and Parmalee (1991). More than half of the specimens recovered from this assemblage were mammals, with the remainder consisting of reptiles, birds, fish, and amphibians (Snyder and Parmalee 1991:4). Smith Bottom's location near the Tennessee River probably accounts for the wide variety of birds, primarily ducks and geese, recovered in this assemblage. The distribution of animals during the almost 8,000 years of the site's human occupation changed very little through time (Snyder and Parmalee 1991:12). Russell Cave also contained faunal remains from deposits dating to the Early Holocene. The most common species recovered include deer, turkey, raccoon, squirrel, and bear (Weigel et al. 1974:81). In addition, the teeth of an extinct peccary were excavated from the lowest deposits of the cave, suggesting that humans occupied the site at the end of the Late Pleistocene. Porcupine remains also were recovered from the lowest levels of Russell Cave.

EARLY HOLOCENE ADAPTATIONS AT DUST CAVE, ALABAMA

Information about regional environmental change is pertinent to an evaluation of Early Holocene adaptations at Dust Cave. The archaeological site of Dust Cave is located in north Alabama in what is the Tennessee River section of the Pickwick Reservoir today. The cave is situated along a limestone bluff and was discovered in 1984 by Dr. Richard Cobb, a local teacher, who brought it to the attention of the Alabama Cave Survey (Goldman-Finn and Driskell 1994). Test excavations were conducted at Dust Cave from 1989 to 1994 by a research team from the University of Alabama Division of Archaeology, headed by Dr. Boyce Driskell. The six years of archaeological excavations revealed approximately five meters of stratified deposits, with abundant faunal (Goldberg and Sherwood 1994; Goldman-Finn and Walker 1994; Grover 1994; Walker 1997, 1998), lithic (Meeks 1994), and botanical remains (Gardner 1994).

Five distinct cultural occupations have been documented at the site of Dust Cave (see figure 2.1). Early Holocene occupations at the site span the Late Paleoindian and Early Archaic periods. The Late Paleoindian component has been radiocarbon dated to between 10,000 and 10,500 years ago (Driskell 1994, 1996). Following the Late Paleoindian occupation, the Early Archaic includes the Early Side-Notched and the Kirk Stemmed components (Driskell 1992, 1994). The Early Side-Notched component has Big Sandy projectile points and dates from 9,000 to 10,000 years ago (Driskell 1994; Justice 1987). The Kirk Stemmed component dates from 7,000 to 8,500 years ago. The Middle Holocene occupation at the site includes the Eva/Morrow Mountain component, which dates between 6,000 and 7,000 years ago, and the Seven-Mile Island phase, which dates from 6,000 years ago until the cave's abandonment around 5,200 years ago.

Taphonomy

The bone recovered from Dust Cave is in excellent condition, but taphonomic factors must be taken into consideration. First, rodent burrows are common in the cave, but it is hoped that careful excavation has controlled the problem. Second, carnivore activities are a taphonomic consideration because of the discovery of two dog burials in the Middle Archaic components and dog or coyote coprolites found in the Early Archaic strata. Observations of carnivore

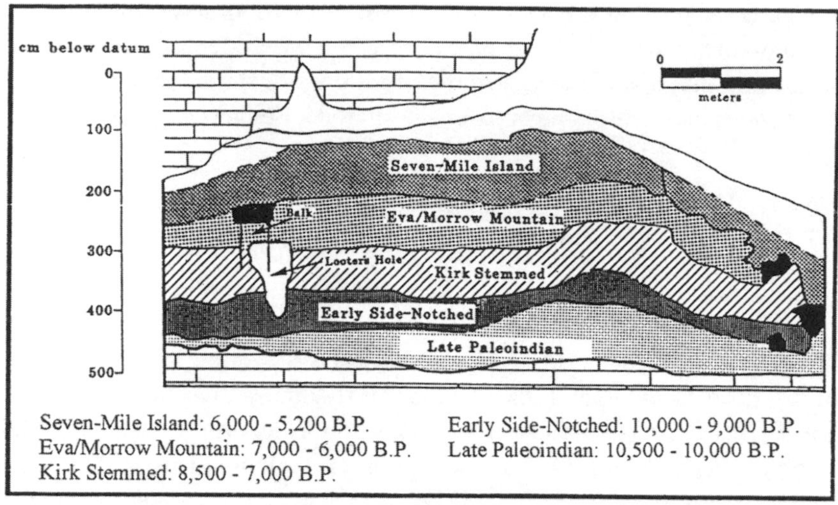

Figure 2.1. Cultural Components and Corresponding Radiocarbon Dates for Dust Cave. (Reprinted from Driskell 1994:20, courtesy of the Alabama Archaeological Society.)

and rodent gnaw marks on bone indicated that only 0.02 and 0.01 percent, respectively, of the faunal remains from the site exhibit this taphonomic activity (Walker 1998). Third, in caves where raptors such as owls are known to roost, large amounts of microfauna can be introduced (Klippel and Parmalee 1982). Such roosts can be recognized through identification of species habitually preyed on by owls (Klippel and Parmalee 1982). In the faunal analysis of the cave, very few of these species (such as mice and rats) were recovered (Walker 1998). Finally, fluvial activity was negligible (Driskell 1992; Goldberg and Sherwood 1994) because the level of the cave was well above the Tennessee River during its human occupation.

The distribution of elements can be used to illustrate taphonomic factors such as differential preservation, butchering practices, and disposal patterns (Binford 1981; Guilday et al. 1962; Lyman 1994; White 1953). The faunal remains of each taxon from the site were separated by class into six body part categories: cranial, vertebra/axial/other, forelimbs, forefeet, hindlimbs, and hindfeet.

Not surprisingly, fish were represented by cranial elements (86 percent) and vertebrae (14 percent), generally the most identifiable elements of fish. Amphibian remains were primarily hindlimbs (50 percent) and vertebrae (33 percent). Many of the reptile remains were placed in the axial/vertebra/other category because of the large quantities of carapace and plastron fragments identified as turtle shell (98 percent). A single forelimb element (2 percent) was identified as an eastern box turtle humerus. Bird remains consisted mostly of wing elements (65 percent) such as the humerus, carpometacarpus, and ulna. Both the large mammal (42 percent) and small and medium mammal (50 percent) categories were composed mainly of cranial elements such as teeth, mandibles, and maxilla that are readily identifiable to genus or species. Also common in the small to medium mammal category were the forelimb (24 percent) and hindlimb (16 percent) elements. However, in the large mammal category the forelimbs and hindlimbs were uncommon (less than 4 percent), whereas the foot elements were often recovered (35 percent total).

In sum, the element distribution for all the components at the site suggests that the faunal remains from the cave are primarily the head, forelimbs and hindlimbs, and forefeet and hindfeet for the mammal and bird classes (Walker 1998). This suggests that, in general, whole mammal and bird carcasses were being brought back to the site, processed, and discarded in the cave. The fish, amphibian, and reptile remains are represented primarily by cranial and axial elements, with the exception of amphibian hindlimb elements (50 percent). These elements may be overrepresented in the assemblage because of the ease of identification and differential preservation of these elements. For example, the cranial elements of fish tend to be larger and better preserved than the thin, easily broken ribs, rays, and spines. In addition, fish bodies may have been cooked as a whole, with the heads removed and discarded (Rostlund 1952).

Faunal remains from the Dust Cave assemblage were examined for any cultural or natural modification (Walker 1998). Approximately 69 percent, or 7,653 faunal remains, were not modified in any discernible manner; 3,164 bones were calcined (28.5 percent), and the remaining modified bones were burned (1.45 percent), cut (0.26 percent), carnivore gnawed (0.03 percent), rodent gnawed (0.02 percent), or fashioned into tools (0.74 percent).

A comparison of animal classes from all the components at the site reveals differences in modification. The mammal and bird remains were predominantly calcined or burned. In addition, only mammal elements exhibited any gnaw marks of carnivores or rodents. Cut marks were primarily on mammal and bird remains, with the exception of several turtle shell fragments that were cut, scraped, or polished. Generally, the amphibian, reptile, and fish remains were subject to very little modification. Humans were responsible for most modification of faunal remains recovered from the site. The high percentages of calcined and burned bones indicate that most of the animal carcasses brought into the cave were heated in or near fires. The low percentage of rodent- or carnivore-gnawed bones suggests that animals rarely used the cave as a den or hibernation site. This could indicate that humans were present at the cave often enough to discourage settlement by other cave-dwelling species (Walker 1998).

Ninety-three bone tools have been recovered from the site (Goldman-Finn and Walker 1994; Walker 1998). The majority of these were bone awls (56 percent). The next most common tool type was antler tines of white-tail deer (11 percent). Indeterminate worked objects were also recovered (7 percent). The remaining bone tools included awl/points (1 percent), bead/tubes (2 percent), fishhooks (1 percent), needles (5 percent), perforated teeth (2 percent), points (5 percent), spatulas (5 percent), polished turtle carapace fragments (3 percent), and wedges (1 percent). The majority dated to the Middle Holocene period of the site (Walker 1998); however, the Late Paleoindian component contained four awls, one perforated tooth, and one worked object. In addition, the Early Side-Notched component contained three awls, one bead/tube, one needle, one point, and one antler tine. Finally, the Kirk Stemmed component contained eight awls, one fishhook, two needles, one perforated tooth, three polished turtle carapace fragments, and one worked object.

Resource Selection

The exploitation of certain animal classes by prehistoric people during the occupation of Dust Cave changed through time (see figure 2.2). The Late Paleoindian component had a much higher percentage (69 percent) of avian remains than later occupations (Walker 1997, 1998). None of the later components had avifauna making up more than 40 percent of the assemblage. In addition, a large proportion of avian remains (47 percent) from the Late Paleoindian component were those of waterfowl. Other animal classes were also represented in the Late Paleoindian assemblage. Nineteen percent of the identifiable remains were mammals, 9 percent were fish, 2 percent reptiles, and only 1 percent of the assemblage was amphibian.

The Early Side-Notched component also had a relatively high percentage of bird remains (38 percent). Fish was the next most abundant class (32 percent). Mammals were also fairly abundant, representing almost a quarter of the assemblage (24 percent). Finally, reptiles constituted 5 percent and amphibians 1 percent. Animal classes in the Kirk Stemmed component were distributed with approximately one-third each of the assemblage made up of mammals (36 percent), birds (32 percent), and fish (27 percent). Five percent of the component was composed of reptile remains, and no representatives of the amphibian class were recovered from the Kirk Stemmed component.

In sum, the use of mammals increased through time, and the exploitation of birds decreased through time. In addition, from the Early Side-Notched component to the Seven-Mile Island phase, use of fish decreased through time.

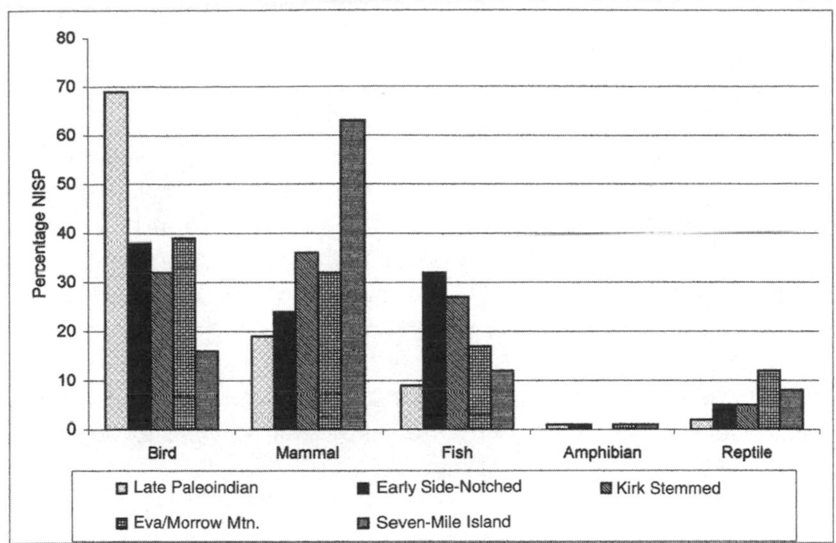

Figure 2.2. Resource Selection of Holocene Hunter-Gatherers at Dust Cave.

Meanwhile, use of reptiles and amphibians was fairly consistent. These trends probably are linked to changes in the environment and reflect adaptations by prehistoric hunter-gatherers at Dust Cave to changes in animal populations.

Habitat Exploitation

A heavy reliance on aquatic species, such as waterfowl, muskrat, swamp rabbit, and pond turtles in the Late Paleoindian component changed in the later occupations to dependence on terrestrial animals such as white-tail deer, turkey, squirrels, and box turtle. In the Late Paleoindian period, 62 percent of the resources were aquatic and 38 percent were terrestrial (Walker 1998). In the Early Side-Notched component, aquatic resources constituted 76 percent of the assemblage, and terrestrial resources constituted only 24 percent. The Kirk Stemmed component contained 65 percent aquatic and 35 percent terrestrial resources.

Between components at Dust Cave, changes also occurred in the relative exploitation of animals from open, ecotone (grassland-forest), and closed habitats (Walker 1998). Species in the cave deposits associated with open environments include prairie chicken and bobwhite (Peterson 1980). Ecotone species include red fox, gray fox, white-tail deer, grackle, cottontail rabbit, and striped skunk (Burt and Grossenheider 1976; Peterson 1980). Closed-habitat species include passenger pigeon, gray squirrel, raccoon, river otter, beaver, woodrat, muskrat, swamp rabbit, barred owl, opossum, and box turtle (Burt and Grossenheider 1976; Conant and Collins 1991; Peterson 1980).

In general, open habitats were exploited least among all habitats; however, the Late Paleoindian and Early Side-Notched components contained the highest percentages of open habitat species. Quantities of white-tail deer and cottontail rabbit remains suggest that ecotone habitats were exploited slightly more frequently. Finally, most resources were exploited from closed habitats, with the exception of the Seven-Mile Island phase, which had a higher percentage of ecotone species. The high numbers for closed habitat species result primarily from the number of gray squirrels in the deposits. Bottomland marsh species such as swamp rabbits, box turtles, and raccoons also were exploited from this habitat. The presence of aquatic and terrestrial animals and animals from open, ecotone, and closed habitats suggests breadth and variation in diet for the inhabitants of Dust Cave.

Seasonality

Seasonality of the cave's occupation can be inferred from species availability, bone growth, and mortality data. Remains of birds that migrate at different times of the year, such as passenger pigeon, have been identified from the cave's faunal assemblage. In addition, species of ducks and geese, such as snow goose, Canada goose, and mallard, have been identified (Walker 1998). The seasonal growth of bones, such as white-tail deer antlers, can also be used to infer seasonality. Finally, certain cold-blooded species such as fish, amphibians, and reptiles can be used to document seasonality in the assemblage. Because the migratory bird, white-tail deer, and cold-blooded taxa are represented in the faunal assemblages for all of the components, seasonality can be summarized for the site as a whole.

The passenger pigeon, now an extinct species, was available in great numbers prehistorically and during early historic times (Schorger 1973). Flocks of passenger pigeons were present in the Southeast during the fall and winter, after which they migrated north to nest in the upper Great Lakes region. In the mid- to late 1800s, passenger pigeons were recorded in western Tennessee and Alabama during October and November (Schorger 1973:269–80). Thus, this bird would have been available to prehistoric hunter-gatherers at Dust Cave during the fall season.

Other migratory birds, such as ducks and geese, would have passed through and perhaps rested in the Dust Cave area on their way south during the fall and again in the spring on their way north. For example, flocks of snow and Canada geese have been observed leaving from James Bay, Canada, in the fall and traveling a distance of 1,700 miles to the Gulf Coast of the United States in approximately sixty hours (Griffin 1962:15). These waterfowl follow the Mississippi flyway, which is one of the most important American flyways (Griffin 1962:128). Other waterfowl, including mallards and Canada geese, follow this route south in the fall to their wintering grounds and again in the spring when they migrate back to their nesting sites.

A large section of white-tail deer antler still attached to the frontals provided evidence of fall-to-winter occupation. This specimen was recovered from the Early Side-Notched component of the cave. The base shows evidence that it was cut from the skull. Male white-tail deer develop antlers, used primarily to compete for females during the fall rut, from spring through the summer. In the fall, the vascular covering of the antler is scraped off and the hard, bony structure of the antler is complete (Brown 1997; Wemmer 1987). Antlers are then shed during the late winter and early spring when a weakened area forms near the base (Brown 1997:183). The presence of the antler with the base still attached supports a fall–early winter occupation of the site in the Early Side-Notched deposit. In addition, mortality data indicate that most (84 percent) of the deer from the site were between six and eighteen months old (Walker 1998). This would place their time of death during the fall as well.

Suckers are bottom-feeding fish that were present in the faunal assemblage at the site and could have been captured during the spring spawning season. During the spring, many suckers species abandon larger rivers in favor of smaller streams to lay and fertilize eggs (Etnier and Starnes 1996:260). The spring spawning of suckers was an excellent opportunity for the inhabitants of Dust Cave to capture these fish. Fishing techniques such as the use of a weir or traps made of rocks would have been conducive to catching suckers in shallow water during the spring (Rostlund 1952). Weirs are successful only when natural movement of many fish occurs, such as during spawning, and weirs are most effective when placed in small, shallow rivers and streams (Rostlund 1952:101). No remains of weirs were recovered from the cave because they are generally constructed of plant fibers, but they have been documented ethnographically as used by Native Americans (Rostlund 1952).

CONCLUSIONS

By providing insight into taphonomic factors, resource selection, habitat exploitation, and site seasonality, the bone remains from the Dust Cave site document the shift in food procurement of prehistoric hunter-gatherers in the southern Appalachian region of Alabama. A study of the bone taphonomy revealed that the animals were brought back to the site primarily as whole units, butchered on the premises, and cooked by roasting (indicated by the high percentage of calcined bone) and that some bones were used to manufacture tools. The earliest occupants of the cave seem to have relied on birds, whereas later hunting efforts emphasized mammals.

Habitat exploitation also changed through time at the site. The percentage of aquatic resources, such as waterfowl, was high during the Early Holocene, whereas terrestrial resources were more important in the Middle Holocene (see figure 2.2). Changes were also observed in the exploitation of open, ecotone, and closed habitats. Most animal resources came from a closed habitat, a third came from ecotone zones, and only a small number came from open habitats. Late Paleoindian, Early Side-Notched, Kirk Stemmed, and Eva/Morrow Mountain people acquired fauna, primarily raccoons and squirrels, from closed habitats. All these patterns are correlated to change in the regional environment from cooler, wetter Late Pleistocene–Early Holocene conditions to a drier and warmer Middle Holocene climate.

Human occupation at the site seems to have occurred in fall to early winter, with the possibility of a spring occupation. The fall and winter occupation is corroborated by the presence of passenger pigeon, waterfowl, and an unshed white-tail deer antler base in the cave deposits. Suckers may have been captured during the spring spawning season, and waterfowl may have been acquired during spring migration northward. Thus, the cave may have been occupied at several times over the course of the year, particularly during the fall and early winter and then later on in the spring.

This interpretation of the faunal remains from Dust Cave suggests a variety of environmental and behavioral adaptations by the prehistoric people who occupied the site. Changes in environment were reflected in the subsistence strategies practiced. People apparently adapted readily when shifts in local vegetation brought on by regional climatic changes affected the animal composition of the area. Although prehistoric inhabitants of Dust Cave began with a reliance on avifauna such as waterfowl, this trend did not continue throughout the site's occupation. The onset of a warming trend during the Middle Holocene prompted a shift in subsistence to a greater reliance on terrestrial fauna. This trend continued until the cave was abandoned around 5,200 years ago.

Because Dust Cave is one of a few stratified Paleoindian and Archaic sites in the Southeast, the faunal remains recovered from it have yielded valuable new information about some of the earliest human inhabitants of the southeastern United States. The analysis of the faunal remains from Dust Cave supports the view that hunter-gatherers in the Early and Mid-Holocene Southeast did not practice a universal subsistence adaptation (Styles and Klippel 1996:115). Rather, they readily adapted to local environmental changes that occurred through time. Some researchers have argued that Early Archaic people were not likely to have relied on small game rather than deer (Cable 1998:184). However, the research on faunal assemblages from sites such as Dust Cave indicates that reliance on a variety of game, including waterfowl and other birds, small and medium-sized mammals, fish, and white-tail deer was the primary subsistence pattern in the Southeast. There are few sites containing information on faunal resources and changes in environment through a time span of several millennia. The Dust Cave faunal remains therefore are an ideal resource for gaining exciting new insights into hunter-gatherer subsistence adaptations to environmental change in southern Appalachia.

References Cited

Anderson, D. G. 1990. "The Paleoindian Colonization of Eastern North America: A View from the Southeastern United States." In *Early Paleoindian Economies of Eastern North America.* Ed. K. B. Tankersly and B. L. Isaac. 163–216. Greenwich, Conn.: JAI Press.

Anderson, D. G., and G. T. Hanson. 1988. "Early Archaic Settlement in the Southeastern United States: A Case Study from the Savannah River Valley." *American Antiquity* 53(2): 262–86.

Anderson, D. G., and K. E. Sassaman. 1996. *The Paleoindian and Early Archaic Southeast.* Tuscaloosa: University of Alabama Press.

Beauchamp, R. 1993. "White-Tailed Deer Crown Height Measurements and Mortality Profiles for the Hayes Site, Middle Tennessee." M.A. thesis, University of Tennessee at Knoxville.

Behrensmeyer, A. K., and A. P. Hill. 1980. *Fossils in the Making: Vertebrate Taphonomy and Paleoecology.* Chicago: University of Chicago Press.

Bennett, J. L. 1996. "Thermal Alteration of Bone: Experiments in Post-Burial Modification." M.A. thesis, University of Tennessee at Knoxville.

Binford, L. R. 1978. *Nunamiut Ethnoarchaeology.* New York: Academic Press.

———. 1980. "Willow Smoke and Dogs' Tails: Hunter-Gatherer Settlement Systems and Archaeological Site Formation." *American Antiquity* 45:4–20.

———. 1981. *Bones: Ancient Men and Modern Myths.* New York: Academic Press.

———. 1984. "Butchering, Sharing, and the Archaeological Record." *Journal of Anthropological Archaeology* 3:235–57.

Bonnichsen, R., and M. H. Sorg. 1989. *Bone Modification.* Orono: University of Maine, Center for the Study of the First Americans.

Brown, L. N. 1997. *A Guide to the Mammals of the Southeastern United States.* Knoxville: University of Tennessee Press.

Burt, W. H., and R. P. Grossenheider. 1976. *A Field Guide to the Mammals: North America, North of Mexico.* Boston: Houghton Mifflin.

Cable, J. S. 1998. "Review of Archaeology of the Mid-Holocene Southeast." *American Antiquity* 63(1): 184–85.

Chaplin, R. E. 1971. *The Study of Animal Bones from Archaeological Sites.* New York: Seminar Press.

Conant, R., and J. T. Collins. 1991. *A Field Guide to the Reptiles and Amphibians: Eastern and Central North America.* New York: Houghton Mifflin.

Davis, S. J. M. 1983. "The Age Profiles of Gazelles Predated by Ancient Man in Israel: Possible Evidence for a Shift from Seasonality to Sedentism." *Paleorient* 9:55–62.

———. 1987. *The Archaeology of Animals.* New Haven, Conn.: Yale University Press.

DeJarnette, D. L., E. B. Kurjack, and J. W. Cabron. 1962. "Stanfield-Worley Bluff Shelter Excavations." *Journal of Alabama Archaeology* 8(1–2): 405–524.

Delcourt, H. R., P. A. Delcourt, and T. Webb III. 1983. "Dynamic Plant Ecology: The Spectrum of Vegetational Change in Space and Time." *Quaternary Science Review* 1:153–75.

Delcourt, P. A., and H. R. Delcourt. 1979. "Late Pleistocene and Holocene Distributional History of the Deciduous Forest in the Southeastern United States." *Veröffentlichungen des Geobotanischen Institutes der ETH* 68:79–107.

———. 1981. "Vegetation Maps for Eastern North America: 40,000 Years Ago B.P. to the Present." In *Geobotany II.* Ed. R. C. Romans. 123–65. New York: Plenum.

———. 1983. "Late Quaternary Vegetational Dynamics and Community Stability Reconsidered." *Quaternary Research* 13:111–32.

———. 1985. "Quaternary Palynology and Vegetational History of the Southeastern United States." In *Pollen Records of Late Quaternary North American Sediments.* Ed. V. M. Bryant and R. G. Holloway. 1–37. Dallas, Tex.: American Association of Stratigraphic Palynologists Foundation.

Delcourt, P. A., H. R. Delcourt, R. C. Brister, and L. W. Lackey. 1980. "Quaternary Vegetation History of the Mississippi Embayment." *Quaternary Research* 13:111–32.

Dillehay, T. D. 2000. *The Settlement of the Americas: A New Prehistory.* New York: Basic Books.

Driskell, B. N. 1992. "Stratified Early Holocene Remains at Dust Cave, Northwest Alabama." In *Paleoindian and Early Archaic Period Research in the Lower Southeast: A South Carolina Perspective.* Ed. D. G. Anderson, K. E. Sassaman, and C. Judge. 273–78. Columbia: Council of South Carolina Professional Archaeologists.

———. 1994. "Stratigraphy and Chronology at Dust Cave." *Journal of Alabama Archaeology* 40:18–30.

———. 1996. "Stratified Late Pleistocene and Early Holocene Deposits at Dust Cave, Northwestern Alabama." In *The Paleoindian and Early Archaic Southeast.* Ed. D. G. Anderson and K. E. Sassaman. 315–30. Tuscaloosa: University of Alabama Press.

Dunnell, R. C. 1990. "The Role of the Southeast in American Archaeology." *Southeastern Archaeology* 9(1): 11–22.

Etnier, D. A., and W. C. Starnes. 1996. *The Fishes of Tennessee.* Knoxville: University of Tennessee Press.

Fladmark, K. R. 1983. "Times and Places: Environmental Correlates of Mid-to-Late Wisconsinan Human Population Expansion in North America." In *Early Man in the New World.* Ed. R. Shutler. 13–42. Beverly Hills, Calif.: Sage Publications.

Frison, G. C. 1991. "Hunting Strategies, Prey Behavior, and Mortality Data." In *Human Predators and Prey Mortality.* Ed. M. C. Stiner. 15–30. Boulder, Colo.: Westview Press.

Gardner, P. S. 1994. "Carbonized Plant Remains from Dust Cave." *Journal of Alabama Archaeology* 40:189–207.

Gifford-Gonzalez, D. 1989. "Modern Analogues: Developing an Interpretive Framework." In *Bone Modification.* Ed. R. Bonnichsen and M. H. Sorg. 43–52. Orono: University of Maine, Center for the Study of the First Americans.

Goldberg, P., and S. C. Sherwood. 1994. "Micromorphology of Dust Cave Sediments: Some Preliminary Results." *Journal of Alabama Archaeology* 40:56–64.

Goldman-Finn, N. S., and B. N. Driskell. 1994. "Introduction to Archaeological Research at Dust Cave." *Journal of Alabama Archaeology* 40:1–16.

Goldman-Finn, N. S., and R. B. Walker. 1994. "The Dust Cave Bone Tool Assemblage." *Journal of Alabama Archaeology* 40:104–13.

Grayson, D. K. 1973. "On the Methodology of Faunal Analysis." *American Antiquity* 38:432–39.

———. 1984. *Quantitative Zooarchaeology: Topics in the Analysis of Archaeological Faunas.* New York: Academic Press.

Griffin, D. R. 1962. *Bird Migration.* New York: Natural History Press.

Grigson, C., and S. Payne. 1982. *Ageing and Sexing Animal Bones from Archaeological Sites.* Oxford: British Archaeological Reports 107.

Grover, J. 1994. "Faunal Remains from Dust Cave." *Journal of Alabama Archaeology* 40:114–31.

Guilday, J. E., H. W. Hamilton, E. Anderson, and P. W. Parmalee. 1978. "The Baker Bluff Cave Deposit, Tennessee, and the Late Pleistocene Faunal Gradient." *Bulletin of the Carnegie Museum of Natural History* 11:1–67.

Guilday, J. E., and P. W. Parmalee. 1979. "Pleistocene and Recent Vertebrate Remains from Savage Cave (15LO11), Kentucky." *Western Kentucky Spelological Survey Annual Report* 1979:5–10.

Guilday, J. E., P. W. Parmalee, and H. W. Hamilton. 1977. "The Clark's Cave Bone Deposit and the Late Pleistocene Paleoecology of the Central Appalachian Mountains of Virginia." *Bulletin of the Carnegie Museum of Natural History* 11:1–67.

Guilday, J. E., P. W. Parmalee, and D. P. Tanner. 1962. "Aboriginal Butchering Techniques at the Eschelman Site (36LA12), Lancaster County, Pennsylvania." *Pennsylvania Archaeologist* 32(2): 59–83.

Hall, E. R., and K. R. Kelson. 1959. *The Mammals of North America.* New York: Ronald Press.

Hesse, B., and P. Wapnish. 1985. *Animal Bone Archaeology.* Washington, D.C.: Taraxacum Press.

Hudson, J. L. 1993. *From Bones to Behavior: Ethnoarchaeological and Experimental Contributions to the Interpretation of Faunal Remains.* Carbondale: Center for Archaeological Investigations Occasional Paper No. 21, Southern Illinois University.

Jacobson, H. A., and R. J. Reiner. 1989. "Estimating Age of White-Tailed Deer: Tooth Wear Versus Cementum Annuli." *Proceedings of the Annual Conference of SEAFWA* 43:286–91.

Justice, N. D. 1987. *Stone Age Spear and Arrow Points of the Midcontinental and Eastern United States.* Bloomington: Indiana University Press.

Klein, R. G., and K. Cruz-Uribe. 1983. "The Computation of Ungulate Age (Mortality) Profiles from Dental Crown Heights." *Paleobiology* 9:70–78.

———. 1984. *The Analysis of Animal Bones from Archaeological Sites.* Chicago: University of Chicago Press.

Klein, R. G., C. Wolf, L. G. Freeman, and K. Allwarden. 1981. "The Use of Dental Crown Heights for Constructing Age Profiles of Red Deer and Similar Species in Archaeological Sites." *Journal of Archaeological Science* 8:1–31.

Klippel, W. E., and P. W. Parmalee. 1982. "Diachronic Variation in Insectivores from Cheek Bend Cave and Environmental Change in the Midsouth." *Paleobiology* 8(4): 447–58.

Klippel, W. E., L. M. Snyder, and P. W. Parmalee. 1987. "Taphonomy and Archaeologically Recovered Bones from Southeast Missouri." *Journal of Ethnobiology* 7(2): 155–69.

Konigsberg, L. W., S. R. Frankenberg, and R. B. Walker. 1997. "Regress What on What? Paleodemographic Age Estimation as a Calibration Problem." In *Integrating Archaeological Demography: Multidisciplinary Approaches to Prehistoric Population.* Ed. R. R. Payne. 64–88. Carbondale, Ill.: Center for Archaeological Investigations.

Lyman, R. L. 1985. "Bone Frequencies: Differential Transport, In Situ Destruction, and the MGUI." *Journal of Archaeological Science* 12:221–36.

———. 1987. "On the Analysis of Vertebrate Mortality Profiles: Sample Size, Mortality Type, and Hunting Pressure." *American Antiquity* 52:125–42.

———. 1988. "Zooarchaeology of 45DO189." In *Archaeological Investigations at River Mile 590: The Excavations at 45DO189.* Ed. J. R. Galm and R. L. Lyman. 97–141. Cheney: Eastern Washington University.

———. 1994. *Vertebrate Taphonomy.* Cambridge, England: Cambridge University Press.

Mead, J. I., and D. J. Meltzer. 1984. "North American Late Quaternary Extinctions and the Radiocarbon Record." In *Quaternary Extinctions: A Prehistoric Revolution.* Ed. P. S. Martin and R. G. Klein. 440–50. Tucson: University of Arizona Press.

Meeks, S. C. 1994. "Lithic Artifacts from Dust Cave." *Journal of Alabama Archaeology* 40:79–106.

Meltzer, D. J. 1989. "Why Don't We Know When the First People Came to North America?" *American Antiquity* 54:471–90.

Monks, G. 1981. "Seasonality Studies." In *Advances in Archaeological Method and Theory,* vol. 4. Ed. M. B. Schiffer. 177–240. New York: Academic Press.

Morey, D. F. 1992. "Size, Shape, and Development in the Evolution of the Domestic Dog." *Journal of Archaeological Science* 19:181–204.

Morey, D., and W. E. Klippel. 1991. "Canid Scavenging and Deer Bone Survivorship at an Archaic Period Site in Tennessee." *Archaeozoologia* 4:11–28.

Parmalee, P. W. 1962. "Faunal Remains from the Stanfield-Worley Bluff Shelter." *Journal of Alabama Archaeology* 8:112–14.

Peterson, R. T. 1980. *A Field Guide to the Birds.* Boston: Houghton Mifflin.

Rostlund, E. 1952. *Freshwater Fish and Fishing in Native North America.* Berkeley: University of California Press.

Schorger, A. W. 1973. *The Passenger Pigeon: Its Natural History and Extinction.* Norman: University of Oklahoma Press.

Snyder, L. M. 1991. "Barking Mutton: Ethnohistoric and Ethnographic, Archaeological, and Nutritional Evidence Pertaining to the Dog as a Native American Food Source on the Plains." In *Beamers, Bobwhites, and Bluepoints: Tributes to the Career of Paul W. Parmalee.* Ed. J. R. Purdue, W. E. Klippel, and B. W. Styles. 359–78. Springfield: Illinois State Museum.

Snyder, L. M., and P. W. Parmalee. 1991. "An Archaeological Faunal Assemblage from Smith Bottom Cave, Lauderdale County, Alabama." Tennessee Valley Authority, Report of Investigations. Knoxville: University of Tennessee Press.

Stiner, M. 1990. "The Use of Mortality Patterns in Archaeological Studies of Hominid Predatory Adaptations." *Journal of Anthropological Archaeology* 9:305–51.

———. 1991. *Human Predators and Prey Mortality.* Boulder, Colo.: Westview Press.

Styles, B. W., and W. E. Klippel. 1996. "Mid-Holocene Faunal Exploitation in the Southeastern United States." In *Archaeology of the Mid-Holocene Southeast.* Ed. K. E. Sassaman and D. G. Anderson. 115–33. Gainesville: University Press of Florida.

Todd, L. C. 1991. "Seasonality Studies and Paleoindian Subsistence Strategies." In *Human Predators and Prey Mortality.* Ed. M. C. Stiner. 217–38. Boulder, Colo.: Westview Press.

Walker, R. B. 1997. "Late-Paleoindian Faunal Remains from Dust Cave, Alabama." *Current Research in the Pleistocene* 14:85–87.

———. 1998. "The Late Paleoindian through Middle Archaic Faunal Evidence from Dust Cave, Alabama." Ph.D. diss., University of Tennessee at Knoxville.

Weigel, R. D., J. A. Holman, and A. A. Paloumpis. 1974. "Vertebrates from Russell Cave." In *Investigations in Russell Cave.* Ed. J. W. Griffin. 81–85. National Park Service Publications in Archaeology No. 13. Washington, D.C.: U.S. Government Printing Office.

Wemmer, C. M. 1987. *Biology and Management of the Cervidae.* Washington, D.C.: Smithsonian Institution Press.

White, T. E. 1953. "A Method of Calculating the Dietary Percentage of Various Food Animals Utilized by Aboriginal Peoples." *American Antiquity* 18:396–98.

Wing, E. S. 1977. "Subsistence Systems in the Southeast." *Florida Anthropologist* 30:81–87.

3 Cades Cove: Reconstructing Human Impacts on the Environment before Euro-American Settlement

CLAIRE JANTZ

Cades Cove is one of the most scenic areas in the Great Smoky Mountains National Park, attracting millions of visitors every year. The appeal lies in its open expanses of fields surrounded by majestic mountains, with small log cabins evoking frontier times. This landscape is the end result of a 10,000-year association with humans. Complex relationships between humans, animals, and plants have resulted in a dynamic history. The purpose of this chapter is to provide a general overview of the environmental history of Cades Cove, to discover how and why Cades Cove has been a center of human activity for the past 10,000 years and how humans have affected the landscape, focusing on the changing vegetation of the cove. However, because the vegetational composition is the result of complex interactions with wild and domestic animals, humans, and competitive relationships between plants, all these factors must be explored.

Although Cades Cove has been the focus of many studies, the majority of the literature deals with the recent past (1818 to the present), and very little has been written about human-land relationships in the cove. Some paleobotanical and archaeological studies have been performed in Cades Cove, but their coverage is limited. However, these studies become more valuable when used in concert with the larger body of literature about the Great Smoky Mountains and the Southeast. In this way, the environmental history of Cades Cove can be interpolated by using what is known about the vegetation and human history of the Great Smoky Mountains as a whole.

PREHISTORIC VEGETATION SURVEY

Before discussing the earliest human inhabitants of the cove, it is important to ask what the cove may have looked like 10,000 years ago. Cades Cove is a geologic fenster. That is, the older Precambrian rocks that surround the cove have eroded to expose the wide, flat limestone base that makes up the floor of the cove (Davis 1993). After the glaciers receded 12,000 to 15,000 years ago, the southern Appalachian mountains became a center of vegetative adaptive radiation (Cain 1930). Silver (1990) describes the early forests as consisting of mixed deciduous hardwoods interspersed with pines. Based on geography, elevation, and current species composition, the Cades Cove forest probably was composed of oaks, hickories, red and sugar maples, chestnut, black gum, poplars, and sweet gum, with various pines distributed throughout. It is very likely that the conspicuous American cane (*Arundinaria gigantea*) grew along the stream banks and in the moist woods at the west end of the cove. Now a rare woody grass, giant cane was once widespread, but needs periodic renewal by fire or grazing (Davis 1993).

To more exactly describe the vegetation of Cades Cove, paleobotanical evidence must be considered. Davidson (1983) conducted such a study in Lake in the Woods, a shallow woodland pond located at the southwestern end of the cove. Using radiocarbon dating of core samples and pollen identification and counts, Davidson provided a vegetation picture of the cove dating from 4600 B.C. to the present. She found that although the species composition remained fairly static, the frequency of the different species has changed over time.

From 4600 to 4300 B.C., oaks (*Quercus*), willows (*Salix*), and sweet gum (*Liquidambar*) were dominant species, their frequencies fluctuating at different times. Other species present include black gum (*Nyssa*), red maple (*Acer rubrum*), ash (*Fraxinus*), hickory (*Carya*), chestnut (*Castanea*), and pine (*Pinus*). From 4300 B.C. to A.D. 1815, the cove was dominated by oak and sweet gum. Within this period, however, Davidson classified three important subzones of secondary dominance: the Nyssa subzone (4300–3300 B.C.), the Castanea subzone (3300 B.C.–A.D. 100), and the Pinus subzone (3300 B.C.–A.D. 1815). During the latter period, pine species made up 12 to 20 percent of the arboreal pollen count. This trend continued from 1815 to the present, where the maximum value for pine species again reached 20 percent.

Although Davidson's study was site specific—a bottomland woodland pond—it does reflect the dynamics of species composition over time. The observed changes are a result of complex environmental fluctuations, sedimentation, changing water levels, and sampling. Changes in species composition may also have been affected by the presence of humans, as discussed later in this chapter.

PREHISTORIC NATIVE AMERICAN ACTIVITIES

By virtue of the significant tenure of habitation, Native Americans in the Great Smoky Mountains caused many changes in the landscape. From the prehistoric vegetation survey, it is clear that the cove was species rich and contained resources that would have been used by Native Americans. It is important to understand their changing subsistence patterns, agricultural practices, and culture to interpret how Native Americans influenced their environment in the Smokies and how they may have affected Cades Cove.

The main archaeological investigation of activities of prehistoric Native Americans in the Great Smoky Mountains dates from 1977, when Quentin Bass conducted minimal pedestrian surveys and evaluated archival holdings to locate sites. Bass documented surface artifacts, including hunting and food-processing implements, which can indicate the intensity of land use.

The earliest signs of human activity in the cove date as early as 10,000 years ago. Chapman et al. (1982) found that the Archaic tradition was established 10,000 years ago in the Little Tennessee River Valley southwest of the cove. In the Great Smoky Mountains, however, Bass uncovered only twenty-five sites with early Archaic artifacts. Of the seven total archaeological sites in Cades Cove and vicinity, only two contained early Archaic artifacts. Although this evidence indicates that people were present in the cove during the Archaic, as early as 10,000 years ago, their activity appears to have been limited. All artifacts retrieved in Bass's survey were used for hunting. The absence of food-processing materials indicates that people during the Archaic probably used these sites strictly as temporary hunting camps and returned to more permanent camps near a river valley (Bass 1977). Because of its geographic proximity, it is reasonable to assume that many of the Native Americans who used Cades Cove came from the Little Tennessee River Valley.

As the Archaic period progressed, the presence of Native Americans in the Great Smoky Mountains continued to increase, and the pattern of seasonal migration became more pronounced. Bass states that by the Late Archaic period, large populations of Native Americans on the floodplains seasonally migrated to the upper valleys, coves, and benches; they used the ridges, gaps, and balds as hunting grounds. Middle and Late Archaic artifacts recovered in Cades Cove reveal activities that point to lengthier occupation of the cove sites: butchering, bone and primary flint-working tools, and hunting implements (Bass 1977).

About 1000 B.C. a new cultural tradition became evident, especially along the Ohio and Mississippi Rivers. The Woodland tradition is rooted in the Archaic tradition but is characterized by a different settlement pattern. Although the Woodland Indians followed the same seasonal migration patterns that were practiced during the Archaic, they created more permanent villages. Though still practicing a hunting and gathering lifestyle, they improved their methods to more efficiently use the resources of a specific area. In the wooded areas of the Southeast, nut harvesting became very important (Hudson 1976). The American chestnut, now practically extinct in the wild, probably was an important source of nutrition for Native Americans during the Woodland period (Davis 1993).

The roots of agriculture in the New World also date to the Woodland period, when Native Americans began to cultivate many of the wild native plants they relied on and some exotic cultigens such as the bottle gourd (*Lagenaria siceraria*), squash (*Cucurbita pepo*), and corn (*Zea mays*). Because the practice of agriculture entails a more sedentary lifestyle and because the most fertile areas generally are around floodplains, the Woodland Indians established settlements in river valleys (Hudson 1976). Bass's findings in the Great Smoky Mountains are consistent with this generalization. Most food processing was limited to the floodplains, and there is evidence to suggest horticulture in these areas. However, there were many base camps throughout the mountains on benches and in coves where food processing occurred, and hunting was still common in the mountains. In Cades Cove, there were three sites containing Woodland artifacts. At all sites, hunting implements were found along with artifacts associated with other activities, including butchering and food processing (Bass 1977).

Around 700 B.C. the Mississippian tradition developed along the Mississippi River. The Mississippians achieved the most organized society to develop in North America to that date and relied heavily on agriculture. Like the Woodland Indians, the Mississippians located villages on the floodplains and valleys, but these were more permanent and centralized settlements. As an agriculturally based society began to develop, distinct cultural differences began to appear between groups of Native Americans. The Native American group associated with the area today is the Cherokee. However, Cherokee origins are still debated. Linguistic evidence ties the Cherokee to ancestors of modern Iroquoians. According to linguists, these northern tribes split perhaps 4,000 years ago, and ancestors of the Cherokee migrated into the southern mountains (Mithun 1984). Although archaeological evidence is scant, archaeologists agree that there is evidence of a split occurring between 3,500 and 4,000 years ago (Snow 1984). For simplicity, I will refer to the Native Americans in the area after A.D. 1000 as Cherokee, although the Cherokee Nation was not formed until after Europeans arrived.

Beginning around A.D. 900, the Cherokee tradition started to emerge, following the general settlement trends of the Mississippians and having much in common with those of other southeastern Indians. In contrast to the seasonal migrations practiced by the Woodland people, the Cherokee were very sedentary, establishing permanent, nucleated settlements on the floodplains of southern Appalachia, hardly needing to venture into the mountains for food as their predecessors had because they relied so heavily on domesticated plants. Bass's research shows that most of the activity was limited to the floodplains and that in the mountains and uplands, hunting was the primary activity. In Cades Cove, three sites contained artifacts indicating food processing as well as hunting (Bass 1977). There was apparently more extensive habitation in the cove than in the rest of the mountains.

PRE-COLUMBIAN HUMAN IMPACT ON THE COVE LANDSCAPE

By using what is known about the culture of Native Americans, we can project their activities onto the landscape of Cades Cove and form hypotheses about how people might have affected the environment. Investigations by Chapman et al. (1982) of human-land interactions in the lower Little Tennessee River Valley are especially pertinent to reconstructing human-land interactions in Cades Cove.

The researchers studied carbonized wood remains, which represent what would have been used for firewood and for building construction and tool manufacturing. They classified the wood according to bottomland wood taxa, upland tree taxa, and disturbance-favored taxa. Several assumptions were made in interpreting the data, but the findings indicate a distinct pattern. From about 10,000 to 4,000 B.P., only 10 percent of the wood remains were disturbance-favored taxa. Four thousand years ago, the Woodland people began to practice slash-and-burn cultivation, and many of their cultigens appear at this time. The abundance of disturbance-favored tree species also increases. By the Mississippian cultural period, disturbance-favored tree taxa make up 51 percent of the wood-charcoal samples.

Chapman et al. (1982) believe that this pattern reflects long-term change resulting from increasingly intensive land use by the Native Americans. During the Archaic time period, much of the landscape probably was close-canopied deciduous hardwood forest. By the Mississippian period, the landscape had been fragmented into croplands immediately surrounding permanent

Indian settlements, forests in the early stages of succession, and virgin forests. This fragmentation would have increased the edge habitat, which is dominated by disturbance-favored taxa.

Without the benefit of such a study, it would be difficult to estimate the degree of disturbance caused by humans in Cades Cove. They certainly would have cleared some of the forests for shelter and firewood. They may have practiced slash-and-burn cultivation. This would have caused an increase in edge habitat, as it has been postulated by Chapman et al. Looking at Davidson's data from Lake in the Woods, which is in the vicinity of some of the archaeological sites, the increase in pine seems to begin around 3600 B.C. This is near the end of the Archaic tradition, and Bass hypothesizes that by the Terminal Archaic, Native Americans were firmly entrenched in the southeastern mountains. In Cades Cove, only one site yielded Late Archaic artifacts, but it seems that the activity was intense: hunting, butchering, and bone and primary flint working (Bass 1977). It is possible that the increase in activity may be partly responsible for the increase in pine and some other disturbance-favored taxa. For example, the herbaceous plant cocklebur (*Xanthium*) began to increase at about the same time. Both cocklebur and pine have increased to the present, becoming especially prolific about A.D. 100 (Davidson 1983).

It is interesting that the most dramatic increase in disturbance-favored species occurred about the same time that the Cherokee tradition arose. Although the Cherokee may have limited their seasonal activities in the mountains in favor of practicing slash-and-burn horticulture, it has been shown that the Cherokee still maintained an intense presence in Cades Cove (Bass 1977). Although there is no evidence that the Cherokee practiced horticulture in the cove before European contact, there would have been abundant resources available for hunting and gathering. It is certain that Cades Cove produced a good seasonal harvest and bountiful hunting for the Cherokee. Seasonal habitation by a substantial group of Cherokee would have resulted in cleared areas for camps and the use of wood for fire. Most researchers believe that the Cherokee practiced burning in the mountains. Reasons for this are not known exactly, but one hypothesis is that the Cherokee burned the forest to produce habitat for desirable species, such as blackberry and blueberry. It is also thought that the Cherokee may have been responsible for creating and maintaining some of the balds in the area, such as Gregory's Bald (Lindsay 1976). Deer and other game would have been attracted to the burned areas for browse and increased the hunters' bounty (Davis 1993).

Lack of evidence does not establish that the Native Americans were not practicing slash-and-burn horticulture in the cove. It may be that the evidence has not yet been discovered because no extensive archaeological study of the area has been undertaken. It is clear that over time, the landscape of the cove was altered by an increase in disturbance-favored species, and that trend has continued into the present.

EUROPEANS ARRIVE: CADES COVE, 1500–1818

When Columbus sailed in 1492, the Native American population in the Appalachian region may have been as high as 30,000 (Silver 1990). Although the Cherokee especially may have had a significant impact on the landscape in Cades Cove, the mark of their actions before European contact in no way compared with what was to come, despite how numerous they were. The Cherokee mythology helped to establish a balance between humans and nature. In addition, their hunting, fishing, gathering, and cropping techniques were not intensive enough to greatly exploit their habitat. Finally, the majority of plants used by the Cherokee were native to North America and therefore already adapted to local ecosystems (Goodwin 1977). The Cherokee lifestyle, settlement patterns, and environment were profoundly affected by the advent of European colonialism in the New World.

The first European explorer to penetrate into the southern mountains probably was Hernando de Soto in 1540. The Spanish established trade with the southeastern Native Americans, mainly along the coast. Because the Cherokee were so far inland, they remained isolated from direct trade with the Spanish for more than 100 years. The isolation of the Cherokee may have continued up to 1670, when the British and French began actively to solicit trade agreements (Goodwin 1977). However, Davis asserts that trade may have begun up to half a century earlier. If this is true, the ecological decline and the decline of the Cherokee began much earlier. However, there is little documentation before 1700 (Davis 1993). In any case, trade with Europeans assaulted the southeast in two ways. First, the exploitation of the southeastern mountain resources for European trade markets caused havoc with ecosystem balance. Second, the Europeans brought many things with them that adversely affected the ecosystem and caused the eventual decline of the Cherokee culture and population.

The Europeans were interested primarily in fur. By 1700, England controlled the fur trade industry and imported thousands of skins each year. Deer and beaver were most coveted, but other hunted animals included fox, raccoon, otter, wildcat, bear, and elk. Beaver were almost completely extirpated from the region by the late eighteenth century (Davis 1993; Silver 1990). The deer population probably was saved by the decline of natural predators being sought by the fur trade and by hunting restrictions implemented in the 1760s (Silver 1990).

Another animal, gone today, may have been present in the cove and would have affected the landscape: the American buffalo. Although they are not generally associated with areas of the country east of the Mississippi, buffalo were latecomers to the Appalachians, arriving in small herds around 1600. Davis (1993) cites many examples of buffalo presence in the east, although their numbers were not large. A pollen sample study by Cridlebaugh (1984) shows an increase in the distribution of ragweed (*Ambrosia* sp.), a disturbance-favored species associated with old fields and roadsides. Davis suggests that clearings created by grazing buffalo and trails created by herd movement may have accounted for the increase in the frequency of ragweed and that these effects would have been evident throughout the southern Appalachians (Davis 1993). Buffalo were known to have been present throughout the area currently encompassed by the Great Smoky Mountains National Park, and the lower end of the cove would have provided an ideal habitat for bison (Linzey and Linzey 1968). They may have been a significant ecological force in the vicinity. Eastern Buffalo eventually were hunted to extinction by long hunters, early settlers, and Native Americans. By 1775, there were no more buffalo in the Appalachians, another casualty of the fur trade (Davis 1993).

Elk were also present in the Great Smoky Mountains National Park. Tennessee made up the southern end of their range, so the mountains probably were only sparsely populated with elk. Although their browsing habits are similar to those of deer, their small population would have minimized their impact on the vegetation. The last elk in eastern Tennessee was shot in 1849, although their numbers had been greatly reduced by the late 1700s (Linzey and Linzey 1968).

The fur trade also affected Cherokee culture. Before European contact, the Cherokee relied on game mainly for food. In fact, they had not developed the hunting technology needed to acquire large numbers of skins. Their participation in the commercial marketing of animal skins was made possible only after the introduction of horses, guns, and steel traps. These hunting implements allowed the Cherokee to hunt more effectively, and they could transport large numbers of skins with horses (Goodwin 1977). Guns and horses were quickly assimilated into Cherokee culture. They were used not only for hunting but also for warfare (Silver 1990). The Cherokee became increasingly dependent on European goods, such as cloth and metal items. Their religious beliefs, which were centered on a reciprocal relationship with the natural world, were jeopardized by involvement in European capitalist practices that changed their entire culture to accommodate the fur trade and European interaction (Goodwin 1977).

Although fur was the major industry in the New World, colonists also traded for medicinal plants. One such plant, snakeroot (*Polygala senega*), had been used by the southeastern Native Americans to treat snakebites and other ailments. The colonists soon adopted this root as a reliable remedy and exported it to England. The extent of this trade is not known, but it is certain that more snakeroot was collected when the Europeans created a demand for it (Silver 1990).

Another plant that was greatly affected by European traders is the valuable plant ginseng (*Panax quinquefolium*), used as a stimulant tonic. The demand for ginseng originated in China, where it was eagerly sought for its supposed aphrodisiac properties. Overharvesting of the plant caused the Chinese to look for an international supplier (Davis 1993). Many traders in the New World desired the plant for the profit to be made by selling it to the Chinese. The Appalachian highland forests provided an ideal habitat for ginseng, where the trade would have encouraged excessive harvesting by the Cherokee and other Native Americans and by Euro-American settlers (Silver 1990). Both ginseng and snakeroot would have been found and harvested by Cherokee and settlers in Cades Cove.

European demand for the exportable resources of the Appalachians caused changes in the ecology, landscape, and native cultures. However, what the Europeans brought to the New World may have caused as much change as what they took. The import of certain European goods, such as horses and guns, has already been mentioned as a factor in Cherokee culture change. A number of exotics, such as new agricultural crops and domesticated livestock, were also incorporated into the Cherokee lifestyle and the environment.

Corn, beans, and squash had been in cultivation for almost 2,000 years by the time Europeans arrived. It is important to note that these and other Native American cultigens had been grown in the Appalachian region for quite some time. Agriculture had developed gradually, and although it involved clearing of the forest, it had probably become an integral and minimally disruptive part of the southeastern ecosystems. The introduction of most European cultigens had little effect on the ecosystems because they were cultivated in the same fields and in the same manner as the native crops (Davis 1993).

Whereas the introduction of exotic American cultivated plants such as maize and squash was in most cases deliberate, the arrival of most European plants was unintentional. The state of West Virginia, which has floristic attributes similar to those of eastern Tennessee, has created a list of nonnative invasive species that numbers in the hundreds. Naming a few off this list that are also common in Tennessee suggests the current state of the exotic invasion that began in the 1500s: yarrow (*Achillea millefolium*), thistle (*Carduus* sp.), English ivy (*Hedera helix*), ox-eye daisy (*Leucanthemum vulgare*), privet (*Ligus-*

trum vulgare), fescue (*Festuca pratensis*), sweet clover (*Melilotus officinalis*), and timothy grass (*Phleum pratense*) (Harmon 1995). Among the cloth, guns, and alcohol shipments from Europe to America were the seeds of European plants, which invaded cleared and disturbed areas, lined trade routes, filled abandoned fields, and followed the destructive path of European livestock into the heart of the mountains (Crosby 1972).

In fact, the introduction of European livestock played an integral role in the establishment of exotic plants. Cattle were brought to Spanish Florida in the sixteenth century. Although animal husbandry was primarily a European activity, Indians in Florida eventually took it up. The practice spread northward, and by the mid-1700s Indians in Alabama and Georgia were also raising cattle. The Cherokee were slow to take up the practice of large-scale cattle raising but kept small, free-ranging herds as early as the last quarter of the eighteenth century (Davis 1993).

Pigs were more common in the area by this time and may account for the Cherokees' late adoption of cattle herding (Davis 1993). Crosby reports that "swine herds were to be found wherever the Spanish settled or even touched" (Crosby 1972:79). They were brought to Florida with de Soto in 1539. By the time he reached the southern mountains, the herd was greater than 300 animals. Some pigs from de Soto's herd may have escaped and spread north into the mountains, becoming feral. The Cherokee did not begin raising them until 1700, keeping them penned during the growing season and harvest and then allowing them to range free (Davis 1993).

Pigs were more attractive to the southeastern Indians than cattle for several reasons. They were easy to care for, bred successfully, and were more self-sufficient. Crosby describes the pig, after arriving in America, as a "fast, tough, lean, self-sufficient greyhound of a hog much closer in appearance and personality to a wild boar than to one of our twentieth century hogs" (Crosby 1972:77). These same characteristics made them popular with the first settlers as well, guaranteeing the extended presence of domesticated hogs in the region (Chapman, personal communication, November 1997).

Because swine were allowed to range free, they had a direct impact on wildlife. They depended primarily on the acorn and chestnut mast, so they competed with black bears for food (Chapman, personal communication, November 1997). Hogs also destroyed the forest understory by rooting, and large, muddy wallows were common in the open areas of the balds and fields (Davis 1993).

The impact of cattle on the mountains cannot be overstated. They were allowed to range freely, foraging for browse and mast, putting them in direct competition with the dwindling deer population. They were attracted to the open areas of the forest: abandoned crop fields, canebrakes, and natural forest openings. They expanded these areas and increased the number of open meadows and forest clearings (Davis 1993). Later, cattle were kept by the Cades Cove settlers and were kept in the cove even in the 1990s, extending the legacy of cattle in the Appalachians that began 200 years ago.

The increase of cleared areas opened corridors for the invasive plants from Europe. A great majority of the plants that came from Europe are "weeds" in the sense that they can spread rapidly, reproduce profusely, and outcompete other plants in disturbed areas. In short, for a weed to be successful and spread over a large area, there must be open, disturbed areas, and there must be corridors to facilitate movement between these areas. Because much of Europe had been cleared for hundreds of years, disturbance-favored species eventually came to dominate the landscape. In contrast, precontact eastern America was still close-canopied forests, with small patches of cleared areas where the Native Americans farmed or the beaver dammed. In the South and the rest of the country, the cattle and swine herds, along with well-traveled trade routes, opened the landscape and provided a sufficiently disturbed habitat for the seeds of exotics to take root. White clover and Kentucky bluegrass seemed to be the forerunners of the exotic invasion, followed by barberry, Saint-John's-wort, common hemp, and many more (Crosby 1986).

While the native flora and fauna of the Appalachians were under siege from European plant and animal invaders, the native people were experiencing a population decline as a result of microbial European imports. Although the Cherokee fell ill from a number of indigenous diseases, they had never been exposed to smallpox, measles, diphtheria, whooping cough, bubonic plague, chicken pox, influenza, or myriad others to which the Europeans had long become accustomed (Crosby 1986). Smallpox is especially devastating to populations that have never been exposed. The disease can easily wipe out 50 percent of a population, and fatalities can reach up to 90 percent (Silver 1990). Traditional Cherokee remedies (such as a cold bath or a visit to the sweat lodge) only exacerbated the disease. This great loss of life had many ramifications. First, with so many ill, the Cherokee could not take care of each other, let alone their crops and livestock. Famine usually resulted when a village was hit hard by the disease (Crosby 1986). Second, when the shaman's remedies failed, the Cherokee lost faith in traditional curing methods, including herbal cures using native flora. The importance of their natural surroundings diminished in the face of so much death (Davis 1993).

In addition to disease and famine, the Cherokee were in the midst of political turmoil. Before the American Revolution, the Native Americans were involved in wars among themselves and with the French and British. British troops burned villages and crops to the ground, and the Cherokee population was decimated. After peace was finally achieved with Britain in 1769, the Cherokee were called upon to help quell the American Revolution (Davis 1993). There was much fighting between the settlers and the Cherokee, mostly for land rights. Finally in 1794, the Treaty of Calhoun created peace between the Cherokee and the white settlers and gave the Cherokee control of the land south of the French Broad River (Frost 1925). By this time, however, warfare and disease had decreased the Cherokee population significantly. As a result, the settlements became more dispersed. Davis (1993) contends that survivors of disease-ravaged villages were unable to reorganize a nucleated settlement pattern. The advent of peace itself may have contributed to the dispersal of the Cherokee villages. Before the Calhoun Treaty, Native American settlements were nucleated and organized to defend against attacks from other tribes and later from white settlers. Because the threat of warfare no longer existed, there was no need for a defensive posture.

How, then, was Cades Cove affected by cattle, swine, exotic plant species, and the changing settlement patterns of the Cherokee between 1500 and 1818? According to archival research of Brett Riggs (personal communication, October 7, 1997), the Cherokee almost certainly grazed cattle in the canebrakes at the lower end of the cove. This would have created sufficient disturbance to invite exotic plant colonization. Corroboration can be found in the travel journals of people exploring the area at this time. Major John Norton traveled through the Cherokee country in the early 1800s. He estimated that the number of cattle in the area equaled the number of people, "as in many civilized Countries" (Norton 1970:132). Norton also mentions that canebrakes were widely used to graze cattle and that cane made excellent fodder.

The area immediately surrounding the cove may have had established populations of exotic species as a result of intense cattle grazing by the Cherokee. Today, there are four grassy balds in the vicinity of Cades Cove: Parson's Bald, Gregory's Bald, Russell Field, and Spence Field. Settlers cleared Russell Field and Spence Field in the late 1800s, but Gregory's Bald has a less certain history. According to oral tradition, it has "always" been there, and balds in the area are mentioned in Cherokee legend. Several theories attempt to explain the existence of the balds. One theory states that they may have been maintained by burning by the Cherokee or earlier inhabitants of the area. In any case, without maintenance, the grassy balds soon begin to revert to forest (Lindsay 1976). It is possible that the balds were maintained first by Cherokee herders and later by Euro-American herders. It is very likely that exotic plant populations were established on the balds, providing a nearby seed bank. When the cove began to be cleared, exotic plants were in the vicinity, ready to invade.

Another related question is whether the Cherokee grew crops in the cove. If they cleared enough land by slashing and burning, they would have left fallow fields, which are ideal for many exotic plants, especially grasses. Riggs maintains that the Cherokee probably intensified their use of the cove after the Calhoun Treaty in 1794, even developing a small settlement. He estimates that around ten households could have been established in the cove. These Cherokee would have kept cattle and cleared land for crops. If this occurred, exotic species would have been firmly established in the cove, and the process of land clearing would have begun before John Oliver arrived in 1818.

EURO-AMERICAN SETTLEMENT TO THE PRESENT

John and Lucretia Oliver were the first Euro-American settlers to Cades Cove, arriving in the fall of 1818. They survived their first winter with help from the Cherokee, who supplied them with dried pumpkin. By surviving the first winter, the Olivers opened the way for others. Although the population fluctuated between 1818 and 1936, it reached a maximum of 709 in 1900 (Dunn 1989).

This dense population was a new environmental force in the cove. The settlers practiced intensive agriculture, especially after the Civil War (Chapman, personal communication, November 1997). The entire floor of the cove was cleared for crops, creating a large, open, disturbed area. Fallow hay fields were seeded with nonnative grasses, such as Timothy grass, fescue, and red clover (Davis 1993). Exotic grasses, especially fescue, continue to dominate the landscape in the cove, causing a decrease in diversity and habitat (Soehn 1997). In addition, many exotic ornamentals were introduced in the cove and can still be found growing at the old homesites (Dyer 1988).

Perhaps the greatest force of environmental disturbance was the large cattle herds. Dunn (1989) states that the number of cattle per farm was four times greater in Cades Cove than in the rest of the area. Russell Gregory, after whom Gregory Bald was named, was a rancher in the cove. He oversaw the care of hundreds of cattle grazing on the bald and surrounding mountains (Dunn 1989). In the late 1800s, Nathan Sparks was grazing at least 700 cattle on Spence Field (Davis 1993). Because cattle were allowed to range free for most of the year, they affected the entire region surrounding Cades Cove. Damage to the soil and forest is still evident. In fact, cattle grazing altered the composition of the forests around the cove. Today, pine-oak forest exists where a cove hardwood forest once stood (Bratton et al. 1980).

One event in settlement history still merits consideration, although it was not the result of direct action by the settlers: the loss of the American chestnut (*Castanea dentata*) to the chestnut blight. The value of the chestnut to the humans who have inhabited the mountains cannot be overstated. Throughout human history in the Appalachians, the chestnut was a significant dietary supplement. It was also a forage crop for wildlife and later for livestock (Davis 1993). Its wood was valuable for many necessities, and it was desirable for tannin extract used to tan leather (Woods 1957).

The blight was caused by a fungus, *Endothia parasitica,* brought to New York in 1904 on Asiatic chestnut trees. The Asian chestnuts are resistant to the fungus, but it is harmful to American and European chestnuts, essentially girdling the stricken trees. Because the fungus can be carried for long distances by animals and by wind and because it happens to be cohosted by oaks, it has yet to be eradicated. Although southern Appalachia was the last area to be infected with the fungus, the loss of the chestnut was complete. In its place are various oaks and hickories, which gradually established dominance after the demise of the chestnut (Woods 1957). Most of the chestnuts in the Appalachians died between 1920 and 1930. Wildlife and the human inhabitants suffered a great loss (Dunn 1989).

Between 1818 and 1936, Cades Cove supported a prosperous settlement. Because of the rich soil in the cove, intensive use of the land produced a bountiful annual harvest and allowed a permanent community to develop. Intensive agriculture, cattle grazing, various small industries, and the permanent presence of a high density of humans altered the landscape of Cades Cove and the surrounding area significantly. Many of these effects are still evident today and pose challenging management questions for the National Park Service.

NATIONAL PARK SERVICE MANAGEMENT OF CADES COVE

In the late 1920s, the National Park Service included Cades Cove within an area to be made a national park. Despite opposition by cove inhabitants, Cades Cove eventually was taken over by the park. Most inhabitants were forced to leave their homes, and by 1936 Cades Cove was officially a part of the Great Smoky Mountains National Park. Some inhabitants were allowed lifetime leases, but most chose to leave (Dunn 1989; Shields 1981).

When the National Park Service took over the management of Cades Cove in 1936, the original management plan was to allow the cove to revert to wilderness. Many of the old homes were destroyed or abandoned, to be burned when they became a hazard. The fields were allowed to turn into forest, erasing the signs of human presence (Dunn 1989). However, in the 1940s the Park Service realized that the appeal of Cades Cove would be lost with the last vestiges of human habitation. The cove was designated a historic district and was to be managed as such (Shields 1981).

This decision created a challenging management problem. During the 1940s, creating an appealing vista took precedence over historical accuracy; park managers decided to allow the area outside the loop road to reforest while the center would remain cleared. The fields have been kept open using a variety of means. Quasiagricultural methods such as cattle grazing and hay production are used. Mechanized mowing is also used as a primary and efficient way to clear the fields (U.S. Department of Interior 1988). These methods are not without problems, nor are they historically accurate.

For example, cattle have extremely harmful effects on soil and water quality. In the late 1990s, the number of cattle in the cove (as opposed to the adjacent balds) was excessive: One permittee had 800 cattle on 800 acres. These numbers of cattle only compound the detrimental effects of grazing and trampling. Historically, cattle were not kept in the cove center. Each settler grazed ten to twenty cattle on the hillsides and balds and in the woodlots (Soehn 1997). Some measures have been taken to alleviate stress on the watershed, such as erecting fences to keep the cattle out of streams. This alone has improved water quality in the cove (Bratton et al. 1980). Hay production removes nutrients from the soil and is devastating to wildlife, especially ground-nesting fowl. By 2000, the National Park Service was phasing out these methods in the interests of conservation as they acquired land from the remaining lessees. Mechanized mowing probably is the least harmful maintenance method, but it compromises the historic value of the cove, creates a homogeneous landscape, and disrupts wildlife (Soehn 1997; U.S. Department of Interior 1988).

More recently, fire management has been proposed to combat the exotic grass fescue. Although fescue was present in the cove during the settlement era, the Park Service and the U.S. Department of Agriculture Soil Conservation Service seeded fescue throughout the cove center in the 1950s, creating a homogeneous field landscape (Chapman, personal communication, November 1997). Fescue provides little cover for wildlife. It is also host to a fungus that causes diseases in mammals. The Park Service is attempting to remove grasses such as fescue and replace them with native grasses such as big bluestem that are adapted to a burn regime. It has been shown that native grasses offer a more diverse habitat and therefore encourage the presence of wildlife. More visible areas would be mowed only after nesting and rearing stages were over (Soehn 1995, 1997). Although native grasses are not part of the historical landscape, they offer a solid alternative to exotic grasses. In the absence of continued farming, historical accuracy is simply not possible. Because conservation is an issue, agriculturally developing the cove again would be too harmful to the ecosystems; however, presenting an environment where historical interpretation is still possible while creating a diverse habitat for wildlife seems to be a viable solution.

This form of compromise is the current trend in management. As well as removing exotic grasses, the National Park Service has proposed creating a mosaic field pattern. This would be more difficult to maintain, but it has many benefits. Historically, it would be more accurate, resembling the patchwork of crop fields (U.S. Department of Interior 1988). The mosaic could be created along old property boundaries, which traditionally were fenced using hedgerows. These would provide more shelter for many forms of wildlife, especially birds and small mammals (Soehn 1997). This is only one example of a management plan in which natural resource preservation and historic interpretation both benefit; an effort to reintroduce red wolves was another indication of changing management policies.

However, providing recreational facilities was another reason the national parks were created. Cades Cove attracts millions of visitors to the Great Smoky Mountains each year, and a great challenge to park management lies in the competing interests of tourism and conservation. For example, during September 1997, almost 400,000 sightseers visited Cades Cove (Gray 1997). The vast majority of these visitors arrived by car and toured the loop by car. According to the park's electronic information system, Smokynet, the Great Smoky Mountains National Park exceeded clean air standards several times in the summer of 1997, and the problem worsened in 1998 and 1999. Pollution is an ever-increasing problem, but the park has done little to offer an alternative to driving through the cove.

The environmental history presented in this chapter contributed to the Cultural Landscape Report (CLR), prepared by the National Park Service in the late 1990s. A CLR inventories and documents the cultural and natural resources of a particular area. Although the cove is managed to showcase the early Euro-American settlement period, accurate historical management of the landscape is difficult because of past management decisions and current management practices. The narrow historical focus also imposes limitations on landscape management. Park historian David Chapman (personal communication, 1997) anticipates that the CLR will be used to create a new management plan tailored to the specific needs and issues in Cades Cove. Ideally, benefits to wildlife, cultural and natural resources, and tourism can be maximized.

The future of Cades Cove lies in the consequences of management decisions the Park Service must make. Preserving wildlife and vegetation does not have to conflict with tourism. In fact, it may enhance a visitor's experience to hear wolves howling and rare birds calling in the evening around a campfire, even though these are sounds that early Euro-American settlers in the cove feared (Dunn 1989). The human history of the cove should not be confined to one particular era because it has spanned thousands of years. Nor should responsible management of the landscape be halted solely for historic preservation. Both the natural and cultural resources of the cove should be available for a visitor to explore so that the tapestry of human history and the evolution of the landscape can be fully appreciated.

References Cited

Bass, Quentin R., II. 1977. "Prehistoric Settlement and Subsistence Patterns in the Great Smoky Mountains National Park." Master's thesis, University of Tennessee at Knoxville.

Bratton, Susan P., Raymond C. Mathews Jr., and Peter S. White. 1980. "Agricultural Impacts within a Natural Area: Cades Cove, a Case History." *Environmental Management* 4(5): 433–48.

Cain, Stanley Adair. 1930. "The Vegetation of the Great Smoky Mountains: An Ecological Study." Ph.D. diss., University of Chicago.

Chapman, Jefferson, Paul A. Delcourt, Patricia A. Cridlebaugh, Andrea B. Shea, and Hazel R. Delcourt. 1982. "Man-Land Interaction: 10,000 Years of American Indian Impact on Native Ecosystems in the Lower Little Tennessee River Valley, Eastern Tennessee." *Southeastern Archeology* 1(2): 115–21.

Cridlebaugh, Patricia. 1984. "American Indian and Euro-American Impact upon Holocene Vegetation in the Lower Little Tennessee River Valley, East Tennessee." Ph.D. diss., University of Tennessee at Knoxville.

Crosby, Alfred W. 1972. *The Columbian Exchange.* Westport, Conn.: Greenwood.

———. 1986. *Ecological Imperialism: The Biological Expansion of Europe, 900–1900.* Cambridge, England: Cambridge University Press.

Davidson, Jean Leighton. 1983. "Paleoecological Analysis of Holocene Vegetation, Lake in the Woods, Cades Cove, Great Smoky Mountains National Park." Master's thesis, University of Tennessee at Knoxville.

Davis, Donald Edward. 1993. "Where There Be Mountains: An Environmental History of the Southern Appalachians." Ph.D. diss., University of Tennessee at Knoxville.

Dunn, Durwood. 1989. *Cades Cove: The Life and Death of a Southern Appalachian Community, 1818–1937.* Knoxville: University of Tennessee Press.

Dyer, Delce. 1988. "The Farmstead Yards at Cades Cove: Restoration and Management Alternatives for the Domestic Landscape of the Southern Appalachian Mountaineer." Master's thesis, University of Georgia at Athens.

Frost, Ralph Walter. 1925. "A History of the Cherokee Indians of the Tennessee Region from 1783 to 1794." Master's thesis, University of Tennessee at Knoxville.

Goodwin, Gary C. 1977. "Cherokees in Transition: A Study of Changing Culture and Environment Prior to 1775." University of Chicago Department of Geography. Research Paper No. 181.

Gray, Nancy. 1997. Great Smoky Mountains National Park press release. October 14.

Harmon, Paul J. 1995. "Checklist of Non-Native Invasive Species of West Virginia." West

Virginia Division of Natural Resources, Wildlife Resources Section. Technical Document 95-6.

Hudson, Charles. 1976. *The Southeastern Indians.* Knoxville: University of Tennessee Press.

Lindsay, Mary. 1976. "History of the Grassy Balds in the Great Smoky Mountains National Park." Great Smoky Mountains National Park, Uplands Field Research Laboratory, Management Report No. 4.

Linzey, Donald W., and Alicia V. Linzey. 1968. "Mammals of the Great Smoky Mountains National Park." *Journal of the Elisha Mitchell Scientific Society* 84(3): 384–414.

Mithun, Marianne. 1984. "The Proto-Iroquoians: Cultural Reconstruction from Lexical Materials." In *Extending the Rafters: Interdisciplinary Approaches to Iroquoian Studies.* Ed. Michael K. Foster, Jack Campis, and Marianne Mithun. 259–81. Albany: State University of New York Press.

Norton, John. 1970. *The Journal of Major John Norton, 1816.* Ed. Carl F. Klinck and James J. Talman. Toronto: Champlain Society.

Shields, A. Randolph. 1981. *The Cades Cove Story.* Gatlinburg, Tenn.: Great Smoky Mountains Natural History Association.

Silver, Timothy. 1990. *A New Face on the Countryside: Indians, Colonists and Slaves in South Atlantic Forests, 1500–1800.* Cambridge, England: Cambridge University Press.

Snow, Dean R. 1984. "Iroquois Prehistory." In *Extending the Rafters: Interdisciplinary Approaches to Iroquoian Studies.* Ed. Michael K. Foster, Jack Campis, and Marianne Mithun. 241–57. Albany: State University of New York Press.

Soehn, Dana. 1995. "Cades Cove Wetlands-Meadow Restoration Project, Great Smoky Mountains National Park." Progress Report for National Park Foundation. Photocopied.

———. 1997. "Proposed Management Plan for Former Hay Lease Area in Cades Cove." Great Smoky Mountains National Park. Photocopied.

U.S. Department of Interior. National Park Service. 1988. "Draft Land Management Plan for Cades Cove Historic District, Great Smoky Mountains National Park."

Woods, Frank. 1957. "Natural Replacement of Chestnut by Other Species in the Great Smoky Mountains National Park." Ph.D. diss., University of Tennessee at Knoxville.

4 Exploring 250 Years of Land Use History in Western Virginia: Viewing a Landscape through Artifacts, Documents, and Oral History

MICHAEL M. GREGORY

A patchwork of forests, croplands, and pasturage, punctuated by homes and urban centers, overlays the mountains and valleys of central western Virginia. Created by natural processes and cultural activities, this landscape records clues about numerous social and economic changes that occurred in the past 250 years. Throughout this period, farming and animal husbandry marked primary land use, and households modified and shaped the countryside in efforts to maintain or improve living standards. An example of this interplay is evident in the documentary and archaeological records related to the rural community of Denmark, located at the edge of the Allegheny Mountains in Rockbridge County, Virginia (figure 4.1).

Members of this almost exclusively white community pursued a combination of economic activities involving neighbors, the iron industry, tourism, and extralocal markets. Involvement with each placed demands on household resources and organization and necessitated responses to changing market, technological, political, and environmental conditions. Besides shaping a picturesque setting, this situation created a unique historical landscape that, when coupled with archaeological and documentary records, offers insights about past and current human behaviors and perceptions (Adams 1990; Yamin and Metheny 1996).

Just as natural and social conditions drew residents to the Denmark area, similar observations brought the community to the attention of historical archaeologists (Adams and McDaniel 1984:221–22, 226). Consideration of personal familiarity, geographic features, surface cover, and apparent social seclusion and economic isolation, among other conditions, influenced the

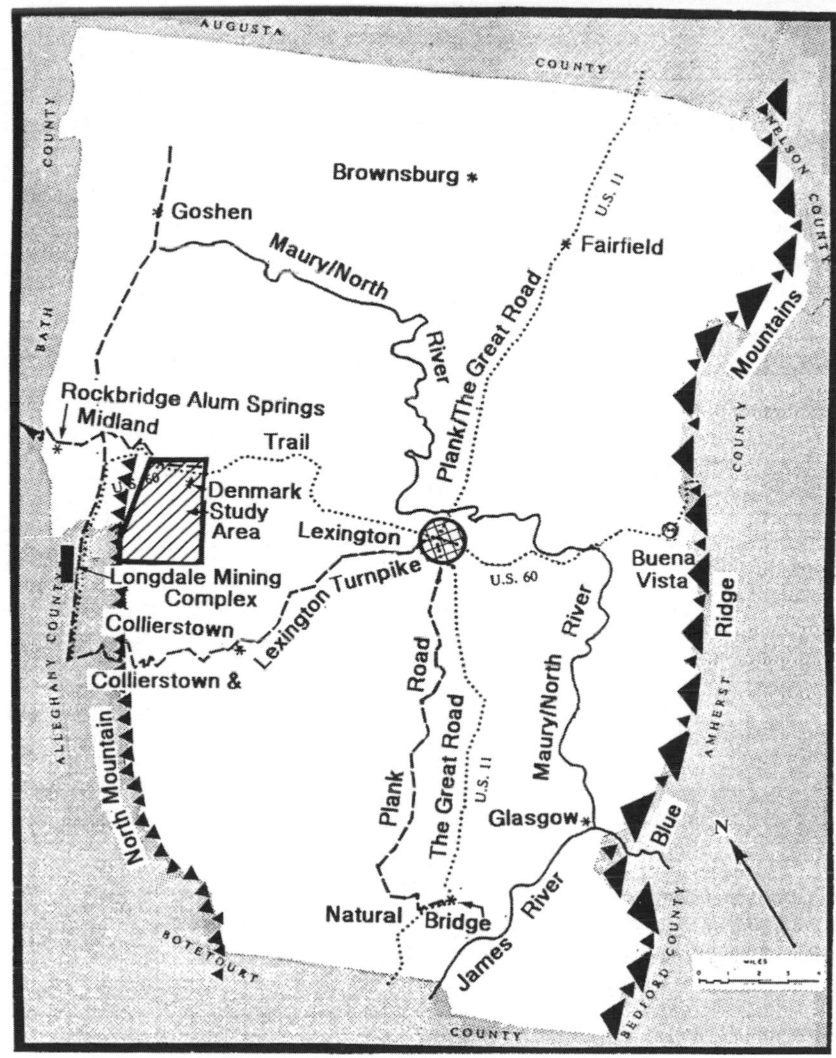

Figure 4.1. Denmark in Relation to Geographic and Cultural Features in Rockbridge County, Virginia. (Adapted from Knapp 1982:226, with permission of the Rockbridge County Historical Society.)

decision to select the area for an intensive examination of regional development (McDaniel and Adams 1984:12; McDaniel et al. 1990:192; McDaniel and Potter 1984:73). The study draws on archaeological fieldwork, archival research, and informant interviews. The resulting data provide in-depth understanding about landscape features, human behavior, and the land's influence on household economies and community networks during the late eighteenth through twentieth centuries.

Similarly, the data reveal researchers' and residents' biases regarding knowledge about local history and data sources (Adams and McDaniel 1984:226–28; Babits 1984:77–78; McDaniel and Adams 1984:16–17; McDaniel et al. 1990:194–96; G. Wilhelm 1977). Research reveals a tremendous amount of information about the roles of community institutions and residents in local, regional, and national affairs. Although seemingly isolated today, in the past the community influenced and reacted to a variety of social movements and economic trends marking America's development. In large and small ways, the landscape reflects this past while reinforcing aspects of southern Appalachia's current mystique.

AN OVERVIEW OF THE DENMARK AREA

Euro-Americans moved into the Denmark area as early as the 1770s, well after the county's initial occupation during the 1730s (Kinnear 1961:9). Native peoples openly resisted the newcomers twice with limited or sporadic raids (Phipps 1993:5), but they could do no more without a large, organized, or settled indigenous group (McDaniel et al. 1994:34). Throughout the prehistoric and early historical periods, the mountains and their drainages appear to have served as settings for little more than Native Americans' transitory activities connected to warring, foraging, hunting, and possibly ceremonial expeditions (Blanton et al. 1992:79–80; Phipps 1993:1). Later, sightings of Native Americans caused settlers to consider safety but did not greatly delay development of newly acquired lands. Archaeological data support these conclusions and suggest that by the early 1780s, the frontier had been pushed further west (McDaniel et al. 1994:137). This situation encouraged fuller regional development, including the expansion and strengthening of economic and social networks (Mitchell 1977:4–7, 175).

Geographically, the Denmark community comprises flood plains, hollows, steep slopes, and ridge tops. Together, these zones provided an abundance of subsistence resources and encouraged residents to practice a range of economic strategies. On floodplains and in limited upland areas, farmers grew corn, oats, wheat, barley, flax, potatoes, tobacco, and vegetables (U.S. Bureau of the Census 1850, 1860, 1870, 1880a, 1880b). Hillsides supported apple, cherry, and peach orchards and provided woodlots and pasturage. Similarly, wooded and grassy areas covered ridge tops, and throughout these and other zones, farmers allowed their pigs, horses, cattle, and sheep to roam. Forest or woodlots provided fuel and yielded wild game, berries, nuts, and other products for home use or exchange (Bennington 1979:5; E. Knick 1979:2). The demand for natural materials, coupled with agricultural and household output, promised a modest or better living for many residents.

In the surrounding area and neighboring counties, community members took advantage of several industries and commercial interests. Over time, these opportunities created conditions that affected the profitability of farms and the availability of jobs. Mineral springs became tourist destinations, attracting many summer visitors during the late nineteenth and early twentieth centuries (Semes 1970:48–49). During the same period, local iron mining and smelter companies operated and created further demand for workers, services, and goods (McDaniel and Ray 1984:240). In addition, towns such as Lexington, Covington, and Millboro provided access to other markets and opportunities. With time, households benefited from existing, new, or expanding market activities and contributed to the short- and long-term development of Denmark and its environs.

With prosperity, nineteenth-century Denmark became a community comprising log, frame, and brick homes; churches; stores; a merchant mill; a temperance hall; and schools. Today, very few of these features, with the exception of homes and churches, remain. Orchards and most open croplands are gone, reclaimed by forest and brush; only minimal animal husbandry, primarily cattle raising, is pursued. An automobile drive through the community reveals little about local history. The trip only reinforces an impression of isolation or seclusion. A walk through the community reveals much more about the landscape and the activities that shaped it, observations that documentary, oral history, and archaeological records enhance.

THE ANTEBELLUM ERA, CIRCA 1780–1860

The exact date when Euro-Americans initially settled the Denmark area remains uncertain, as does the nature of the occupation. The British Crown issued local land patents as early as 1771 (Rockbridge County Records Land Book [RCR LB] 1849 AA:357), and the first land transaction recorded between private parties dates to 1777 (RCR LB 1779 A:222–24). Unfortunately, land ownership and occupation may not go hand in hand; whether squatters, patentees, tenants, or later grantees initiated settlement is unknown.

Archaeological and documentary data indicate that the Denmark community began to take shape during the late eighteenth or very early nineteenth century. Dated archaeological deposits reveal the presence of settlers who participated in local and regional trade networks, and public records identify some inhabitants' early efforts to modify the landscape. Court cases involving real estate claims highlight "improvements" such as the removal of 200 trees from a disputed parcel (RCR Plat Book [PB] 1802:55–62), and land deeds reference stumps (RCR LB 1778 B:289), fields (RCR LB 1806 E:515), and fences (RCR LB 1815 J:163).

Material Culture

At the beginning of the nineteenth century, commercial networks, a degree of self-sufficiency, and community stability or growth characterized the area. The Cunningham Site (Site 44-RB-89), which yielded thousands of late eighteenth- and early nineteenth-century artifacts (Adams and McDaniel 1984:222–23; McDaniel et al. 1990:192–93), provides the first clues about local trade and commerce. Occupied as early as the mid-1770s, the site was abandoned before about 1820, when owners built a nearby brick home. Left behind is an artifact assemblage including porcelain sherds; broken cream, pearl, cane, and red paste earthenware vessels; decorated metal buttons and furniture hardware; glass goblet fragments; pipe bowl pieces; scythe parts; a thimble; and miscellaneous brass artifacts. The assemblage emphasizes day-to-day activities as well as social and consumer values. In particular, the refined ceramics highlight a rapid spread of fashionable tastes from established, eastern regions. The presence of decorated cream and pearl ware ceramics and engraved metal buttons, in the relative absence of firearm-related items (McDaniel and Adams 1984:17), signals a decreased concern for personal safety and a greater interest in comfort or fashion. This shift, together with increased farm improvements, reflects a maturing community that is producing for itself and tightening ties to eastern centers.

Communities such as Denmark achieved a high degree of self-sufficiency; however, members rarely produced items meeting acceptable fashion standards. Although the archaeological record often reveals extralocal trade and the consumer demands from which it arose, relying on the record to identify levels of household or community self-sufficiency is more problematic. Artifact preservation, reuse, or discard patterns often account for this observation. Fortunately, public records such as probate inventories and deed trusts provide at least a partial list of goods a household would have needed to function and prosper in newly settled tracts.

Although an inventory of possessions for Cunningham Site occupants has not been identified, neighbors' inventories recorded between 1806 and 1848 (Gregory and McDaniel 1996:8–9) exhibit great consistency and probably identify the basic possessions needed or desired. Excluding the presence of pewterware and the absence of ceramics, a typical inventory is that of Dennis Donahoo (table 4.1). Donahoo owned at least 176 acres near Denmark (RCR LB 1805 E:403). Like many of his neighbors, he headed a household with minimal home furnishings and farming implements (Donahoo 1806).

Specific tool kits, professional equipment, or household production implements listed in inventories such as Donahoo's suggest that households and the community furnished goods and services to neighbors. As an example, spinning wheels or looms are strong indicators of yarn or fabric production. Many home manufacturing activities probably served household and community needs rather than generating commercial goods. Women who spun, wove, or gained reputations as seamstresses resided in the area until at least the early twentieth century (Cunningham and Knick 1979:4; C. Knick 1979:5; Teaford 1962–79:62). Commercially produced fabrics were bought, as were sewing notions, but home production enjoyed a long life. This home activity is exemplified by the recovery of pins and thimbles at sites such as the Cunningham plantation. In addition, wool and flax or other raw materials were needed and, when produced locally, resulted in additional modifications to the landscape. Local wool and flax production is described in mid-nineteenth-century census and later documentary sources (C. Knick 1979:7; E. Knick 1979:5–6).

Table 4.1. 1806 Probate Inventory for Dennis Donahoo

2 mares	Seven pewter plates
2 wedges	1 bed, bedstead, & clothing
1 horse	3 quart Basons
Cutting knife & steele	1 felling ax
1 colt	3 pewter dishes
1 sheep	1 large box
2 cows	1 large pot
5 sows & pigs	1 pot & hooks
2 calves	2 pair pot hooks
1 [unreadable] iron	2 chains
1 mans saddle	1 log chain
1 pair wool shears	2 chains
2 old saddles	3 drawing chains
Notes & bonds (some for wheat & rye)	5 tins
1 spinning wheel	1 plow shovel
1 hammer	3 tins
1 large skillet & lid	1 mattock
1 spike [giblet?]	1 pepper mill
1 frying pan	2 hoes
1 auger	1 spice box
1 pewter Bason	Maul rings
2 bottles	

Source: Dennis Donahoo, Appraisal of Personal Property, Rockbridge County Records Will Book No. 2, Rockbridge County Courthouse, Lexington, Va., 1806, p. 244.

Settlement and Development

With time, documentary and archaeological records provide further evidence of evolving landscapes and economic networks. Land deeds often reference houses, buildings, fences, fruit trees, stumps, and fields. Viewed graphically, deed parcels initially reveal a mosaic of overlapping and disjointed adjacent tracts. Only after about 1840 do boundaries begin to stabilize and align with one another to reflect farms or tracts with well-defined borders that are maintained through the early twentieth century. Occupation, more intensive use of parcels, and tax considerations necessitated identification of clearly determined property lines.

During the late antebellum period (1840–60), settled areas expanded (Adams and McDaniel 1984:227). Archaeological and documentary data identify households moving up tributaries and into hollows from lower slope and bottomlands adjoining major creeks. Based on limited ceramic data from sites such as the Knick-Hughs farmstead (Site 44-RB-121), ridge hollows became attractive homesites during the 1820s through the 1850s. By the 1840s, a large population inhabited the hollows. Land deeds bear this out, as does an 1859 county map (Gilham 1859), which identifies many family names that also begin to appear in a local store ledger maintained from 1841 through 1871 (Bowen 1983).

The store ledger records a variety of transactions, identifying customers and their purchases of local and nonlocal goods. Items acquired during 1841–42 include fur hats, combs, flour, coffee, cloves, nutmeg, nails, teacups, fish, madder, books, paper, flints, indigo, bagging, hand saws, files, draw knives, and shot (Bowen 1983). Despite this commercial activity, people do not appear to have relied heavily on extralocal suppliers for goods, except to purchase luxury or exotic items. Rather, the household or the community met most subsistence needs. Community self-sufficiency existed through the antebellum era into the 1890s and perhaps a few decades longer. Home manufacturing, a cornerstone of self-sufficiency, is documented through 1880 in census manuscripts (U.S. Bureau of the Census 1850, 1860, 1870, 1880a, 1880b) and for later decades with oral histories (E. Knick 1979:9; C. Wilhelm 1979:2).

As the community developed through the late antebellum era, many farm improvements occurred and are identified by documentary records. One of the most informative sources is nonpopulation, agricultural census schedules (U.S. Bureau of the Census 1850, 1860), which provide quick overviews of household and landscape conditions. Between 1850 and 1860, the number of area farms does not fluctuate greatly, decreasing from twenty-nine to twenty-seven, but numerous changes are recorded for farm output and improvements (table 4.2). The average farm size dropped from 235 to 219 acres. Similarly, farm productivity declined, or rather fewer bushels of wheat, corn, and oats were harvested, a situation that was attributed to poor weather conditions in 1859–60.

Between 1850 and 1860, orchards were planted or matured to the point that they became a financial asset to households. The 1850 census attached no value to fruit production, but ten years later, orchards represented $545.00 in earnings to the community, or an average $20.16 for each of the twenty-seven households listed. As a source of fruit and the basis of brandy and cider vinegar production, orchards remained a component of the economy and landscape until the early twentieth century. As late as the mid-1930s, aerial photographs (U.S. Department of Agriculture 1936, 1937) revealed numerous orchards, which are not seen in later air photos (U.S. Department of Agriculture 1980).

Similarly, home manufacturing made important contributions to incomes. Whether items produced by a family served immediate household needs, entered exchange networks, or served both functions has yet to be determined. In 1850, twenty-nine area families earned an average of $30.83 each from home manufacturing, an average that more than doubled by 1860. Whether the rising value reflects an increase in the quantity or quality of goods remains unknown. After the Civil War, home production decreased, although as late as the twentieth century households continued to make shoes, leather goods, alco-

Table 4.2. Selected Agricultural Production Averages and Totals for Denmark Households, 1850–80

Census Category	1850		1860		1870		1880	
Number of households	29		27		17		59	
Total acres	235	(6,803)	219	(5,902)	331	(5,628)	176	(10,410)
Improved	86	(2,495)	105	(2,830)	222	(3,770)	93	(5,488)
Unimproved	149	(4,308)	114	(3,072)	109	(1,858)	83	(4,922)
Wheat (bu.)	151	(4,380)	128	(3,444)	389	(6,610)	135	(7,941)
Corn (bu.)	332	(9,640)	327	(8,825)	251	(4,275)	237	(13,962)
Oats (bu.)	187	(5,415)	125	(3,371)	95	(1,611)	40	(2,372)
Fruit ($)	0	(—)	20.16	(545)	22.94	(390)	9.61	(567)
Butter (lb.)	261	(7,575)	177	(4,775)	170	(2,892)	142	(8,381)
Hay (tons)	3.69	(107)	5.14	(139)	8.65	(147)	4.85	(286)
Home manufactures ($)	30.83	(894)	64.37	(1,738)	11.18	(190)	—	(—)
Meat ($)	88.10	(2,555)	90.15	(2,434)	247.70	(4,211)	—	(—)

Sources: U.S. Bureau of the Census, *Seventh Census of the United States,* Schedule 4 (Washington, D.C.: Government Printing Office, 1850), 189–96; idem, *Eighth Census of the United States,* Schedule 4 (Washington, D.C.: Government Printing Office, 1860), 92–95; idem, *Ninth Census of the United States,* Schedule 3 (Washington, D.C.: Government Printing Office, 1870), 1–4; idem, *Tenth Census of the United States,* Schedule 2 (Washington, D.C.: Government Printing Office, 1880), 799–824 and 825–52.

Note: Total acreage or production is shown in parentheses.

hol, sorghum molasses, furniture, tool handles, clothing, cloth, baskets, and coffins (Bennington 1979:3; Cunningham and Knick 1979:4; E. Knick 1979:2–3, 5; Offenbecker 1983:1; C. Wilhelm 1979:2). Unfortunately, archaeological byproducts of these activities have not been recognized in local context; however, several activities, especially sorghum molasses production, were captured on film for the period 1931–40 (Hoyt 1989).

External demand for area goods and produce existed before 1860, but the specific role of nearby business and industry, such as spas and mining complexes, in the local economy is unclear. Commercial exploitation of local iron deposits (McDaniel et al. 1997) and alum springs began in the late antebellum era, but before the benefits of either could be fully realized, the Civil War intervened. The war curtailed development of the springs but encouraged limited expansion of iron production for the Confederate cause. Before 1860, the economic and visual impact of mining and resort interests on the countryside probably was minimal. Farmers appear to have geared their production to other markets.

Resident farmer Madison Dunlap (1859) alluded to unnamed markets in a brief letter. Writing to a person who was seeking to purchase 300 bushels of corn, Dunlap stated that because of a harvest shortfall, little corn was available at the offered price (not given) because a local mill was offering eighty-five cents per bushel. Residents were not suffering great hardship from the shortage, but harvests, which in prior years yielded surpluses, were being managed more carefully. Although brief, the letter makes two implicit points: Dunlap had an eye on the market, expecting to hold his surplus until a certain profit could be made, and some local farm improvements were commercially motivated.

Regardless of how local farmers became part of the commercial market system, by the late 1850s or sooner, an adequate transportation system existed that allowed goods to be transported profitably over short and long distances (Knapp 1982). Using roads, turnpikes, rail lines, and river locks and canals, a farmer or broker could move produce from Denmark to a number of market centers. After completion of the North (now Maury) River canal and lock system in 1860 (Gilliam 1982:122), a shipment could be transported from Lexington eastward to the James River, through the James River and Kanawha canal system to Lynchburg, a rail center; to Richmond, a major flour milling center; or on to the Chesapeake Bay for more distant destinations.

If marketed for regional consumption, a crop could be transported east or west along the Collierstown and Lexington Turnpike or along the Midland Trail, among other maintained routes (Knapp 1982:224–26). Once in Lexington, goods could be sent north, down the Great Valley to Stauton or other towns via the Great/Plank Road. Despite not being directly linked to other parts of the state by rail during the antebellum or postbellum periods, Denmark residents enjoyed easy access to numerous communities and markets to the east, west, and north. The flow of goods and produce to and from the community indicates that geographic features and distance did not interfere with the local pursuit of commercial activities.

Summary: Expectations Postponed

On the eve of the American Civil War, established and expanding commercial markets stood to strengthen the Denmark economy and stimulate further improvement of the landscape. Such promise was delayed a decade or more because of the war and its aftermath. Numerous postbellum changes arose from economic opportunities created by locally generated demand dependent on extralocal conditions, such as the price of iron. With resorts, mining enterprises, and other interests demanding local produce and services, residents who put the war behind them could be optimistic about their futures and hope to improve their quality of life.

THE POSTBELLUM PERIOD: 1865 TO CIRCA 1920

The local economy rebounded and remained healthy during much of the late nineteenth century; however, by the turn of the twentieth century, the Denmark community began to experience a series of economic set backs. Prosperity had brought growth, and residents of the 1880s could boast of their several churches, schools, and stores; a mill; and a temperance hall. Construction of the mill probably occurred immediately after the war (Hotchkiss 1863; *Lexington Gazette and Citizen* [*LGC*] 1875a), when its owner anticipated better economic times as farms, neglected during four years of war (J. Knick 1864), began once more to prosper. In 1875, Ananias Smith took possession of the facility (RCR LB 1878 QQ:439–40), which included a "merchant" mill, a store house, a cooper, a dwelling, and outbuildings. Smith owned and managed the operation successfully until his death in 1897 (*Rockbridge County News* [*RCN*] 1897a).

Construction of Smith's mill did not fill a vacancy created by the failure of another mill; rather, anticipation of increasing grain production coupled with expanding markets made the location appealing. The mill filled a niche. Its position along upper Kerrs Creek, above the nearest competitors, offered readier access to commercial enterprises in northwestern Rockbridge and western Alleghany counties. Similarly, the mill benefited from more distant demands; twenty miles to the north at Millboro, Virginia, Smith's products were "handled by merchants and sold to dealers . . . from the grazing regions of Bath, Highland and Pocahontas counties [in Virginia and West Virginia] where little grain was raised" (*RCN* 1927b). Closer to home, Smith sold meal, flour, and feed to the Rockbridge Alum Springs, in addition to hauling materials, such as shingles, for the resort (Rockbridge Alum Springs 1892). Similar services may have been provided to the mines, another source of revenue.

The social and economic advantages the mines and spa offered the community were recognized throughout the late nineteenth century. These opportunities and other happenings are often mentioned in a regular community column that Ananias Smith wrote for the *Rockbridge County News* during February 1885 through mid-February 1897. Often on the road conducting business and interacting with residents, Smith was well informed about events taking place across the region. The columns—penned under Smith's name and pen names "Denmark" and "A Little Girl"—were included in a Smith family scrapbook (Smith Family Book 1861–1941; this rich source of local history will hereafter be cited as "Smith column" followed by a publication date).

Ten years after acquiring the mill, Smith (column, February 27, 1885) reported that the Victoria mines suspended operations, as did the furnace at Goshen, "very much to our [the Denmark area] regret and also to their employees." There would be no reason to regret a shutdown unless operations provided employment, a market, or both to area people. Two years later, "the people of this community [Denmark] are looking forward to a more prosperous future this year. . . . The Victoria Mines . . . will resume work in a few weeks . . . [which] will be a little bonanza to this part of old Rockbridge" (Smith column, March 18, 1887). By late 1888, county people remained interested in seeing the furnace return to operation (Smith column, December 14, 1888). Whether the furnace and certain other mining complexes ever experienced a long, uninterrupted period of operation or ran only on a sporadic basis during the 1880s has yet to be determined. Fortunately for the area, the Longdale complex, which Smith writes of less frequently, ran continuously throughout the period beginning in 1869 (Smith column, April 18, 1889).

The different mining complexes operated into the early 1920s, prompting Denmark residents to further modify the landscape with structures, roadways, and paths. The mines needed laborers, and at the Longdale complex, local men sought full- and part-time employment. Some local men worked their week, came home for the weekends (Bennington 1979:6), and returned to the job carrying enough food to last the new week. Others worked the period between harvest and planting, when the demands of farming decreased. In both cases, wagon roads and mountain footpaths facilitated travel.

Where one path and road intersect on North Mountain, an unidentified person supposedly established a bar. Here, the road makes a sharp bend, called the Barroom Bend. Archaeological survey located the Barroom Site (Site 44-RB-

193), and subsequent recovery of tumbler fragments, a shot glass, and pieces of ginger soda and alcohol bottles (Gregory 1999:197–98) identified it as a place where a person could get a drink. Leaving the barroom, the path hugs the ridge slope and is wide enough for pedestrian travel to or from the Longdale mines. Today the path may be walked a few hundred feet before it is lost from view under a graded dirt road. Together, the old road, the footpath, and the site define a specific instance of landscape modification brought about by past conditions and opportunities.

In addition to wage work, the mines gave Denmark residents an outlet for their goods and services. John U. Wilhelm, a stonemason, did a "great deal" of work throughout the late nineteenth century at many furnaces in Rockbridge and Alleghany counties (Smith column, August 8, 1895). At the turn of the century, Lee Vest sold tool handles made at his home (Site 44-RB-121) below the Barroom Site to workers at the Longdale mines (Offenbecker 1983). Farmers such as Henry Hughes, who occupied the Hayslett farm (Site 44-RB-117) and was a neighbor of Vest, sold apples and potatoes to the miners (Teaford 1962:64). Once more, the local network of roads and paths facilitated trade, linking supply with demand by efficient ridge routes, which are shorter than established lowland gap roads.

Together with the mines, the Rockbridge and Jordan Alum Springs made additional contributions to the region's prosperity. In 1880, the two springs joined under one management, becoming the Rockbridge Alum Springs (Semes 1970:49), and soon experienced a golden era spanning the 1880s through the early 1900s. Yearly, the resort hired a substantial seasonal labor force and served guests local produce. In 1888, the springs employed "a corps of good attendants and servants" (Smith column, June 8, 1888), some of whom no doubt came from Denmark and its vicinity. Two years later, management expressed a desire to spend its money with Rockbridge people (Smith column, May 1, 1890), a practice it had probably pursued for years. A news column printed four years later (Smith column, April 1894) is less ambiguous about benefits derived from the spring, stating that a good season at the spa meant a "heap of money distributed through Rockbridge county."

To operate, the Alum Springs needed a variety of services that local and nonlocal people provided (C. Knick 1979:1; Offenbecker 1983; Smith column, June 25, 1896). These included a livery proprietor, meat suppliers, a physician, a bookkeeper, a room clerk, a gardener, domestics, other suppliers, and skilled and unskilled employees. During the 1894 season, A. Smith contracted to do the huckstering. Similarly, H. T. Lindsay of lower Kerrs Creek agreed to furnish roasting ears, watermelons, and cantaloupes; his melons were renowned for their quality (Smith column, April 1894). As a result of its popularity and related needs, Alum Springs enhanced the agricultural image of the area through the early twentieth century. For example, an advertisement (RCR Chancery Causes 1896 278:81) for a Denmark farm listed the property in "a good neighborhood" within seven miles of the "celebrated Rockbridge Alum Springs . . . [which] offers a good market during the summer for farm products." Similarly, the article assures the reader that the property possesses a "good orchard."

At best, the new owner enjoyed benefits of proximity to the resort—and the mines, for that matter—for only a few years. In 1919, after a number of troubled years, Rockbridge Alum Springs closed it gates. Possibly the spa fell victim to improved sanitation conditions in southern cities, where waterborne diseases began to be controlled, and former or potential spa guests no longer felt a need to escape to cooler, healthier mountain settings. Perhaps the automobile and the personal mobility it afforded took visitors to more accessible vacation destinations rather than the out-of-the-way mountain resort reached more easily by train. Maybe the draw of the springs had run its course, and the resort fell out of fashion (Semes 1970:52–54). Examination of the topic probably will reveal multiple causes for the closing, which struck a blow to the area's established economy.

Although closing spas and mines marked a turning point in the area's economy, earlier trends foreshadowed the erosion of established subsistence and market practices. Nowhere would these events have been more recognizable than on the shelves of local stores, as now inferred from the archaeological record. Postbellum prosperity encouraged increased consumerism and participation in greater numbers of markets. Locally, goods could be acquired at several stores operating along Kerrs Creek (Bennington 1979:3; Cunningham and Knick 1979:1; E. Knick 1979:2; Smith columns, March 6, 1885 and April 3, 1890). These enterprises competed for patrons and often were short-lived (Smith column, September 1, 1892) but gave residents greater access to consumer goods close to home. Archaeological sites (Gregory 1999) have yielded decorated and undecorated refined ceramicware, coarse ceramic vessels, patent medicine bottles, nails, jewelry, buttons, horse tack, footwear, flatware, musical instruments, stove parts, farm tools, and a variety of other domestic and agricultural materials probably purchased locally or perhaps from peddlers.

Certain goods, such as vinegar bottles, ceramics, and canning jars, document changing consumer behavior and community exchange practices. By the turn of the century and certainly later, the archaeological record shows a marked increase, in both quantity and diversity, of commercially produced, nonlocal items. This is significant because previously community members had produced some of these goods. An example of this commercial replacement is cider vinegar. A person with access to a press and apples could easily produce vinegar for household use and neighborhood exchange. Sometime during the early twentieth century this practice was abandoned, like other practices reflecting self-sufficiency, and brand name vinegar gained wider acceptance. Vinegar bottles that identify brands such as "White House" suggest deterioration in the community's exchange network between 1903 and the 1930s.

Even earlier, the local earthenware and stoneware industry may have fallen victim to large commercial producers. The majority of coarse wares produced before 1870 are believed to be of local or regional manufacture (Russ 1994). These wares were distributed by canal boat (J. D. Anderson and Company 1869–70) and cart and enjoyed local patronage because of their low cost. Major commercial potteries may not have been able to compete with area potters until the arrival of rail service and subsequent lowering of freight costs. In addition, the Civil War may have altered the balance of production, permitting commercial manufacturers to enter a market where local supply could not match demand. The death of local and regional potters further reduced the availability of traditional wares. Whatever the causes, the local ceramic tradition experienced a significant reduction in scale during the 1870s through the 1880s and practically disappeared by the turn of the century (Russ 1990:466, 474, 479–83). With the demise of the traditional potter, a suite of sights and sounds—kilns, road traffic, and long-standing vessel shapes and designs—passed from the countryside, and certain ties between communities weakened.

In turn, large commercial potters may have watched their market share decrease during the late nineteenth and early twentieth centuries as canning jars became more popular. Locally, canning jars may have entered households as early as the 1870s, certainly by the turn of the century; however, their introduction did not signal an immediate threat to the traditional reliance on ceramic vessels. Conservative behavior, often a characteristic of rural life (Arpaia 1982:8; Martin 1989:23), probably ensured a transitional period before widespread acceptance. By the 1920s and 1930s, the popularity of the jars, judged by archaeologically monitored distributions, appears to have been widespread; numerous Ball, Mason, and Hazal Atlas jars, among other brand names, shared pantry space with anonymously produced stoneware crocks (Gregory 1999).

These illustrative material culture patterns highlight technological and marketing advances and possible social or demographic trends that influenced consumer decisions and selections. Throughout the period, the availability of traditionally crafted goods decreased as new products evolved, as proposed health and licensing codes became law, and as residents died or left the area for new opportunities. These conditions in turn changed features within the countryside as residents adopted new items and associated behaviors. Systems for transporting and transferring goods had to be expanded or revised, possibly reorienting the focus of transportation networks. In addition, new technologies and products may have emphasized different services, foodstuffs, and crops, allowing some established practices to survive while others were abandoned.

Because of the long-standing need for traditional skills and services, a rich supply of natural resources, and prosperity encouraged by local industrial demands, Denmark's land-poor residents who desired to live an agriculturally based lifestyle could do so. A variety of circumstances allowed these residents to pursue farming on a full- or part-time basis as tenants or hired help (Hardbarger 1898–1902; Smith columns, September 19, 1895 and February 18, 1897). Perhaps to an even greater extent than their landed neighbors, tenants and farm laborers could supplement their livelihood by peeling tan bark (Smith column, June 1, 1893; Walsh 1893); selling wild game (Smith column, December 3, 1891); picking or gathering berries and nuts, including bushels of chestnuts before the blight (Bennington 1979:5; Cunningham and Knick 1979:4; C. Knick 1979:4; *LGC* 1875b; Smith column, June 4, 1896); making handicrafts (Offenbecker 1983); and, if necessary, taking positions with local businesses. Without much effort, land-poor residents wanting to farm could cobble together a comfortable income when they gained access to woodlots, cropland, pasturage, and commercial networks.

Life as a tenant could be precarious, but some residents pursued the practice much of their lives. In actuality, leasing land may have been easy given the large size of some farms, family or social connections, and the needs of inheritors, older landowners, and the widowed. The availability of land with good terms could make tenancy an attractive way to earn a living. For the lessor, a renter or sharecropper generated income and maintained a parcel's value as long as use did not damage the soil or ground cover.

The little evidence that exists suggests that tenancy did not reduce people to substandard living conditions but allowed some families to achieve a respectable living standard (Smith column, April 11, 1895). The presence of households dependent on farm labor or tenancy added more nodes to the community's social and economic network, further modifying the landscape and placing sites and activity areas in unsuspected or unpredictable locations. Identifying these sites from surviving materials becomes a challenge (Orser 1993) important to rural landscape studies.

Whereas people willingly or by circumstances chose to remain landless or owners of marginally productive farms, some community members—prosperous and otherwise—decided to move west. This movement decreased social and economic pressures to develop unimproved land, intensify existing land use activities, construct additional homes, and organize new, perhaps smaller farms. Smith's columns relate the departure of numerous residents during the 1880s through the mid-1890s. During early 1894 (Smith column, March 15, 1894), three young men departed Denmark for Yeats City, Illinois, to farm. They brought the number of Denmark males who relocated to the Yeats City area to eight. Several months later, the youths returned to Denmark describing Fulton County, Illinois, as "the Garden of Eden for farming," a place to which they intended to return in early spring (Smith column, January 3, 1895).

Other native sons and daughters left or thought of leaving to pursue farming, business, or milling further west in Virginia, Ohio, or Illinois (Smith columns, March 29 and late June 1894). Smith identified the community of Jamestown in Green County, Ohio as "the headquarters" for Rockbridge people (Smith column, March 21, 1895) because many former county residents settled there. In some, perhaps most cases, departing people had job offers or were moving nearer to relatives and friends who left Rockbridge County. Similarly, declining farm produce prices toward the end of the century may have driven farmers west in search of more productive land and higher profits. By early 1897, Rockbridge farmers were selling meal to a local mine for approximately thirty cents per bushel, not a "big" price (Smith column, February 4, 1897), to keep a market share against western suppliers.

Throughout the late nineteenth century, people's mobility, together with their commercial interests and social relations, ensured that this headwaters area did not become a backwater community developing in isolation. For all its ruralness, Denmark enjoyed strong connections to a wider, dynamic world. Visits and letters from family and friends maintained bonds extending across the nation and throughout the region. These ties kept knowledge and news current. A. Smith received the *Chicago Herald* from the Agner brothers, who established themselves as contractors and builders in Chicago (Smith column, June 5, 1890). One can be certain that Smith followed western wheat harvests, as well as other topics, with great interest. From him, news reported in the *Herald* passed to other households as he interacted with acquaintances and customers of his mill.

Within the community, a well-developed communication network further facilitated the spread of news or gossip. The efficiency of the network is attested to by the numerous deaths Smith reported. Funeral services usually followed a death by one or two days, and services, whether held at community churches or in Lexington, often were described as well attended. For example, A. Smith's death occurred late in the evening on April 7, 1897, and the funeral service was held on April 9. Attendance at the service, performed several miles from Smith's home, was described as the largest ever seen at a similar service and included a number of members from the Lexington Lodge of Odd Fellows (*Lexington Gazette* [*LG*] 1897; *RCN* 1897a and 1897b); Smith belonged to the Denmark Lodge.

If funeral descriptions are accurate, they indicate that news spread quickly by word of mouth. Footpaths, roads, scheduled events, and day-to-day activities assisted the exchange of information about social conditions, fashion trends, market prices, political movements, technological advances, economic opportunities, and many other topics. Acting on news and gossip, community members could prepare for developing situations and shape aspects of their environment to advance or maintain their social and economic positions.

Because of a variety of advantages, the members of the Denmark community enjoyed a great deal of economic prosperity based on farming and household resources during the late nineteenth century. By the turn of the century, the agricultural or rural basis of the economy was in decline because of shifting markets (Smith column, February 4, 1897), decreasing demands (*RCN* 1927a), and government regulations (Chittum 1979:8). As the century closed, farmers were selling low in an attempt to keep their market share. Production costs eventually outstripped returns, and many residents abandoned farming. With this passing, the character of the countryside began to take on a new appearance as cropland was allowed to return to natural cover or saw new uses, and community services combined with those of other localities. The local milling industry declined until it ceased to exist in the 1930s. Smith's Mill closed during the 1920s—if not sooner—and in 1927 the mill stood "deserted," a reminder of "a past industry of the neighborhood . . . [that] will possibly go down with the work of improving the Midland Trail [US Route 60]" (*RCN* 1927b). Although these events greatly modified the visual character of the countryside, more importantly, they created a new perception of the area's past, one that does not necessarily foster the recognition of its earlier nature.

SUMMARY AND CONCLUSIONS

Changes in the landscape never came overnight; rather, they took time to express themselves and accommodated adjustments in response to changing social, political, and economic conditions. Although no single factor can account for the majority of changes influencing the historically white, Euro-American community of Denmark, greater and greater participation in nonlocal markets had a significant impact on members' wants, needs, and ability to satisfy these desires.

Throughout much of the nineteenth century, market involvement did not threaten the economic independence of the community or its households. Community self-sufficiency remained largely intact through social relations and residents' practice of diversified economic strategies. With time, indirect—barely recognizable—assaults to independence occurred, and the sum of these actions became clear in the early twentieth century when markets and technology worked in unison to sweep aside residents' false sense of economic independence.

Together, a variety of conditions reduced farmers to wage workers and, more importantly, attracted sons and daughters from farming to nonagricultural jobs. As wage-earning consumers, they exhibited little resistance to changing economic and social conditions that meant more dependable income, additional free time or entertainments, greater consumer power, and a better living standard. The landscape captured and expressed these ongoing changes: more homes, smaller farms, fewer crops, withering orchards, invading brush and secondary growth, increasing utility lines, and indoor plumbing. The countryside retained a rural feeling, but one largely divorced from its agricultural potential or former working character.

The Denmark area's shifting fortune is tied significantly to the demise of mining enterprises and resort spas, all of which failed by about 1920. Afterward, livestock raising and crop production continued to be pursued, but immediate markets shrank. Towns such as Clifton Forge and Covington provided outlets for agricultural products (C. Knick 1979:1; E. Knick 1979:6) but eventually offered more attractive work opportunities and imported foodstuffs more cheaply by rail. With these changes, land did not offer the economic security it previously held.

In addition, the automobile, the great transformer of the American scene, put draft animals to pasture, and with them went a need for grain and other feed. During the 1930s, mechanized farming retired many remaining draft teams. With these changes, the area needed filling station attendants, mechanics, salespeople, and a host of other services, which satisfied new needs and introduced new images and demands.

Today, a variety of signs record these events. Traces of a more active past use of the area are distributed across or embedded in the landscape; however, they are not always easily understood or recognized without the aid of oral history, archives, or archaeological data. Spring boxes, tree stumps, fence segments, chestnut saplings, and many other features reflect an intensive use and occupation, which mark a community that for many years remained largely self-sufficient while integrated into a larger society.

Perceptions arising from a drive through the community tell us more about ourselves than about the area's history. From an automobile, a sense of isolation marks the area, but in the past, the community was well connected to a variety of markets, movements, and ideas. Only after walking the land, talking with long-time residents, and reviewing historical records does one begin to recognize the former life of the community and the use members made of the countryside.

References Cited

Adams, James T., Jr., and John McDaniel. 1984. "A Research Design for Archaeological Interpretations of Upland Historic Sites: The Opportunities and Challenges." Proceedings of Upland Archeology in the East: A Symposium, 1981. *Cultural Resources Report* 5:221–30. Atlanta: USDA Forest Service, Southern Region.

Adams, William Hampton. 1990. "Landscape Archaeology, Landscape History, and the American Farmstead." *Historical Archaeology* 24(4): 92–101, 110–26.

Arpaia, Paul Thomas. 1982. "The Reed Organ in the Hollows." Manuscript on file, Laboratory of Anthropology, Washington and Lee University, Lexington, Va.

Babits, Lawrence. 1984. "Locating Archaeological Sites in Space, Time, and Society." Proceedings of Upland Archeology in the East: A Symposium, 1981. *Cultural Resources Report* 4:76–87. Atlanta: USDA Forest Service, Southern Region.

Bennington, Mary. 1979. Interviewed October 29 in Rockbridge County, Va. Transcript on file, Washington and Lee Anthropology Laboratory, Lexington, Va.

Blanton, Dennis B., Joseph Schuldenrein III, and Eric E. Voigt. 1992. *Phase III Archaeological Data Recovery at Site 44RB281, The Dryfoot Site, Route 602 Bridge Replacement, Rockbridge County, Virginia Project: 0602-081-151, C501*. Williamsburg, Va.: William and Mary Center for Archaeological Research.

Bowen, David C. 1983. "The Moore/Dunlap Account Book Analysis." Manuscript on file, Washington and Lee Anthropology Laboratory, Lexington, Va.

Chittum, Clyde. 1979. Interviewed November 6 at unknown location. Transcript on file, Washington and Lee Anthropology Laboratory, Lexington, Va.

Cunningham, Hattie Entsminger, and Vera Knick. 1979. Interviewed on October 30 and November 1 in Covington, Va. Transcript on file, Washington and Lee Anthropology Laboratory, Lexington, Va.

Donahoo, Dennis. 1806. Appraisal of Personal Property. Rockbridge County Records Will Book No. 2:244. Rockbridge County Courthouse, Lexington, Va.

Dunlap, Madison. 1859. Letter. Rockbridge Historical Society Manuscript Collection. Special Collections, James G. Leyburn Library, Washington and Lee University, Lexington, Va.

Gilham, William. 1859. "Map of the County of Rockbridge, Virginia Drawn by Cadet W. N. P. Otey." Baltimore: A. Hoen & Co.

Gilliam, Catharine M. 1982. "Jordan's Point—Lexington, Virginia: A Site History." *Proceedings of the Rockbridge Historical Society* 9:109–38.

Gregory, Michael M. 1999. "Transitions to Capitalism as Reflected in Archaeological and Historical Records of Rockbridge County, Virginia." Manuscript on file, Washington and Lee Anthropology Laboratory, Lexington, Va.

Gregory, Michael M., and John M. McDaniel. 1996. "The Material Culture of the Southern Backcountry: Beginnings, Growth, and Change." Paper presented at the 1996 Southern Backcountry Conference, Staunton, Va.

Hardbarger, T. W. 1898–1902. "Settlement of David Ruley Accounts." Privately owned. Facsimile of manuscript in author's possession.

Hotchkiss, Jedehiah. 1863. *Confederate Engineers Map of Rockbridge County, Virginia.* Special Collections, James G. Leyburn Library, Washington and Lee University, Lexington, Va.

Hoyt, William D. 1989. *Valley Views: Lexington and Rockbridge County, Virginia, 1924–1940.* Privately printed, n.p.

J. D. Anderson and Company. 1869–70. "J.D. Anderson and Co. Freight Blotter." Canal Records. Rockbridge County Court House, Lexington, Va.

Kinnear, D. Lyle. 1961. "Some People and Events in the Early History of Timber Ridge Community." *Proceedings of the Rockbridge Historical Society* 5:8–14.

Knapp, John W. 1982. "Trade and Transportation in Rockbridge: The First Hundred Years." *Proceedings of the Rockbridge Historical Society* 9:211–31.

Knick, Clara. 1979. Interviewed October 31, at unknown location. Transcript on file, Washington and Lee Anthropology Laboratory, Lexington, Va.

Knick, Elmer. 1979. Interview conducted on unspecified date at unknown location. Transcript on file, Washington and Lee Anthropology Laboratory, Lexington, Va.

Knick, James. 1864. Letter from Camp Champ [Chonp?] dated February 21. Hand copied and privately owned. Facsimile in author's possession.

Lexington Gazette [Va.] (*LG*). 1897. Obituary: Ananias Smith. April 14.

Lexington Gazette and Citizen [Va.] (*LGC*). 1875a. "Property Sale." July 2.

———. 1875b. "Good News for Timber Ridge." July 2.

Martin, Ann Smart. 1989. "The Role of Pewter as Missing Artifact: Consumer Attitudes toward Tablewares in Late 18th Century Virginia." *Historical Archaeology* 23(2): 1–27.

McDaniel, John, and James Adams. 1984. "The Research Area Approach to Historic Sites in Western Virginia." In *Historical Archaeology West of the Blue Ridge: A Regional Example from Rockbridge County.* Ed. John M. McDaniel and Kurt C. Russ. 12–22. The James G. Leyburn Papers in Anthropology, No. 1. Lexington, Va.: Liberty Hall Press, Washington and Lee University.

McDaniel, John, James T. Adams Jr., and Randall Ray. 1990. "Archaeological Interpretations of Upland Historical Sites in Rockbridge County: The Opportunities and Challenges." *Proceedings of the Rockbridge Historical Society* 9:191–202.

McDaniel, John M., and Parker B. Potter. 1984. "A Review of Historic Site Work Conducted by Washington and Lee University over the Last Decade." Proceedings of Upland Archeology in the East: A Symposium, 1981. *Cultural Resources Report* 4:67–75. Atlanta: USDA Forest Service, Southern Region.

McDaniel, John, and Randall Ray. 1984. "Economic Insights from the Archaeology in the High Hollows." Proceedings of Upland Archaeology in the East: A Symposium. *Cultural Resources Report* 5:238–45. Atlanta: USDA Forest Service, Southern Region.

McDaniel, John M., Kurt C. Russ, and Parker B. Potter Jr. 1994. "An Archaeological and Historical Assessment of the Liberty Hall Academy Complex, 1782–1803." The James G. Leyburn Papers in Anthropology No. 2. Lexington, Va.: Liberty Hall Press, Washington and Lee University.

McDaniel, John M., Katharine C. Stroh, Chase A. Karsman, and Charles E. Mason. 1997. "Archaeological Investigation of Longdale Iron Mining Complex and Outlying Features, Alleghany County, Virginia." Manuscript on file, Washington and Lee Anthropology Laboratory, Lexington, Va.

Mitchell, Robert. 1977. *Commercialism and Frontier, Perspectives on the Early Shenandoah Valley.* Charlottesville: University Press of Virginia.

Offenbecker, Alice Vest. 1983. Interviewed on February 26 at Covington, Va. Notes on file, Washington and Lee Anthropology Laboratory, Lexington, Va.

Orser, Charles E., Jr. 1993. "Profits in the Fields: Farm Tenancy, Capitalism, and Historical Archaeology." Paper presented at the School of American Research Advanced Seminar on the Historical Archaeology of Capitalism, Santa Fe, N.Mex.

Phipps, Sheila. 1993. "'In the Excited State of Public Feeling': Cornstalk and the Virginia Backcountry." Manuscript on file, History Department, College of William and Mary, Williamsburg, Va.

Rockbridge Alum Springs. 1892. Ledger. Rockbridge Historical Society Collection: Rockbridge Alum Springs Papers. Special Collections, James G. Leyburn Library, Washington and Lee University, Lexington, Va.

Rockbridge County News [Va.] (*RCN*). 1897a. "Death of Ananias Smith." April 8.

———. 1897b. untitled. April 15.

———. 1927a. "Shenandoah National Park to Be a Magnet to Attract to Virginia." January 20.

———. 1927b. "Twelve Living Children Attend Family Reunion of Mrs. Ananias Smith." Circa September 13.

Rockbridge County Records (RCR) Chancery Causes. 1778–1980. "Decided Cases" with separate index. Rockbridge County Courthouse, Lexington, Va.

Rockbridge County Records Land Books (RCR LB). 1778–1980. "Deed Books" A–Z, AA–ZZ, and 53–384 with separate indices. Rockbridge County Courthouse, Lexington, Va.

Rockbridge County Records Plat Books (RCR PB). 1778–1811. "Plat Book" 1 unindexed. Rockbridge County Courthouse, Lexington, Va.

Russ, Kurt C. 1990. "Traditional Pottery Manufacturing Industry in Virginia: Examples from Botetourt and Rockbridge Counties." *Proceedings of the Rockbridge Historical Society* 10:453–90.

———. 1994. Personal Communication: coarse ware ceramic identifications. Recorded by Michael M. Gregory; notes in author's possession.

Semes, Robert Louis. 1970. "Two Hundred Years at Rockbridge Alum Springs." *Proceedings of the Rockbridge Historical Society* 7:46–54.

Smith Family Book. 1861–1941. Family Scrap Book. Privately owned. Facsimile of news articles, photos, and official documents in author's possession.

Teaford, Cleopatra. 1962–79. Recollections of life on the headwaters of Kerrs Creek, also referred to as the Teaford Diary. Privately owned. Facsimile of handwritten and typed manuscripts in author's possession.

U.S. Bureau of the Census. 1850. "Schedule 4: Productions of Agriculture in District 51½ in the County of Rockbridge State of Virginia during the Year Ending June 1, 1850." *Seventh Census of the United States.* 189–96. Washington, D.C.: Government Printing Office.

———. 1860. "Schedule 4: Productions of Agriculture in the 5th District in the County of Rockbridge in the State of Virginia." *Eighth Census of the United States.* 92–95. Washington, D.C.: Government Printing Office.

———. 1870. "Schedule 3: Productions of Agriculture in Kerrs Creek Township in the

County of Rockbridge in the State of Virginia." *Ninth Census of the United States.* 1–4. Washington, D.C.: Government Printing Office.

———. 1880a. "Schedule 2: Productions of Agriculture in Buffalo Township in the County of Rockbridge, State of Virginia." *Tenth Census of the United States.* 799–824. Washington, D.C.: Government Printing Office.

———. 1880b. "Schedule 2: Productions of Agriculture in Kerr's Creek Dist. in the County of Rockbridge, State of Virginia." *Tenth Census of the United States.* 825–52. Washington, D.C.: Government Printing Office.

U.S. Department of Agriculture. 1936. "Rockbridge County Aerial Photographs": Series BV-3-96 and BV-3-98. Soil Conservation Service, Lexington, Va.

———. 1937. "Rockbridge County Aerial Photographs": Series BV-21-28, BV-21-30, BV-21-31, BV-21-37, BV-21-38, and BV-21-40. Soil Conservation Service, Lexington, Va.

———. 1980. "Rockbridge County Aerial Photographs." Soil Conservation Service, Lexington, Va.

Walsh, Patrick. 1893. "He Fought with Jackson." *Chronicle,* n.d. Augusta, Georgia. Reprinted in the *Rockbridge County News,* June 29. Lexington, Va.

Wilhelm, Clarence. 1979. Interviewed during October at unknown location. Transcript on file, Washington and Lee Anthropology Laboratory, Lexington, Va.

Wilhelm, Gene, Jr. 1977. "Appalachian Isolation: Fact or Fiction?" In *An Appalachian Symposium.* Ed. J. W. Williamson. 77–91. Boone, N.C.: Appalachian State University Press.

Yamin, Rebecca, and Karen Bescherer Metheny, eds. 1996. *Landscape Archaeology: Reading and Interpreting the American Historical Landscape.* Knoxville: University of Tennessee Press.

PART 2 Sense of Place

Loyal Jones included love of place in a now-classic enumeration of Appalachian values first published in 1972. During the intervening years, human geographers, folklorists, cultural anthropologists, and environmental psychologists have produced a rich literature that explores how physical space is transformed into culturally constituted place as humans use it, structure it, and attach meaning to it in the course of everyday activities. Traditions bind the members of families and communities to forebears who have called the same places home, but place making encompasses additional layers of meaning beyond the genealogical and historical. Individual members of place-based communities are socialized into a shared ethnoecology as they gain intimate knowledge of their physical surroundings and attach cultural meanings and valuations to their surroundings: landforms that have become landmarks, flora and fauna of utilitarian or intrinsic interest, pure air and water, and the land itself.

Each ethnographic account in this section illustrates some part of the multifaceted dimensions and processes through which geographic space and natural resources become a culturally meaningful place. But on a darker note, each also describes struggles to maintain local claims to place in the face of extralocal counterclaims that would appropriate space and resources for other purposes. These counterclaims include government stewardship of park resources to benefit a national constituency, state support for West Virginia's coal industry and corporate plans for postindustrial economic development, and American Electric Power's exporting electricity from Appalachia to satisfy desires of urban consumers in eastern Virginia and the nation's capital.

Michael Ann Williams describes the enduring nature of place attachment that is renewed annually in homecoming rituals. Rather than diminishing through the years as people who lived in Cades Cove, Cataloochee, and other vacated communities passed on, a transgenerational stewardship of homeplace has emerged, and the contest between that stewardship and bureaucratic stewardship continues. In reciting the history of displacement from the Great Smoky Mountains National Park and its legacy, Williams makes it clear that the sentiments outsiders attribute to anti-environmentalism are in reality a protest against the bureaucratic arrogance that erases local culture to refashion "natural" space.

Mary Hufford offers a revealing glimpse at local environmental stewardship in the mixed mesophytic forest of West Virginia. She adds her voice to the voices of citizen activists who challenge the use of mountaintop-removal strip mining to "improve" sites for postindustrial commercial use, seemingly without compunction, regret, or even awareness that cultural survival is at issue. A case in point is the multiple symbolic and utilitarian ways in which ginseng intersects the lives of West Virginia collectors. Bureaucratic conservation regulations are ironic, to say the least, in that government regulates traditional harvest while ignoring wholesale destruction of ginseng and ginseng habitat through strip mining and development. The proposal to reverse this "undevelopment" of local commons serves as a powerful parable, for flourishing ginseng is an index of forest health just as lively canaries in underground mines once assured miners of breathable air. Hufford observes that heritage preservation is a counterpoint to development; both are undergirded by narratives of progress that discount or denigrate Appalachian people's attachment to place.

Along the pathway of power transmission lines from the West Virginia coal fields to the Atlantic seaboard are deeply rooted southwest Virginia farming communities whose integrity is threatened by population growth and development in distant cities. Melinda Wagner describes ethnographic studies of cultural attachment to place and land that were used to contest another narrative of progress: classic modernization theory's construction of polar oppositions between modern cosmopolitan societies and traditional rural communities, whose rootedness in place becomes a symptom of backwardness and isolation. This framework assumes that modernization breaks down local traditionalism as mobility increases, social networks expand, and national reference groups eclipse local social ties. Place attachment, conceived within this framework, becomes the mental dimension of being place-bound through lack of physical, social, and economic participation, another symptom of deprivation and pathologically underdeveloped capacity to cope with modern life.

Each chapter in this section counters this simplistic equation of rural life with backwardness by offering insight into sentiments and values via the ethnographer's account of what people say and what they do. It becomes clear that attachment to the Great Smokies remains a central part of personal identity for descendants who never lived in North Carolina or Tennessee. West Virginia coal miners have been caught up in industrialization and the ebb and flow of the global economy while retaining intimate knowledge and relationship with the nearby forest. Craig and Giles County citizens participate in an urban world of work and public affairs while remaining rooted in the ecosystem of their rural homeplace. Systematic collection and analysis of verbal accounts—conversational exchanges, formal interviews, and traditional oral genres—is a crucial component of the cultural sciences. Verbal communication in storytelling and less structured talk dominates the symbolic interaction through which cultural insiders express, teach, share, and renew their ties to one another. This is the primary avenue through which offspring, newcomer residents, and outsider researchers can become steeped in the cultural heritage of unfamiliar places.

5 "When I Can Read My Title Clear": Anti-Environmentalism and Sense of Place in the Great Smoky Mountains

MICHAEL ANN WILLIAMS

Cultural stereotypes of southern Appalachians often are contradictory. This is certainly the case in portrayals of Appalachians' attitudes toward the natural environment. Appalachians, or at least non-Cherokee Appalachians, sometimes are represented as being exploiters of the environment; at the same time, they also may be characterized as having a strong sense of place. In the past half century, local anti-environmentalist sentiments have developed in parts of the Great Smoky Mountains region of southern Appalachia. Although these sentiments may be based to some degree in traditional attitudes toward the natural environment, they also develop because of, rather than despite, a strong sense of personal affiliation with the mountains. An examination of local history and federal policy can help illuminate the interplay between sense of place and the development of anti-environmental sentiment.

The cultural history of the Great Smoky Mountains region is marked by two major removals of the local population: first, the erosion of Cherokee claims to the mountains beginning in the late eighteenth century and culminating with the Cherokee Removal of the 1830s, and then, a century later, the removal of the local population to create the Great Smoky Mountains National Park, the largest park removal in the history of our country. Coming hard on the heels of the park removals was yet another removal of the local population with the Tennessee Valley Authority's (TVA's) construction of the Fontana Dam in the 1940s. Most families who have lived in the Smokies for generations, Cherokee or non-Indian, have been touched in some way by these federally sponsored removals.

The environmental attitudes of the white usurpers of Cherokee land have been directly contrasted with those of the native population. It should be noted, however, that the pressure of white settlement was only one of the federal government's motivations in the Cherokee Removal and that the region adjacent to the Smokies was considered the least desirable of the Cherokee lands. The relative lack of desirability of mountain land was a factor in the federal government's permitting a small fraction of the Cherokee to stay in western North Carolina, both in exempting the Qualla Indians from removal and in not finding it cost-efficient to seek out every fugitive hidden in the mountains (Neely 1991:20–22; Finger 1984:28–29). At least some of the white settlers of the Smokies came into direct contact with the native population, and some aspects of their traditional stewardship were passed from one cultural group to the other.

Stereotypes of the "Scotch-Irish" have often been used to characterize the white settlers' attitudes toward the environment. This cultural group has often been portrayed as wild and restless, drawn inexorably to marginal lands they were intent on conquering. However, people of Northern Irish heritage made up only a quarter to a third of the European-American settlers in the Smokies. The cultural heterogeneity of this group alone is enough to defy easy stereotypes. More broadly, the belief system of all the European-American settlers might be contrasted with traditional Cherokee beliefs. Certainly Christianity does not preach harmony with nature to the extent of the native belief system, although many Cherokee have reconciled both belief systems (Albanese 1984; Neely 1991:64). If the European-American settlers felt that they were masters of their environment, the reality of living in the mountains must have soon tempered these beliefs.

More to the point, even if the non-Indian settlers had wanted to exploit the environment, their ability to do so was limited by the difficulty of transportation. During the nineteenth century extraction of natural resources was limited. Only in the final years of the century did the construction of the railroad, long delayed by terrain and politics, allow more than local timbering and mining (predominantly of copper). However, as the potential for these industries developed, the land exploited passed quickly out of local hands to those of large northern-based industries (see Eller 1982:86–127). Most local people, both Cherokee and non-Indian, participated in the timber boom only as laborers. For the first time many were earning cash wages. Although they temporarily had more money than ever before, many were ultimately left poorer by the boom-and-bust economy of the timber industry.

In the southern mountains, commerce and tourism developed hand in hand. The opening of the Buncombe Turnpike in 1827 not only permitted goods to be transported in and out of western North Carolina but also brought the first summer people from the lowland South into the region. Commerce and tourism developed exponentially with the coming of the railroads in western North Carolina and eastern Tennessee. During the early twentieth century the timber companies built lines deep into the mountains. Excursion cars sometimes were attached to these railroads, and tourist accommodations were developed in tandem with the timber camps.

As visitors and tourists began to flock into the mountains in the late nineteenth century for reasons of health (particularly the treatment of tuberculosis) and recreation and to view the stunning scenery, concern for the preservation of the Smokies grew (Carpenter 1985). However, the movement for a national park, which began in earnest in the 1920s, was also fueled by business concerns. One of the most effective groups of park promoters was the Knoxville-based Great Smoky Mountains Conservation Association, made up predominantly of businesspeople and professionals with ties to the local chamber of commerce and automobile association (Campbell 1960:12–24). Many of these businesspeople must have seen the demise of the timber boom on the horizon, and they sought the region's economic salvation in the tourists who could be brought not by the railroad but by the automobile. The creation of the park was linked strongly to the "Good Roads" movement.

The linking of environmental conservation with commerce had consequences. Its legacy is felt today as the National Park Service struggles to manage what is now the country's most popular national park. The irony of this linkage probably was not lost on one park supporter, writer Horace Kephart. Troubled by ill health and alcoholism, Kephart fled St. Louis in 1904 and settled in "this wild east," the Great Smoky Mountains. When Kephart first settled along Hazel Creek in Swain County, North Carolina, he found almost nothing written on the Smokies. His work, *Our Southern Highlanders,* first published in 1913, was instrumental in piquing interest about the region and about southern Appalachia in general. In 1910, the timber industry, in the form of the W. M. Ritter Lumber Company, followed Kephart into his little corner of the Smokies, setting up operation along Hazel Creek. Kephart himself resettled in Bryson City, the county seat, and during the 1920s became one of the major advocates for the creation of the park. Kephart warned that a "leviathan," the timber industry, would consume the mountains. However, he did recognize that the park would also disrupt the lives of the "highlanders" he wrote about and bring the type of progress that he himself felt the necessity to flee. In a letter to his son, Kephart wrote, "Within two years we will have good roads into the Smokies, and then—well, then I'll get out" (Ellison 1976:xlv). Horace Kephart died in an automobile accident in 1931 before he could escape the coming of the new roads.

If the creation of the park could preserve, or rather reinvent, wilderness, at the same time making it tamer and more accessible, promoters believed it could also better the lives of the people in the region by bringing business to the Smokies. Less consideration was given by the majority of the park promoters to those whose families had lived for generations within the proposed boundaries of the park. More than 700 farm families and an uncounted number of tenants lost their homes in the subsequent park removals.

As the park histories insist, by the time the park was authorized, the majority of the land within the Smokies was owned by a few timber companies (Campbell 1960:12). They would not have relinquished the land so readily if the industry had not already peaked in the region. Much of the prime timber had already been hauled out of the mountains. The farm families tended to live at lower elevations in the coves and valleys that provided the best agricultural land. Many, such as those in Cades Cove, were promised by promoters that their lands would not be acquired for the park. Many felt powerless to fight when their land was taken by eminent domain. In some cases, the borders of the park were deliberately manipulated, taking the homes of those who were seen as "undesirable" (Brown 1990). Ironically, despite the motives of local promoters who wanted to bring business to the region, among those whom the Park Service deemed "undesirable" were local people who wanted to establish commercial enterprises at the park's gates (Becker 1998:428–31).

A few landowners with means fought back. Among them was John Oliver, a descendant of one of the first white settlers in Cades Cove. As a progressive businessperson, Oliver was expected to go along with the park plans. However, not only did he not happily relinquish his several hundred acres in Cades Cove, but he fought the loss of his land through the legal system for years (Dunn 1988:248–54). Sixty years later, the college-educated Oliver was portrayed by a park interpreter in an evening campground program as an ignorant hillbilly who could not accept progress (Williams 1995:152).

Progress, in the form of the railroad and timber industry, brought environmental degradation of the Smokies, but those who paid the greatest price for the creation of the park were accused of not being progressive enough. It was the local landowners, many of whom continued to farm their properties in a manner largely unchanged over the generations, who lost their homes. The hardship was exacerbated by the fact that the removals took place in the early years of the Great Depression, and little relocation support was offered by the federal government (Whittle 1934). Some, of course, were just as happy to sell out. Sixty years later, former Smokies resident Celia Baxter recalled, "We was glad to get out. Didn't get much for it. We didn't have many acres. . . . [My husband] just wanted to get out somewhere where he could make a living. Because we just had a little rocky farm" (C. Baxter 1994). However, disbelief, a sense of betrayal, and bitterness were also common emotions. Bonnie Meyers, who sixty years later worked in the Visitor Center in Cades Cove, where she was raised, recounted her mother's feelings. "My mother even cooked meals for these people that were dealing for the state. She put them up in her house, fed them, cooked meals for them, and all the time they were saying that we don't want your homes and your farmland. Betrayal, yes, it's sad." However, Meyers adds her own coming to terms with the park, "But as it comes on down to the end of the line, I'm glad that, you know, it's like this for people to see" (Meyers 1993).

Tenancy was offered as an option to some landowners in exchange for a reduced price for the land. Some clung to their land by accepting this deal from the government. However, with the removal of businesses, schools, and the support of neighbors, life in the Smokies was no longer feasible for many families, and many of the tenants soon left. One of the few groups that benefited from the deal were the owners of summer homes at Elkmont, on the Tennessee side of the park. With access to greater legal expertise and political clout, these tenants negotiated and renegotiated their leases for the summer homes they built at two social clubs along the rail lines of the Little River Lumber Company. Only in 1992 did these "cabin holders" lose their leases at Elkmont (Thomason and Associates 1993).

One manifestation of the park removals was distrust of the federal government. Southern Appalachians are apt to be stereotyped as distrustful and less than law-abiding. However, the historical and political experience of many in the region shaped these attitudes. In the Smokies, local landowners discovered that their government could, and would, take the land that had been in the family for generations, even if they did not want to sell. Tenants and those who remained near the park boundaries also found a plethora of new regulations controlling their relationship with the natural environment. The tenant within the park could no longer shoot the bear raiding the chicken house. Not only were hunting and fishing regulated or prohibited, but so was the digging of ginseng and the gathering of ramps and other wild plants within the park boundaries. Is it any wonder that many local people came away with the feeling that the animals and plants of the forest had more rights than they did?

To the people who for generations saw the wilderness as both a resource and an adversary, the natural order of things was being destroyed. For some, this sense of order, of human over animal, was confirmed by their religious beliefs. This sense of order is clear in the most famous poem written by vernacular poet Louisa Walker. Louisa Walker was one of the five Walker sisters of Little Greenbrier, Tennessee, who became the best known lessees in the park. By persisting in their traditional lifestyle in the log home in which they were raised, they became tourist attractions. The sisters, in turn, made a modest income by peddling crafts and poems to the visitors.

In the final verses of her poem, "My Mountain Home" (Madden and Jones 1977:18–19), Louisa Walker finds solace in having a title in heaven, drawing perhaps on the sentiments of the hymn "When I Can Read My Title Clear," found in *The New Harp of Columbia,* the most commonly used shape-note songbook on the Tennessee side of the Smokies. Despite this solace, her bitterness is evident:

For us poor mountain people
They don't have a care
But must a home for
The wolf the lion and the bear

But many of us have a title
That is sure and will hold
To the City of peace
Where the streets are pure gold

There no lion in its fury
Those pathes ever trod
It is the home of soul
In the presence of God

When we reach the portles
of glory so fair
The Wolf cannot enter
Neather the lion or bear

And no park Commissioner
Will ever dar
To desturbe or molest
Or take our home from us there.

Other former residents needed no religious justification. They were simply astonished that human concerns were taking second place to concern for the creatures of the woods. In 1950, Robert H. Woody, a professor at Duke University who was born in Cataloochee, wrote in the *South Atlantic Quarterly,* "The birds and beasts of the forest needed a home. In short, the people were to be moved and improved; the land returned to the bear, the fox, the wild turkey, not to mention the copperhead and the rattler" (Woody 1950:8).

For many the grief of losing a home could not be assuaged. Some refused to set eyes on their former homes, even when they relocated to communities just outside the park. However, a more common reaction was to make a ritual of homecoming. The act of homecoming began soon after the park removals. Linguist Joseph Hall, who studied the speech and stories of the Smokies, described such homecomings in 1940: "Great numbers return for the homecoming held in each cove or other districts where a settlement once existed. This yearly event draws many people from distant places. The good attendance bears witness to their affection for their former homes. In Cades Cove I was told by the local fire-guard that a certain family returned frequently, as often as every two or three weeks in the summertime, and sat on the site of their former mountain-side home drinking water from the nearby spring and eating wild strawberries which run rampant over the place" (Hall 1940). In some cases, homecoming was a private act carried out by individuals or nuclear families. However, homecomings also took more institutionalized shape in the form of large family reunions within the park and in annual church homecomings.

Annual community homecomings also began soon after the park removals. In 1941, according to a park superintendent's report, 678 people attended a homecoming at Cataloochee; another 600 people held a reunion at Smokemont the same summer day. In the years that followed, the gas rationing of World War II took its toll on the homecomings. Still, attendance stayed above 200 at the Cataloochee homecoming in 1942 and 1943, and the event found renewed life in the postwar years. Not all attendees were pleased with what they found. Of the 1950 homecoming at Cataloochee, Professor Woody (1950:17) writes, "Homecoming on Cataloochee strikes a contrast between happy memories and the drab present. The Palmers and the Caldwells, the Messers and the Bennetts have departed. . . . Only when those with the happy memories are gone will the present Cataloochee seem better than the old." As those who intimately knew the community passed away, Woody believed that the "time approaches when these reunions must cease" (Woody 1950:10).

Professor Woody was wrong in his estimation. More than fifty years later, the homecoming at Cataloochee rivals the size of the 1941 reunion. Hundreds of people attend, despite the fact that the reunion is not publicized, and the National Park Service itself is protective of the event in an attempt to discourage the casual visitor. Unlike the far better-known Cades Cove, Cataloochee itself is far from the main park entrances. Its current isolation belies the fact that Cataloochee was once a prosperous community located on the first major wagon road through the Smokies. Today the long winding road up to Palmer Chapel does not seem to discourage the hundreds of former residents and park descendants from making an annual pilgrimage. On a date earlier in the year, a smaller number travel even further up a dirt road (on other days of the year access to the road is barred by a locked gate) to the homecoming at Little Cataloochee. Aged former residents are helped up the steep hill to the church that is the center of the homecoming.

If the various forms of homecoming were once a means of coming to terms with grief and dislocation, they are now a celebration of place and family. The majority of those who now attend are direct descendants of park families but did not themselves live in the former communities. The bitterness of the removals, though still held in the hearts of some of the surviving former residents, has dissipated among the generations of most park descendants. At the homecoming, attitudes toward the federal government, the park service, and environmentalism are as disparate as they are in the general public. What draws those in attendance together is their strong sense of place.

If the attitude of the former residents of the Smokies toward nature were as antagonistic as stereotypes would have us believe, how did they bequeath to their families such an abiding connection to this place? Most former residents would insist that they loved the mountains and loved the nature that surrounded their former homes. However, they do not feel that stewardship of the land warranted that their homes be taken from them. It was not traditional attitudes but the federal government's act of redefining their homes and communities as wilderness that pitted the former residents against environmentalism (though not necessarily against the environment itself). Those who profited from the creation of the park were not just the birds and the beasts but also the largely urban and affluent tourists who needed to seek a bit of wilderness in the eastern United States and the businesspeople in the cities and towns immediately outside the park's boundaries.

Although their sense of place encompasses the mountains and the more immediate natural environment, the former residents and the park descendants cling especially to the cultural remnants left behind in the national park. In creating the three eastern parks authorized in the 1920s, the National Park Service intended to return the formerly occupied land to wilderness, removing evidence of human occupation. Only the most sensitive cultural artifacts, the cemeteries and some churches, were likely to be given a reprieve from destruction. In the Smokies (unlike in Mammoth Cave and Shenandoah), there was some backing away from this official stance. Although initially houses were burned or salvaged, by the mid-1930s claims were being made within the Park Service for the "unique" culture of the Smokies, and efforts were made to preserve and present traditional culture. Still, this interpretation was highly selective, preserving an image of the pioneer past, not life as it was lived during the time of the removals.

The "past" portrayed by the Park Service in the Smokies is a mythic American past, not the highly personalized past celebrated at the homecomings. Most evidence of twentieth-century habitation was swept away and with it the majority of old homes and other structures. As Bonnie Meyers notes of Cades Cove, "All those [frame] houses were torn down. They left the cabins, you know, more pioneerish. . . . [Visitors] can't believe that people used to be here and you had schools and stores and churches and stuff like that" (Meyers 1993). As Joseph Hall observed, empty homesites became the sites of some family homecomings. As unnatural as the park removals were in themselves, visiting homesites where the dwelling itself had been torn away became an accepted part of regional tradition. Affection for the "homeplace" tended to focus on the place, not the physical structure (Williams 1991:135–36). Still these were cultural, not natural places. Old fencerows, the remaining signs of fields and gardens, and the daffodils that bloom around homesites lingered and marked the presence of former homes.

Even for the few families who have a physical structure to visit, the dwelling alone is not the sole focus of homecoming. As unsentimental as Celia Baxter remains about her and her husband's relocation from the Smokies to central Kentucky, Mrs. Baxter and some sixty members of her family now gather in the Smokies every fall for a family reunion. Part of the family ritual is the visit to Paper Baxter's homeplace, a small log home located near the Maddron Bald Trail. In the past the children were shown the former location of the garden, the pigpen, and the structures that made this place a farmstead. The family still visits the site of the home of James and Celia Baxter nearby, now marked just by a hedgerow. A few members of the family take the arduous hike to the "upper place," where Granny Baxter's family lived before she was born. An old chimney, the foundation of an apple cellar, and a family cemetery mark this site. Even in her eighties, Mrs. Baxter has made this hike, with her family carrying a lawn chair so she could rest along the way. As her daughter-in-law, Lee Baxter (1994), explains, "There wasn't going to be anything that would hinder her from going up there. . . . It was just like her heart's desire to once more—one more time, see that gravestone. Her brother Philip's gravestone."

Although none of Celia Baxter's children or grandchildren has ever lived in the Smokies region, the sense of place has been transferred from one generation to another in the act of homecoming. The sentiment of John Baxter (1994), Celia Baxter's youngest son, speaks for many who make this sort of pilgrimage: "And yet, when we get that close, in terms of miles, to the log cabin and to the apple cellar . . . the hedgerow, the graveyard, we want to just go back up there and stand there and look and think, 'My Daddy, he lived right here. And he walked and played right here. And people that have been kin to people that I know—this has been part of their home.'"

As the park descendants pass away and wilderness reclaims the cultural landscape of the Smokies, some families lose touch with the specific location of their family homes but not with the sense of connection. The larger community homecomings attract many who have no idea where their family once lived. The surviving churches serve as stand-ins for the former homes, even if a particular family did not worship there. Church and family cemeteries are also enduring touchstones for homecoming. As in rural congregations throughout the South, church homecomings are a time of cleaning and decorating graves, although the Park Service now takes responsibility for clearing much of the grounds before the larger homecomings.

The importance of homecoming in healing the wounds of dislocation is demonstrated in instances where this simple act has been obstructed. One of the longest festering disputes between former residents and the Park Service in the Smokies has been over access to cemeteries and homesites in the former communities along the north shore of the Little Tennessee River in Swain County, North Carolina. Ironically, although it resulted in some of the bitterest anti-environmental sentiments among former residents, the removal of the north shore residents was not ostensibly for environmental reasons. The original boundary of the Great Smoky Mountains National Park was to include this area, but the expense of acquiring certain tracts of land spared residents of the north shore the park removals of the 1930s. However, with the advent of World War II, the long-planned dam at Fontana finally became a reality. The TVA not only inundated a number of communities along the Little Tennessee but also flooded the access road to the communities along the upper reaches of Hazel Creek.

Today one of the most remote parts of the Great Smoky Mountains National Park, Hazel Creek was not an isolated mountain community. When the W. M. Ritter Lumber Company began timbering along the creek in 1910, Proctor developed into a boomtown complete with railroad depot, pool hall, movie theater, and more than a thousand residents. Like most timber booms, Ritter's occupancy of Hazel Creek was short lived. In 1928 the company pulled out, taking the railroad and many families' source of income. The families who stayed behind struggled through the Depression years, and many subsequently found work with the TVA building the largest dam east of the Mississippi.

By the time of the construction of Fontana Dam, the TVA had learned its own lessons about population removal. Compared with the National Park Service, the TVA offered greater assistance to those removed by their construction projects, and generally the policy was to acquire the minimum amount of property necessary. However, during World War II it was not considered expedient to build a new road to the north shore. Instead, the north shore lands were acquired by the TVA and then given to the Great Smoky Mountains National Park, a plan that park historian Carlos Campbell wrote was "received with great joy on all sides" (Campbell 1960:133).

The 163 families who lost their land to the National Park were not so joyful. They lost not only their land but also access to their former homes and communities. The former residents were promised that "all diligent efforts" would be made to build a park road along the north shore. They waited many bitter years. In the two and a half decades after the war ended, a road was built that extended from Bryson City, the county seat, to the park boundaries and into the park several miles, petering out in the middle of a tunnel. In the late 1960s construction of the road was abandoned in the face of environmental concerns, which ended plans for a loop road along the circumference of the park. Along this road today, immediately before it crosses into the park, is a hand-painted sign that reads,

Welcome to
The Road To No-Where
A Broken Promise
1943–?

The Road to No-Where became a local symbol of the bad faith of the federal government and the elitism of environmentalists who transformed former homes and communities into an inaccessible wilderness. Only with the realization that the road was not likely to be built did the act of homecoming begin. The first reunion of local residents was held in 1976 at the Deep Creek campground. Organized grave decorations began two years later. Hoping to assuage bitter feelings, the Park Service accommodated former residents and their families by aiding in transportation (now available by boat and Park Service vehicles within that portion of the park) and by playing a more active role in cemetery maintenance. However, some former residents continue to fear that environmentalists could block not only completion of the road but also the limited access now available for acts of homecoming (Oliver 1989:96–99).

The anti-environmentalism spawned by the Road to No-Where and other issues of access in the park bled into a larger "No More Wilderness" campaign opposing all wilderness designations. The anger was fueled not just by the original taking of homes but also by the changing federal policies after the park's creation. If the original motivations behind the creation of the park were about creating access to nature as well as building "good roads," fears for the environment have led to a policy of limiting access. However, no matter how much the land changes and how difficult it is to get there, former residents of the Smokies and their descendants imbue this "wilderness" with human meaning. The former farms and communities are cultural places, not just natural places.

Anti-environmentalism—or rather, opposition to federal environmental policy—and sense of place are tightly intertwined in the Smokies. The conflict over the Road to No-Where spawned not only some to the most rabid anti-wilderness campaigns but also one of the most active historical associations of the region. The former residents and park descendants who make up the North Shore Historical Association, which publishes the award-winning journal *The Bone Rattler,* have explored their connection to place in a way that far exceeds the annual act of homecoming.

Perhaps it is all too easy for environmentalists to dismiss local attitudes. Negative Appalachian stereotypes can be invoked, or the attitudes can be characterized as emanating from only a troublesome few. However, it is time to look at the historical realities that contribute to local sentiment and critically assess the imposition of values from outside the region. Just as the historic preservation movement has found that no matter how good its intentions, it cannot succeed without consideration of local sentiment and economic realities (as well as a constant check on elitist attitudes that may emerge from within), this lesson must be learned by those who advocate or administer environmental policy. If we are to sustain southern Appalachia's environment, it must be with the support, not the opposition, of those who ascribe cultural values to the place.

References Cited

Albanese, Catherine L. 1984. "Exploring Regional Religion: A Case Study of the Eastern Cherokee." *History of Religion* 23:344–71.

Baxter, Celia. 1994. Tape-recorded interview with David Baxter. Keavy, Ky.

Baxter, John. 1994. Tape-recorded interview with David Baxter. Somerset, Ky.

Baxter, Lee. 1994. Tape-recorded interview with David Baxter. Lexington, Ky.

Becker, Jane Stewart. 1998. *Selling Tradition: Appalachia and the Construction of an American Folk, 1930–1940.* Chapel Hill: University of North Carolina Press.

Brown, Margaret. 1990. "Power, Privilege, and Tourism: A Revision of the Great Smoky Mountains National Park Story." M.A. thesis, Department of History, University of Kentucky.

Campbell, Carlos. 1960. *Birth of a National Park in the Great Smoky Mountains.* Knoxville: University of Tennessee Press.

Carpenter, David E. 1985. "The Great Smokies: Diverse Perceptions of the Park as a Resource." In *The Many Faces of Appalachia: Exploring a Region's Diversity.* Ed. Sam Gray. 169–81. Proceedings of the Seventh Annual Appalachian Studies Conference. Boone, N.C.: Appalachian Consortium Press.

Dunn, Durwood. 1988. *Cades Cove: The Life and Death of a Southern Appalachian Community, 1818–1937.* Knoxville: University of Tennessee Press.

Eller, Ronald D. 1982. *Miners, Millhands, and Mountaineers: Industrialization of the Appalachian South, 1880–1930.* Knoxville: University of Tennessee Press.

Ellison, George. 1976. "Introduction." In *Our Southern Highlanders: A Narrative in the Southern Appalachians and a Study of Life among the Mountaineers* by Horace Kephart. ix–xlvi. Knoxville: University of Tennessee Press.

Finger, John R. 1984. *The Eastern Band of Cherokees, 1819–1900.* Knoxville: University of Tennessee Press.

Hall, Joseph. 1940. "Folk-lore and Folk History in the Great Smoky Mountains." Manuscript, Great Smoky Mountains National Park Archives.

Madden, Robert R., and T. Russell Jones. 1977. *Mountain Home: The Walker Family Farmstead, Great Smoky Mountains National Park.* Washington, D.C.: U.S. Department of Interior.

Meyers, Bonnie. 1993. Tape-recorded interview with Michael Ann Williams. Cades Cove Visitors Center, Tenn.

Neely, Sharlotte. 1991. *Snowbird Cherokees: People of Persistence.* Athens: University of Georgia Press.

Oliver, Duane. 1989. *Hazel Creek: From Then Till Now.* Maryville, Tenn.: Stinnett Printing Co.

Thomason and Associates Preservation Planners. 1993. *The History and Architecture of the Elkmont Community.* Report prepared for the National Park Service Southeast Region.

Whittle, W. O. 1934. *Movement of Population from the Great Smoky Mountain Area.* Knoxville: University of Tennessee Agricultural Experiment Station Bulletin.

Williams, Michael Ann. 1991. *Homeplace: The Social Use and Meaning of the Folk Dwelling in Southwestern North Carolina.* Athens: University of Georgia Press.

———. 1995. *Great Smoky Mountains Folklife.* Jackson: University Press of Mississippi.

Woody, Robert H. 1950. "Cataloochee Homecoming." *South Atlantic Quarterly* 49:8–17.

6 Reclaiming the Commons: Narratives of Progress, Preservation, and Ginseng

MARY HUFFORD

If the world is to contain a public space, it cannot be erected for one generation and planned for the living only; it must transcend the life-span of mortal men.

—Hannah Arendt, *The Human Condition*

I'll tell you what's dying here: the concept that the forest itself was open. . . . It didn't dawn on me until a couple of years ago when that began to change, that concept that the Native Americans had, that the land was like air or water—who could own it?

—Doug Stover, Mullens, W.Va.

The Sundial Tavern, known up and down Coal River as Kenny and Martha's, is a mom-and-pop beer joint on Route 3 just north of Naoma, West Virginia. Retired coal miner Kenny Pettry and his wife, Martha, now in their sixties, have been the proprietors for nearly thirty years. By day the bar's modest facade belies the often uproarious vitality of its evenings. On weekend nights the music of Hank Williams, Bill Monroe, and Dolly Parton flows out of the jukebox to mingle with the haze of cigarettes, the clangor of pinball, the crack and clatter of pool, and the jocular talk and teasing of friends from neighboring hollows and coal camps.

Like many taverns, the Sundial Tavern is a dynamic museum of local history, its walls covered with photographs, artifacts, and trophies that register local perspectives on national events, the triumphs of patrons, and the passing of eras. Among the items displayed are photos of Dolly Parton (who is Martha's second cousin), an ingenious trigger-and-funnel mechanism for planting corn, and a souvenir cap that registers the present struggle of the United Mine Workers for survival on Coal River. On another wall hangs a photograph of John Flynn, a science writer and forest advocate, deemed one of the three best pool players on Coal River. After thirty years of writing for midwestern metropolitan newspapers he returned to Coal River in 1991 to study and publicize the effects of acid rain on the Appalachian forests. He spent many nights here talking, sympathizing, arguing, joking, and shooting pool. I had begun working with John on a study of the cultural implications of forest decline when an aneurysm claimed his life in March 1996. He is buried not far from Sundial in his family cemetery on Rock Creek, the hollow he was born in nearly six decades ago.

Tucked into the display on the wall that faces you as you sit on a barstool is a set of framed and laminated leaves. Most citizens of the United States would have trouble identifying this specimen, but for many of the tavern's regular patrons it represents an extraordinary trophy and object of desire: the stalk from a rare six-prong ginseng plant, *Panax quinquefolia*. Above the large specimen is a lesser but still remarkable five-prong. The display speaks to the continuing status accorded to ginseng in life and thought on Coal River.

Diggers call it "seng," and on Coal River the passion for seng runs deep. In 1994, for example, the state of West Virginia exported 18,698 dry pounds of wild ginseng root from its fifty-five counties (Fritsch 1996). Although ginseng grows wild throughout the mountain state, more than half of the wild harvest came from eight contiguous counties in the state's southwestern corner (Kanawha, Boone, Fayette, Raleigh, McDowell, Wyoming, Mingo, and Logan). "It's always been like that," says Bob Whipkey, who monitors the export of ginseng for the state's Division of Forestry. "There are more diggers there because of the culture. People there grow up gathering herbs and digging roots."[1]

Because of wild ginseng's limited range and extraordinary value (diggers are averaging $450 per pound for the dried wild root), the federal government has been monitoring the export of ginseng (both wild and cultivated) since 1978 under the Convention on International Trade in Endangered Species. Of nineteen states authorized to export wild ginseng,[2] West Virginia came in second, behind Kentucky, which certified 52,993 pounds. Tennessee came in third, with 17,997 pounds. In 1994 these three contiguous states certified more than half of the 178,111 pounds of wild ginseng reported among nineteen states (Fritsch 1996).

THE COMMONS

There is a story in these figures of a vernacular cultural domain that transcends state boundaries. Anchoring this domain is a geographic space, a de facto commons roughly congruent with two physiographic regions recognized in national discourse. One is the coal fields underlying the ginseng, most of which are controlled by absentee landholders (Appalachian Land Ownership Task Force 1983). The other is the mixed mesophytic forest, known among ecologists as the world's biologically richest temperate-zone hardwood system (Braun 1950; Loucks 1998).

This multilayered region is increasingly the focus of debates pitting the short-term economic value of coal and timber against the long-term value of a diverse forest system and topography. While the long-term effects of clear-cutting and mountaintop removal on the commons of air, water, and soil are hotly debated, the immediate impacts of ecosystem destruction on the local commons and the collective memory it sustains are not recognized. The geographic commons is local, but its loss is of national significance. As Beverly Brown (1996) points out in her writing about the rural working class in the Pacific Northwest, the widespread loss of access to the geographic commons occurs in tandem with a shrinking civic commons.

Nationally, indeed globally,[3] such loss of access is one effect of the increasing privatization and enclosure of land that for generations has been used as commons (Brown 1996; Shiva 1992; Kovaleski 1998). This commons has supported a patchwork of strategies for survival typically found in rural areas, including seasonal employment, barter, hunting, gathering, and various forms of relief (Halperin 1990). Over the past decade, processes of gentrification, preservation, and intensified extraction of timber and minerals have depleted lands in which communities have exercised fructuary rights for generations.

In his effort to publicize and reverse the effects of acid rain on central Appalachia's mixed mesophytic forest, John Flynn cast the mixed mesophytic forest as a globally unique ecosystem worthy of recognition as national and global patrimony (Hufford 1998). My part of this project was to document the extent of local knowledge and use of the forest. Our initial premise was that if the mixed mesophytic forest is radically diminished by air pollution, a way of life with roots in antiquity will be diminished as well.

It quickly became clear that on Coal River the impacts of air pollution are eclipsed by processes of extraction on a Faustian scale. In fact, the Clean Air Act of 1990, which set acceptable levels for emissions of sulfur dioxide and nitrous oxide from coal-fired utility plants, heightened the demand for West Virginia's low-sulfur bituminous coal. Since the passage of that act, more than 500 square miles of West Virginia have been approved for mountaintop removal and reclamation. Mountaintop removal is a method of mining that shears off the top of a mountain, allowing the efficient recovery of multiple seams of coal. When the topped mountains are "reclaimed" under the terms of the Surface Mining Control and Reclamation Act of 1977, the rich soils essential to ginseng and hardwood cove forests will be gone. Moreover, because the highly compacted reclaimed sites are unreceptive to native hardwood plant communities, species that thrive in habitats like the Gobi desert are planted to begin the process of rebuilding the soil. No one knows yet what effect the introduction of these species at the highest elevations will have on the undisturbed forests below. Added to the disturbance of ridges is the practice of filling in adjacent valleys with excess rock and spoil, permanently altering the structures of watersheds (figure 6.1).

For projects that radically transform ecosystems, the checklist approach of federal legislation designed to protect air, water, wildlife, prime farmland, and a narrow range of cultural resources is inadequate. In fact, this approach assists the displacement of local commons by a national commons. Conferring protected status on resources tends to lift them out of local life, into the province of national patrimony. Where rarity provides the rationale, the species and structures protected by federal legislation, such as snail darters and spotted owls, tend to be irrelevant to local ways of life. On Coal River, knowledge and appreciation of the forested commons is fostered by sustained engagement, not detached viewing.

Ginseng is an alternative to the rare and arcane species around which preservationists pitch their battles. Commonly found within its shrinking habi-

Figure 6.1. Aerial View of Mountaintop Removal and Reclamation. Photo by Lyntha Scott Eiler. Courtesy of the American Folklife Center, Library of Congress.

tat, ginseng could anchor both national and local interests. Dollar for pound, ginseng probably is the most valuable renewable resource on the central Appalachian plateaus.[4] To protect the habitat for ginseng is to protect the mixed mesophytic forest and by extension the seasonal round that is integral to a way of life. Ginseng is a mainstay of the seasonal round, for reasons that are cultural as well as economic. "I'd rather ginseng than eat," says Dennis Dickens, eighty-five, of Peach Tree Creek. "Every spare minute I had was spent a-ginsenging." "If you can't go ginsenging," says Carla Pettry, thirty, of Horse Creek, "it totally drives you crazy."

Ginseng's etymology and economic value derive from China and other Asian countries, where the root has long been prized for conferring longevity and vigor of all sorts on its users. The term *ginseng* is an Americanization of the Chinese *jin-chen,* meaning "manlike." The Latin term, *Panax quinquefolia,* alludes to the five whorled leaves on each branch and the plant's function as a panacea. The active ingredients in the fleshy, human-shaped root are ginsenocides, chemical compounds celebrated for their capacity both to stimulate and soothe. Whether ginsenocides warrant such claims is a matter of continuing controversy among scientists and physicians (Fritsch 1996).

According to Randy Halstead, a Boone County buyer, "stress rings," which give the wild root its market value, are linked with a higher concentration of ginsenocides. Nearly impossible to reproduce in cultivation, stress rings are produced as the root pushes through soil just compact enough to provide the right amount of resistance. The ancient, humus-laden soils in the mixed mesophytic forests of Tennessee, Kentucky, and southern West Virginia are ginseng's ideal medium. "The most prolific spreads of wild ginseng," writes Val Hardacre in *Woodland Nuggets of Gold* (1968:x), "were found in the region touched by the Allegheny Plateau and the secluded coves of the Cumberland Plateau." Through centuries of interaction with this valuable and elusive plant, residents of the plateaus continue to conjure a rich social imagery, anchored in the space of the de facto commons (figure 6.2).

HISTORICAL BACKGROUND

The history of human interaction with ginseng lurks in the language of the land. Look at a detailed map of almost any portion of the region and ginseng is registered somewhere, often in association with the deeper, moister places: Seng Branch (Fayette County), Sang Camp Creek (Logan County), Ginseng (Wyoming County), Seng Creek (Boone County), and Three-Prong Holler (Raleigh). The hollows, deep dendritic fissures created over eons by water cutting through the ancient tableland to form tributaries of the Coal River, re-

Figure 6.2. Randy Sprouse Gathering Ginseng in Tom's Hollow. Photo by Lyntha Scott Eiler. Courtesy of the American Folklife Center, Library of Congress.

ceive water from lesser depressions that ripple the slopes. These depressions are distinguished in local parlance as coves (shallower, amphitheater-shaped depressions), swags (steeper depressions, "swagged" on both sides), and drains (natural channels through which water flows out of the swag or cove). The prime locations for ginseng are found on the north-facing, wet sides of these depressions. "Once in a while you'll find some on the ridges," says Denny Christian, fifty-six, of Dry Creek. "But not like in the swags there." "You just go in the darker coves," says Wesley Scarbrough, twenty-five, who grew up on Clear Fork, "where it just shadows the ground so it'll be rich for ginseng."

Occupying higher and drier ground are sandstone "camping rocks," formed on the bottoms of ancient seas. These natural ledges have sheltered people hunting and gathering in the mountains since prehistoric times, and during centuries of corn-woodland-pastureland agriculture such ledges sheltered stock as well. Named according to local tradition by nineteenth-century settlers, sites such as Jake Rock, John Rock, Turkey Rock, Crane Rock, and Charlie Rock served as bases for ginsenging expeditions. "My granddad and all them used to go and lay out for weeks, ginsenging," says Kenny Pettry. "A rock they stayed at, they called it the Crane Rock, and they stayed back in under that. They'd be gone for weeks ginsenging." "Did you ever hear tell of Charlie Rock?" asks Woody Boggess of Pettry Bottom. "That's a famous place." "I've camped out many a night under Charlie Rock," says Randy Sprouse of Sundial. "People used to live under Charlie Rock two or three months at a time, camp out and dig ginseng."

The harvesting of ginseng (as well as other wild plants) flourished within a system of corn-woodland-pastureland farming with Celtic and Cherokee antecedents (Evans 1969; Hart 1977). Crucial to this system was recourse to a vast, forested commons rising away from the settled hollows, which supplied the community with essential materials and staples: wood for fires, barns, fences, homes, and tools; coal for fuel; rich soil for growing corn, beans, and orchards; wild nuts, herbs, mushrooms, berries, and game; an open range for hogs and cattle; and places for distilling excess corn into liquor. Because of the abundant supply of tree fodder (wild nuts and fruit), the central Appalachian plateau in the nineteenth century furnished some of the best pastureland in the country (Otto 1983; Salstrom 1994; Appalachian Land Ownership Task Force 1983).

The system of coves, hollows, and streams overlaid by history is as legible to old-timers as the grid of any city. By many accounts, every wrinkle rippling the mountains has been named for people, flora, fauna, practices, and events both singular and recurrent. "Each hollow has a name," says eighty-six-year-old Dennis Dickens. "These different little hollows or branches or creeks," says Howard Miller of Drew's Creek, "they had a name for each one, so when a neighbor talked to another neighbor about a certain thing that happened at this holler, they knew exactly where it was at, from Beckley down to Racine."

Onto a scrap of drywall Ben Burnside of Rock Creek fixed the names of the hollows along Rock Creek so they wouldn't be forgotten. The names index and weave together elements of corn-woodland-pastureland farming and community life: Calf Hollow, Bee Comb Hollow, Big Lick Hollow, School House Hollow, Paw-Paw Hollow, Mill Hollow, Stockingleg Hollow, Coon Hollow, Canterbury Hollow, Sugar Camp Hollow, and Hollow Field. There was Bee Light Holler, named for the practice of tracking wild bees to their hives, known as "lining." "They would cut out the trees so they could bait bees and see where they went to," recalls Howard Miller. Up the hollow from Miller's home is Quill Holler, named for the reedy plants that provided straws for extracting sugar water from "sugar (maple) trees."

During the Civil War many families, seeking refuge from plundering Yankee and Confederate soldiers, fled the valleys and settled on the ridges. After several generations, people moved off the mountains, either lured by jobs in the coal mines or forced out by land companies. The remains of those settlements serve as important landmarks for people working the seasonal round.

History, deeply lodged in the mountains, is recovered along with plants and animals. Mae Bongalis, who recalls meeting Mother Jones when she was a young girl, grew up in a coal camp on Montcoal Mountain. She learned of her Cherokee ancestors while gathering greens, bark, and roots with her grandmother. Charred flat rocks and rocks pocked with cone-shaped mortars marked the places where her Cherokee ancestors ground corn and baked corn bread.

As practice and concept, the commons is ancient, predating the idea of private property. Beryl Crowe (1977:54) writes, "The commons is a fundamental social institution that has a history going back through our own colonial experience to a body of English common law which antedates the Roman conquest. That law recognized that in societies there are some environmental objects which have never been, and should never be, exclusively appropriated to any individual or group of individuals." Development of commons by absentee investors is a recurrent capitalist process epitomized in the parliamentary enclosures that cleared the commons for grazing sheep in England during the seventeenth and eighteenth centuries. The social and environmental legacy in England includes irreversible deforestation, degradation of soils and water, homelessness, and the emergence of the world's first industrial working class from the displaced rural population that found work weaving wool at the looms of Birmingham and Liverpool. Social and ecological effects were ignored and sustainable agriculture displaced in the name of efficiency and higher production (Snyder 1993).

In southern West Virginia a variant of this sequence has played out over the past century. Initially the system of corn-woodland-pastureland farming dovetailed nicely with the industry's need for a large work force. The rich soils and diverse forests helped industry to keep its wages low.[5] W. D. Ansted (1885:129–30), a nineteenth-century British prospector, described the mixed mesophytic commons on the Cabin Creek Plateau to entice industrialists of the late nineteenth century:

> There are on the plateaus, intersected by the valleys, many thousand acres of good land, admirably adapted for cultivation. These lands are nowhere far from settled habitations, and would supply everything required for a colony of emigrants. The climate is delightful for the greater part of the year, and the winters moderate and short. There is excellent water and deep soil, well adapted to the growth of wheat, Indian corn, potatoes and other crops. The pastures where the trees have been removed are excellent, and the cattle are left to graze far into the winter. By offering allotments of moderate extent on easy terms, reserving the minerals, population could be secured and the whole district improved. The reserved allotments would soon increase in value. The cost of placing emigrants on these lands, from Liverpool, would not exceed $45 per head.

What Ansted observed, even as he articulated the formula for its destruction, was a corn-woodland-pastureland system of small, independent farmers arrayed around a mutually agreed-upon commons. Subsequent deeds of ejectment on record at the county courthouse measure land as the distance between particular trees, in language registering the rich diversity of mixed mesophytic species.

Throughout central Appalachia in the late nineteenth century, newly formed land companies surreptitiously subverted the system of the commons, taking out deeds on its unclaimed portions, offering small amounts of money and the right to continue using the surface resources in exchange for mineral rights.[6] Memories of these transactions are vividly recalled. "My daddy had a farm in the head of this creek," says one retired miner. "The land company men went on top of that mountain, and they got up there where he was hoeing corn on top of the mountain, and they said, 'Mr. Peters, we come up to make a deal with you.' Said, 'You make us a deed to the mineral rights, and we'll make you a clear deed to the surface.' And right there a big fight took place. But they got it all anyway. That's the way the Rowland Land Company got it all. The old people didn't know what they was doing." Under the terms of the Broad Form Deed, the owner of the surface rights had to guarantee the land company access to the minerals, regardless of what that access might do to the surface.

Historians such as Salstrom and Corbin argue that coal companies exploited the local system of corn-woodland-pastureland agriculture to subsidize their low and intermittent wages. Yet however weakly, the historical agreements that allowed companies access to underground reserves of coal upheld the culturally imbued integrity of mountains and valleys. This integrity emerges not from abstract definitions of ecosystems but from the institution of the commons and the seasonal round. Consequently, residents do not view the closing of the mountains in the 1990s as the simple closing off of private property; the closings are widely experienced as pressure to empty out the valleys. This pressure is felt because a whole comprising people, mountains, and valleys is being violated.

Curiously, in contrast to the preservation ethos that evicted residents and separated national park lands from the everyday lives of tourists, the mixed mesophytic terrain controlled by industry depended in a sense on the population of workers it supported. This landscape has been thoroughly tended from ridge to bottom. One cannot travel far without encountering old rock piles that signal former "newgrounds": rich land on small flat "benches" once cleared for growing corn and beans and "let go" into forest fallow in a cycle that took generations to complete. Ginseng and ramps are propagated, both in the woods and in backyards. Certain kinds of trees, such as "den trees," "bee trees," and hickories, were avoided when cutting timber. Consequently some people explicitly link forest health with a corn-woodland-pastureland system of use. I have heard residents observe that cows grazing in the woods helped control rattlesnakes and copperheads, that hogs grazing in the woods aided in the dispersal of native red mulberry seeds, and that old apple orchards scattered throughout the woods provide the perfect medium for morel mushrooms, locally known as molly moochers.

"The mountains are our history," says Randy Sprouse, a United Mineworker who has taken over where John Flynn left off. An elementary school teacher from Clear Fork echoed this point at a recent meeting that Randy Sprouse convened on mountaintop removal. Arguing that strip-mining erodes not only hillsides but the heritage locked up behind gates, she cited a child's ignorance about "paw-paws." The child thought paw-paws were grandfathers, not custardlike fruits (also known as West Virginia bananas). The child wondered whether "maw-maws" also grew on trees.

In a sense it could be said that this commons has existed at the behest of land companies and the coal industry. What is of great interest here is industry's representation of reclamation—which displaces the mixed mesophytic system and commons with an industrially designed ecosystem—as an end that serves the public good. Thus in an op-ed piece for the *Huntington Dispatch* (November 28, 1997), Ben Greene, president of West Virginia Surface Mining and Reclamation Association, and William B. Raney, president of the West Virginia Coal Association, emphasized that mining is actually only an interim process in a giant remodeling project. "Through careful and thoughtful sculpting of the earth in these rural settings the more intense needs of the state are being met by leaving the area in a more environmentally stable, near level, developable condition than prior to mining. Sensible planning has permitted the construction of schools, prisons, recreational facilities, shopping centers and other projects on reclaimed mine sites."

How is it that industry has found such a *tabula rasa* for its projects, in a space so intensely occupied and inscribed with history? This statement epitomizes what Foster calls "symbolic depopulation," erasing not only the geographic commons and its occupants but also the civic commons. It slams the door on public debate by telling the public what industry is preparing for it. Symbolic depopulation is one of the forms of cultural representation industry uses to accomplish its ends in southern West Virginia. It is compatible with the state's compensatory narratives of preservation, which are codified in the elaborate, sanitizing apparatus of environmental review.

NATIONAL NARRATIVES OF PROGRESS AND PRESERVATION

The coal fields of central Appalachia exemplify a kind of space created by our system, one that is, as anthropologist Kathleen Stewart (1996) puts it, "doubly occupied" both by people whose families have been there for generations and by absentee land companies and transnational corporations that appropriated the minerals and timber a century ago. For these corporate occupants the narrative of the coal fields is one of development and economic growth. But for many who live there the narrative is one of chronic undevelopment, exile, and cultural disappearance. The state's efforts to temper this contradiction are set within narratives of preservation, which sift out and preserve aspects of mountain culture in spaces set apart from the path of development, in portions of a larger national commons of forests, parks, and rivers.

National narratives of progress and preservation, which Batteau (1990) calls "the twin ideological pillars of Jacksonian expansionism," hark back to the process of literal and figurative enclosure set in motion by the Enlightenment. Anthropologist Keith Thomas (1983) has shown how the enclosed system of scientific discourse that validates environmental assessment grew out of the systematic assessment of common knowledge in the seventeenth and eighteenth centuries. What was left over after science carved up the world became the domain of culture. Robert Cantwell (1993) argues that we have never recovered from this cataclysm, citing the seventeenth- and eighteenth-century enclosures of the commons in England and the landscape gardens cultivated around the ruins of the common life anchored in the commons. These gardens, Cantwell argues, gave rise through the Romantic painters and poets to an object of contemplation that is the unbridgeable distance created by progress between the heart and its objects of desire. Cantwell suggests that capitalism's continual reproduction of that structure of feeling gives rise to a host of modern "landscape gardens": national parks, folk festivals, hotel lobbies, deep suburbs, golf courses, heritage corridors, and other constructs designed to screen out industrial capitalism's visual blight.

The net effect is a checkerboard landscape of preservation and progress. A narrative of Appalachia as domestic enclave and font of traditional craft is materialized in such tourist attractions as pioneer villages, heritage trails, and wilderness preserves and parks. A narrative of Appalachia on the path of progress is crystallized in industrial sites where clear-cutting and surface mining clear the slate (so to speak) for "economic growth." In both narratives, an imagined population will benefit, either through the preservation of its past for touristic consumption or through its movement out of economic backwardness into future prosperity.

Consider, for instance, how the *New River Gorge Newsletter* (National Park Service 1989) relates the region's folk culture to tourism: "By 1900 the folk culture typical of the Appalachians was submerged under an enormous transition to the exploitation and transportation of coal. Handicrafts were replaced by cheap manufactured products from stores or mail order houses; live music was replaced by phonographic records and, eventually radio. . . . Popular American Traditions of the industrial age were a pervasive force which eroded the traditional culture rapidly. . . . As tourism grows and people earn an income from restoring the older customs, there will be more opportunity for visitors to experience them through fairs, festivals, and craft shops."

Here a master narrative of loss and rescue constitutes the National River as a refuge from the industrial contamination of nature and culture. (In fact, legislation explicitly bans surface mining that would be visible anywhere from the center of the New River, where a lucrative whitewater industry is staged in view of the ruins of early coal mining history.) The narrative's historical frame, which contextualizes the New River as a fragment of the ancient Teays river system, screens out the industrial and postindustrial landscape created in the coal camps (while the postmodern headquarters models the *idea* of coal company housing). This screening out is echoed on maps for tourists that do not feature the coal camps through which tourists must drive to get to the river. For instance, the rapids, named by whitewater rafting companies, are on the maps, but not the coal camps that line the river's approaches.

Elsewhere in the state, we find the same temporalizing practices at work but in a private heritage display. The Pete Dye Golf Course is a stunning monument to coal heritage constructed on a reclaimed strip mine. The private, invitation-only club has become the site for annual golf tournaments of coal executives. In various interpretive texts the course's five hundred acres are made to represent a complete evolutionary sequence of development, beginning with the carboniferous era when coal was formed, moving through Indian hunting ground (indicated by a mound), through pioneer farming (a plow and haystack), to coal extraction through deep mining, stripping, and reclamation, culminating in the leisurescape of the golf course constructed around ruins and directed by the Burning Embers Corporation. I cite a text that appeared in *Greenlands,* the magazine of the West Virginia Surface Mining and Reclamation Association (n.d.): "The heritage of the land as a former coal property is readily apparent. Lumps of coal serve as tee markers. Cart paths are paved with red dog. From the 5th tee, the red and white towers of the coal-fired Harrison Power Station are visible at a distance of more than three miles. The 6th, 7th, 8th, and 10th holes will utilize crushed coal in place of sand traps. Between the 6th green and the 7th tee, golfers can pass through a 140 foot stretch of an authentic underground mine shaft. The 10th fairway is defined by 22 coal-filled rail cars on an old track."

Here the state's narrative of loss and rescue gives way to an unmistakable narrative of conquest, with the same effect of cultural disappearance for coal field residents and workers. This space anchors a timeline in which the future is "members" playing golf in what a club brochure describes as "an environment of seclusion and exclusivity." The *Greenlands* article concludes that "After previous lives as the home of [Native American] hunters, coal miners and farmers, [playing golf] is what the valley behind Smith chapel is all about."

A QUESTION OF TIMING: ISSUES OF INTEGRITY AND SIGNIFICANCE

The national narrative of progress and preservation is a transcendent one, situating its sites in geological and industrial time and naturalizing the National River as the outcome of an economic sequence that moves from industrialization to tourism. The explosion of time into geological ages is echoed in reclamation planning, which turns on the assumption that the soils can be built up over time to support forest habitat. No one knows how many generations this could take and how the attendant breach in collective memory could be mended.

In contrast to the spectatorial time of national narratives, the time that frames the commons in local narrative is inhabitable, comprising "the human unit of time as the space between a grandfather's memory of his own childhood and a grandson's knowledge of those memories as he heard about them" (Mead 1972:284).

It is significant that coal camps in their postindustrial incarnations don't fit into the state's grand narrative. We could say that it has something to do with conflicting notions of integrity and significance written into National Register criteria and assigned during environmental review.

The coal camp landscape exhibits an immanent integrity, that of a pastoral-industrial hybrid wrought by people through and despite the exigencies of life in a place taken over and occupied by industry for more than a century. The logic of cultural production—whether of cooking, architecture, motor vehicles, quilts, or gardening—is hybridity: the effort to recombine in novel ways things that have been used up and that become saturated with meaning as the history of reuse lengthens (Stewart 1996). In gardens, to use a small but telling example, we may find tomatoes supported by roof bolts scavenged from abandoned mines side by side with the traditional arrangement of pole beans supported by corn stalks, one of a number of farming practices with Cherokee antecedents found on Coal River (Finger 1995:42).

The double occupation was enabled by systems of measurement that severed mineral and timber rights from Appalachian farmers. That system of measurement persists with much the same effect through environmental impact assessments, which formulaically state that the premining use is forest and wildlife and propose a postmining reclamation plan such as wildlife refuge or range land. The impact assessments generally go on to state that there are no historic artifacts worthy of inclusion on the National Register, no prime farmland, and no endangered species. Onto a historically and biologically rich commons the environmental impact assessment writes a deteriorated and empty space ready for improvement.

The cultural portions of environmental impact assessments generally are grounded in acts of looking, in windshield and pedestrian surveys, and in consultation with maps. Consultation with local communities is rare and desultory. One archaeologist points out that the coal companies paying for environmental assessments would be unlikely to pay for the extra time needed to consult with local residents. Significance and integrity are conferred on artifacts and land forms that illustrate official narratives of progress and preservation. Meanwhile, local narratives, material constructions, and acts that we might think of as rites of reappearance take issue with this vision of the world and provide a starting point for reclaiming the commons.

SENG TALK AND GINSENG TALES: CONJURING THE COMMONS

For seng aficionados, the ongoing prospect of ginseng makes the mountains gleam with hidden treasure.

> "It's like catching a big fish," said Randy Halstead. "You're out here all day and you find this big fish, and you know it's everybody's desire to catch this big fish in the lake. You find this big enormous plant and you know everybody that's out there digging, this is the one that they'd like to find. So you get an adrenalin rush when you find them, and when you find a big one it's like showing off your daily catch. You bring it in and say, 'Look what I found today.'"
>
> "You can't get out and dig it for the money," said Joe Williams. "It's like looking for Easter eggs. You're always looking for the big one. If I found one eight ounces, I believe I'd quit."

"The one that boy brought in up at Flats weighed a pound," said Randy Sprouse.

"I'd like to have seen that one," said Williams.

"It was a monster," Sprouse emphasized.

"That's what you get out for," Williams mused. "Always looking for the big one."

On Coal River, ginseng plays a vital role in imagining and sustaining a culture of the commons. Among the means of keeping the commons alive is talk about ginseng: where to hunt it, its mysterious habits, the biggest specimens ever found, and the difficulties of wresting the treasure from an impossibly steep terrain shared by bears, copperheads, rattlesnakes, and yellow jackets. The ability and authority to engage in this discourse are indeed hard won.

Over generations of social construction in story and in practice, places on the commons accrue a dense historical residue. Every wrinkle rippling the mountains has been named for people, flora, fauna, practices, and events both singular and recurrent: Beech Hollow, Ma Kelly Branch, Bear Wallow, Board Camp Hollow, and Old Field Hollow. "I guess there must have been a newground in there at one time," said Ben Burnside, of Rock Creek, alluding to the old-time practice of clearing woodland to grow corn and beans.

Overlooking the valley from its giant, tightly crimped rim, places such as the Head of Hazy, Bolt Mountain, Kayford Mountain, the Cutting Box, Chestnut Hollow, and Sugar Camp anchor the imagery spun out in a conversation that Woody Boggess videotaped in Andrew, West Virginia. In one exchange, Cuba Wiley and Dave Bailey conjure and coinhabit a terrain so steep that seng berries would roll from the ridge to the hardtop.

"You know where the most seng is I ever found up in that country?" asked Cuba Wiley. "I'm going to tell you where it was at. You won't believe it."

"Chestnut Holler, I'll bet you," guessed Dave Bailey.

"I found one of the awfulest patches of it, lefthand side of Chestnut Holler," Cuba continued. "I never seen such roots of seng in my life, buddy. And where I found all my seng, the good seng, come right this side of Clyde Montgomery's, and come down that first holler, and go up that holler and turn back to the right. Buddy, it is steep."

"Going toward the Cutting Box?" asked Dave Bailey, referring to a place named for a mining structure.

"I senged through there," said Cuba, "from there to Stickney, and I have really found the seng in there. One time me and Gar Gobel was in there, and Clyde would start up the mountain, and we just kept finding little four leaves, all the way up the mountain.

"Gar says, 'Cuba, there's a big one somewhere. It seeded downhill.' We senged plumb to the top of the mountain, Cutting Box, got on top, and that old big nettleweed was that high, Gar had him a big stick, was hunting for the big one. Right on tip top the mountain, directly beneath them, it was about up to my belt, buddy. It didn't have such a big root on it, and I still wasn't satisfied. Gar, he dropped over the Cutting Box, and I still searched around up on top, parting the weeds, and directly, I found them about that high [indicates a height of about three feet], two of them right on top of the mountain. It was so steep, [the berries] rolled plumb down next to the hard road, buddy. I got more seng in there than any place I ever senged in that part of the country. It's steep, buddy."

"It's rough too, ain't it?" said Dave Bailey.

"It's rough, buddy," Cuba agreed. "But I swear I dug some good seng in there, buddy. And I dug some good seng in Sugar Camp."

Cuba's amazing account reminds Woody Boggess of a tall tale he heard from his brother, Bud. "You remember that time Bud and French Turner was . . . up there sawing timber for Earl Hunter? Remember Bud telling you about that? He said he was sawing that big tree. Thought it was a buckeye. And stuff like tomatoes started hitting him in the head."

"It was seng berries," laughed Dave.

"It was seng berries," Woody dead-panned.

"Said it was big as tomatoes," said Dave, still chuckling.

"Boy, that was some stalk of seng," allowed Cuba, his eyes twinkling.

Through narrative the commons becomes a public space, its history played out before audiences who know its spaces intimately whether they have been there together or not. Inhabiting the commons through practice and narrative confers social identity and makes a community of its occupants. "I work in construction," wrote Dennis Price, forty, of Arnett, on a petition to document the cultural value of the mixed mesophytic forest. "But really I consider myself a ginsenger."

In the realm unfolded through ginseng stories and other tales of plying the woods, the commons becomes a proving ground on which attributes of courage, loyalty, belonging, stamina, wit, foolishness, stewardship, honesty, judgment, and luck are displayed and evaluated. However, this narrative session does more than simply model values to live by. The glimpse of gigantic ginseng exemplifies the way in which people reoccupy the confiscated commons in which political presence is grounded.

Narrative "lies" of the gigantic counter the state's narratives that miniaturize and contain the region and its people and the industrial narratives that laminate a biologically diverse commons under a green veneer of lespedeza (a variety of grass locally known as sawgrass). The mountains of local narratives, like Bakhtin's carnivalesque body, are continually becoming. Gleefully exaggerated accounts of giant ginseng berries, a potato the size of a car, a rattlesnake "so big it had hair on it," or a molly moocher so big that twenty pounds of meal wouldn't cover it symbolically shatter the state's efforts at containment, creating what Stewart (1996) calls "room for maneuver."

Through incessant conversational practices of genealogizing, etymologizing, naming, nicknaming, and telling stories, people lay cultural claim to land flooded with significance and integrity. Seeds that you can't get from catalogs are traced to founding families: Bill Dickens beans, Aunt Liz apples, ox-heart tomatoes. A discussion about the chestnut blight triggered a story of how John Flynn's grandfather foraged his hogs all through the woods, rounding them up with a dog named Bounce. As a mountain feist, Bounce was specifically bred to run the hills. A conversation about trees prompted a Civil War story of how Dennis Dickens's grandmother planted a peach orchard on a ridgetop to hide it from Yankees. The orchard replaced itself sixty years later when someone timbered there and exposed the dormant seeds to sunlight.

The impulse to re-piece what has been torn apart through development unifies a host of verbal and material practices that might otherwise seem idiosyncratic. In this vein, Woody Boggess built a log cabin out of the dismantled bridge to Edwight, a structure of oak timbers that for sixty years connected the once populous hub to Route 3. "A lot of trucks have driven over this house," he quipped when he showed it to me. It houses artifacts he salvaged from the mountains and hollows that have been systematically depopulated by the coal industry: Hobart Clay's spoke shave for harvesting hickory bark; a pair of leather leggings worn by an uncle for protection against snakes on Bradley Mountain; and the fiddle of old Joe Pettry, who lived and made music on Shumate's Branch. A family cemetery that was finally the only obstacle to the creation of a slurry pond on Shumate's Branch (slurry is sludge from the coal cleaning process impounded in deep valleys) is moved to a "commercial cemetery" ten miles away. Some tombstones are rejected by that cemetery, and the Baileys have one made for their parents that reconstitutes Shumate's Branch where it flowed past the cemetery, now buried hundreds of feet deep in sludge: a dead place, transformed into a powerful and unattainable space of desire in the moment of its destruction. Descendants of those buried on "Graveyard Hill" overlooking the sludge converge from Detroit, Cleveland, Philadelphia, and New York each year to tend that cemetery on Memorial Day. This is not only to honor their loved ones but also to keep the company from destroying the cemetery.

On Kayford Mountain the Stanley Family heirs form an association and create a park near their family cemetery in full view of a mountaintop removal project. Having rejected the company's aggressive efforts to acquire the mountain, they stage public reunions on all national holidays, centered around traditional music and food, hoping to keep the company from closing the private road that is the only access to their park.

These efforts are at heart a defense of the commons, of a relationship between community and landscape that is not registered in terms such as *forest* and *wildlife refuge*. Their verbal and material constructions are platforms from which to begin reclaiming both a geographic commons that models an ideal relationship between people and environment and the suppressed civic commons of public debate. This is the commons on which industry and the state encroach when building new ecosystems without disclosing the social and ecological impacts of their massive designs.

GINSENG AND THE FUTURE OF THE COMMONS

"Understanding the commons and its role within the larger regional culture," writes Gary Snyder (1990:37), "is one more step toward integrating ecology with economy." What is missing in West Virginia's environmental planning process is any recognition of the commons and its critical role in community life. The commons, a multigenerational achievement, models an interdependence of culture, ecology, and economy, which it should be the state's duty to defend.

The postcoal economy of the doubly occupied coal fields is in the hands of land companies, now considering whether to raise poultry, open ski resorts, or store the nation's waste in their exhausted lands. Although the present practice of reclamation is ostensibly for the public good, alternatives are not publicly considered. John Flynn dreamed of building a small plant for packaging and processing ginseng right on Coal River, where the digging of wild ginseng might be supplemented through the cultivation of "virtually wild ginseng" (Fritsch 1996).

Ginseng, like the commons, falls through a crack between preservation and progress. Because ginseng is not classified as an endangered species, its harvest is permitted, and its presence is unacknowledged in environmental review. Because of its economic value, its harvest by individuals is monitored. Heavy fines and possible imprisonment are levied on anyone possessing green ginseng out of season (August 15 to November 30).

Ginseng's immunity to environmental review helps keep the impact of mountaintop removal on ginseng—and an associated way of life—off the record. I asked Bob Whipkey how much ginseng is uprooted off-season in the course of mountaintop removal. No one is tracking this information. "They're not *harvesting* it," he pointed out. "They're destroying it, but the law only regulates the harvest!"[7]

Ginseng could provide a focus for the defense of a commons anchoring both national and local interests. The central Appalachian coal fields are the nation's most prolific source of wild ginseng. As a renewable resource with a high dollar value, ginseng merits a prominent place in planning for a postcoal economy. Given ginseng's predilection for native hardwood forest and rich soils, planning for forests that support wild ginseng would nurture a globally significant hardwood forest and the cultural landscape to which it belongs.

Notes

1. All quoted speech is from conversations tape recorded during the Appalachian Forest Folklife Project, a project of the American Folklife Center, the Lucy Braun Association, and Trees for the Planet, from 1994 to 1998.

2. Ginseng can be cultivated, and cultivated ginseng makes up more than 90 percent of American ginseng exports. However "tame seng," as diggers call it, commands an average price of $30 a pound. That sector of the industry is concentrated in Wisconsin, which in 1994 certified more than a million pounds of the 1,271,548 pounds reported nationally (Fritsch 1996).

3. In Central America, for instance, the drama is replayed around the new cattle ranches of investors from the United States, abetted this time around by international treaties such as the General Agreement on Tariffs and Trade and the North American Free Trade Agreement (see Kovaleski 1998).

4. According to a study directed by scientist Albert Fritsch (1996), who heads the Center for Science in the Public Interest, the Chinese market alone will bear $12 billion worth of ginseng annually. To provide a basis for comparison, according to the West Virginia Mining and Reclamation Association in Charleston, the coal industry meets a direct annual payroll of $1 billion for the state of West Virginia.

5. Paul Salstrom (1994) argues that this use of the land for farming and hunting ultimately subsidized the coal industry. Compensating for depressed wages, it kept the union out of southern West Virginia longer than in other areas (see also Corbin 1981:37–38).

6. Consequently, according to a study by the Appalachian Land Ownership Task Force (1983), roughly 80 to 90 percent of the land is controlled by absentee owners. For more detailed documentation of the often illegal means of land acquisition, see Corbin (1981) and Eller (1982). An abundance of stories persist in oral tradition on Coal River about how the company "took" the land. Two local land companies have publicly accounted for the recent enclosures by citing instances of lawsuits brought against them by people injured while gathering wood on the property.

7. Whipkey's comment calls to mind a quatrain from an unknown medieval satirist: "The law locks up both man and woman / Who steals the goose from off the commons / And lets the greater felon loose / Who steals the commons from the goose."

References Cited

Ansted, D. T. 1885. "The Cabin Creek Coal Company Lands." *The Virginias: A Mining, Industrial and Scientific Journal* 6(9): 129–30.

Appalachian Land Ownership Task Force. 1983. *Who Owns Appalachia?: Landownership and Its Impact.* Lexington: University Press of Kentucky.

Batteau, Allen. 1990. *The Invention of Appalachia.* Tucson: University of Arizona Press.

Braun, E. Lucy. 1950. *Deciduous Forests of Eastern North America.* New York: Macmillan.

Brown, Beverly. 1996. "Fencing the Northwest Forests: Decline of Public Access and Accustomed Rights." *Cultural Survival Quarterly* 20 (Spring): 50–52.

Cantwell, Robert. 1993. *Ethnomimesis: Folklore and the Representation of Culture.* Chapel Hill: University of North Carolina Press.

Corbin, David Allen. 1981. *Life, Work, and Rebellion in the Coal Fields: The Southern West Virginia Miners, 1880–1922.* Urbana: University of Illinois Press.

Crowe, Beryl. 1977. "The Tragedy of the Commons Revisited." In *Managing the Commons.* Ed. Garret Hardin and John Baden. 53–65. San Francisco: W. H. Freeman.

Eller, Ronald. 1982. *Miners, Millhands, and Mountaineers: Industrialization of the Appalachian South, 1880–1930.* Knoxville: University of Tennessee Press.

Evans, E. Estyn. 1969. "The Scotch-Irish: Their Cultural Adaptation and Heritage in the American Old West." In *Essays in Scotch-Irish History.* Ed. E. E. R. Green. 69–86. London: Routledge & Kegan Paul.

Finger, John R. 1995. "Cherokee Accommodation and Persistence in the Southern Appalachians." In *Appalachia in the Making: The Mountain South in the 19th Century.* Ed. Mary Beth Pudup, Dwight B. Billings, and Altina L. Waller. 25–49. Chapel Hill: University of North Carolina Press.

Fritsch, Albert. 1996. "Ginseng in Appalachia." ASPI Technical Series, TP 38. Mt. Vernon, Ky.: ASPI Publications.

Halperin, Rhoda. 1990. *The Livelihood of Kin: Making Ends Meet "The Kentucky Way."* Austin: University of Texas Press.

Hardacre, Val. 1968. *Woodland Nuggets of Gold.* New York: Vangate Press.

Hart, John Fraser. 1977. "Land Rotation in Appalachia." *Geographical Review* 67(2): 148–65.

Hufford, Mary. 1998. "Weathering the Storm: Cultural Survival in an Appalachian Valley." In *An Appalachian Tragedy: Air Pollution and Tree Death in the Eastern Forests of North America.* Ed. Harvard Ayers, Jenny Hager, and Charles Little. 147–59. San Francisco: Sierra Club Books.

Kovaleski, Serge F. 1998. "'There Is No Law Here': Fear in Rural Costa Rica: Landowners Terrorized by Squatters." *Washington Post,* March 2, A11, A18.

Loucks, Orie. 1998. "In Changing Forests, A Search for Answers." In *An Appalachian Tragedy: Air Pollution and Tree Death in the Eastern Forests of North America.* Ed. Harvard Ayers, Jenny Hager, and Charles Little. 85–97. San Francisco: Sierra Club Books.

Mead, Margaret. 1972. *Blackberry Winter: My Earlier Years.* New York: Simon & Schuster.

National Park Service. 1989. "New River Gorge Newsletter." Glen Jean, W.Va.: New River Gorge National River.

Otto, John Solomon. 1983. "The Decline of Forest Farming in Southern Appalachia." *Journal of Forest History* 27(1): 18–27.

Salstrom, Paul. 1994. *Appalachia's Path to Dependency.* Lexington: University Press of Kentucky.

Shiva, Vandana. 1992. "Resources." In *The Development Dictionary.* Ed. Wolfgang Sachs. Atlantic Highlands, N.J.: Zed Books.

Snyder, Gary, 1990. "The Place, The Region, and the Commons." In *The Practice of the Wild.* Essays by Gary Snyder. 25–47. San Francisco: North Point Press.

———. 1993. "Understanding the Commons." In *Environmental Ethics.* Ed. Susan J. Armstrong and Richard G. Botzler. 227–31. New York: McGraw-Hill.

Stewart, Kathleen. 1996. *A Space on the Side of the Road: Cultural Poetics in an "Other" America.* Princeton, N.J.: Princeton University Press.

Thomas, Keith. 1983. *Man and the Natural World: A History of the Modern Sensibility.* New York: Pantheon Books.

West Virginia Surface Mining and Reclamation Association. n.d. "Greenlands." Charleston, W.Va.: West Virginia Surface Mining and Reclamation Association.

7 Space and Place, Land and Legacy

MELINDA BOLLAR WAGNER

It's more than just the land; it's our legacy. It's our heritage.

From my house, when I look out one way, I see where my ancestors lived, and when I look out the other way, I see where my husband's lived.

These quotes from rural Virginia natives are examples of physical space transfigured into culturally meaningful place; they show the relationships between space and place, land and legacy. Anthropologists and folklorists observe that a sense of place enveloped in a person's identity or definition of self "provides a reassuring sense of the world's continuity and stability" (Ryden 1993:252; see also Low 1994; Relph 1976).

Attachments to land that turn space into place might be based on "orientations to the environment" that are instrumental (based on economic benefit), symbolic (based on aesthetic enjoyment and moral or religious meaning), or sentimental (Cohen 1976). For residents of the two rural Virginia counties where my students and I worked, economic attachments are not missing. But in the residents' talk, these footings take a back seat to genealogical, historical, aesthetic, and even spiritual foundations.

The talk we heard was elicited in interviews conducted by the Radford University Cultural Heritage Research Team of anthropology and Appalachian Studies students and their professor.[1] The team used the ethnographic methods of cultural anthropology to discover whether there is cultural attachment to land in these counties and, if so, on what it is based and how it is played out in people's daily lives. Although this ongoing research is valuable in its own right, the impetus to begin it in May 1994 was a proposed 765,000-volt power line routed across these counties. Residents requested that we undertake this study as a supplement to an environmental impact assessment in which cultural attachment to land was a significant issue (Hedrick 1997; Wagner et al. 1995a, 1995b, 1997; Wagner 1996).

To answer the research questions, ethnographic interviews were conducted with 131 residents; most hailed from two contiguous valleys in the two counties. From this talk, anthropologists learn what is salient in a native culture. In ethnographic interviews, the ethnographers are careful not to ask leading questions or make leading comments. (For example, questions and comments such as "Would you say you loved your land?" or "I'll bet you love your land" would never be used.) No answers were implied in the questions we asked, and no multiple-choice answers were supplied. The questions were used when necessary to elicit talk. Sometimes it was not even necessary to rely on them. For example, if a person shows you her home, pointing out the family photographs and describing all the people in her family and where they live, it isn't necessary to then ask, "How many members of your family live nearby? Where else do members of your family live?"

The eighty-seven separate tape-recorded interviews with the 131 different residents were from one-half to six hours long, yielding more than 2,500 pages of interview transcriptions and field notes and more than 2,000 pages of computerized analyses of every word used in the transcriptions, from which the findings in this chapter are derived. We also attended church services, subscribed to the local newspaper, and collected archival materials (booklets of local history and the like) that residents gave us.

Analysis of the text of each interview discovered what is significant to people by finding what they talk about *first,* what they talk about *often,* what *kinds* of things they talk about, what things they talk about in *detail,* and what kinds of things they *could* talk about but *don't.* The analyst is seeking themes and patterns.

As is typical in anthropological reports, the residents' names are not used in citations to their interview transcriptions; in quotations, names of people and places have been replaced by pseudonyms. In this chapter, quotes from interviews are indicated by quotation marks, and specific transcript citations are omitted.

Translated into the specifics that apply to these counties, the land attachments the residents have are based on cultural continuity founded on their knowledge of the past, their life in the present, and their vision of the future on the land; and they are based on the link between their culture and the nature that surrounds and penetrates that culture.

A farm family in these counties may earn their living—or at least a part of it—from their land. But they are rooted in their place in many other ways. They are rooted by their genealogical tie to their land that was owned by their ancestors. They are rooted by the work they have done to maintain the buildings these ancestors built. They are rooted by the cemetery at the top of the hill that contains their relatives' bones and where they know their own and their spouses' will one day be. They are rooted by the sight of the huge "sugar trees" that they planted as saplings when they first moved there and by the taste of the apples from the trees they began grafting fifty years ago. They are rooted by the past, present, and future on the land. They are living in a "genealogical landscape" (Allen 1990).

LIVING IN THE GENEALOGICAL LANDSCAPE

> *He goes back to the Eastmans who settled here right at 1800, and I go back to the Grahams who were here in 1754. So the two families, his family and my family, lived side by side.*

Time and again, as residents swept their hands across a landscape, they said something like, "From here to here, this has been in the family for generations." The number of generations that can be accounted for goes back to nine for the young people of some families.

"You know when you look around that you're seeing the same things they saw" (Allen 1990:161). This is how folklorist Lynwood Montell explains the importance of living in the genealogical landscape where the land is a "historical anchor that reaches several generations into the past" (Hicks 1976:50). This "history is a representation that provides a matrix of meaning for the present" (Foster 1988:36; cf. Manzo and Nagy 1979). As a resident put it, "It means something to put down roots and to know your family—your people—have been here all this time."

The detailed and long-ranging knowledge of county history and family genealogies that residents demonstrated illustrates the inseparable link between land and culture in the county. Even residents who did not grow up in the county and who have no relatives there know the genealogies of their neighbors and the "genealogies" of the homes they have purchased.

For many residents, the genealogical landscape is both historical and contemporary: Their ancestors lived there; their relatives live there. "Everybody that I own in the world except my nephew is in [this] county." "All of [the members of the family] live nearby; they live within two miles of us." "Everybody around I'm related to unless they just moved in."

Such longevity in one place tends to make the tie to the land a familylike attachment. "Every tree, every creek, every building is not just a structure or a piece of nature, but a part of their family history. . . . When land has been owned by a family for so many generations, it ceases to be simply property: it moves from commodity to family member" (Usack 1994:5, 8).

Another clue to the familial attachments weaving together the land and the people who inhabit it is the practice of what anthropologists call fictive kinship. Fictive kinship is constructed for those who take on the needs and obligations of a kinship role but who are not biologically related. For example, some outsiders who moved in bought the house of an elderly woman—and moved in with her. The two families in the household cared for each other, physically and emotionally, as if they were kin and came to see each other as kin. Residents reported calling older neighbors "aunt" and "uncle." Although that practice is less common today, diminutives that symbolize bonds of familiarity are used: Iona is Onie, Lida is Lidie, Charles is Charlie.

ORIENTING BY THE SOCIAL MATRIX

> *Unless someone's moved in I can drive down the road and tell you who lives in almost every house.*

The land in these valleys functions for its inhabitants as social space. Anthropologist Tom Plaut (1979) describes various relationships between humans and land by constructing a continuum. On one end are societies who view land as sacred space and who see themselves as part of nature. Plaut uses the North American Indian as an example. Black Elk, an Oglala Sioux holy man, tells of the two-leggeds, the four-leggeds, the wings of the air, and all green things living in peace and harmony on the earth (Neihardt 1961).[2] This perspective, which includes identification with place—seeing the land as a place where one belongs—is common in nonindustrialized societies. In fact, in the history of humankind, the idea of land ownership did not exist until the onset of the kind of agriculture that allowed production year after year on the same piece of land. On the other side of the continuum is land as property. Here land is to be bought and sold for gain, or used. It is seen as useful for what it can produce, as infrastructure for development, as investment, or as useless "overburden" (as in strip mining).

The view of land in these counties seems to fit neither end of this continuum. Unlike a preagricultural society, here people do own the land and treasure it as theirs and pass it down. Yet the Navajo Indian and the county native sound alike when they decry activities that they see as harmful to their homelands. The Navajo person speaks of the sacredness of the land, the county native of his or her family's ties to the land and of its beauty. "Land had a special meaning for mountain residents which combined the diverse concepts of utility and stewardship. . . . While land was something to be used and developed to meet one's needs, it was also the fiber of daily existence, giving form to personal identity, material culture, and economic life. As such, it defined the 'place' in which one found security and self-worth" (Eller 1979:105).

So Plaut (1979) makes a place for the Appalachian view of land in the middle of the continuum. Here land is social space; it is a crucible for the social world, a carrier of social history (Hicks 1976:50–62). Here, the land is identified with the people who have lived there; the land is given meaning by the human activities that have happened and are happening on it.

The genealogical landscape extends beyond knowing the link between one's ancestry and the chain of title to one's land. As Barbara Allen (1990) notes, when mountain natives are talking to one another, route numbers and intersections never come up. They navigate by, and identify with, named geological features and historical circumstances that have marked the land with cultural meaning. The human connection to the land is the orienting force to be reckoned with.

Of course, when a native is giving directions to a stranger, he will use route numbers if he can recall them. Otherwise, he is more likely to use a part of the social matrix such as "the old red barn": "This old barn down here was kind of a landmark. They call it the old red barn; it's not red anymore because the paint is off of it, but anybody's askin' directions they'd say, 'Go to the old red barn.'"

Even when giving directions to a stranger, residents fall back on the social matrix. A resident drove the principal investigator around a section of one county, knowing that she did not know the roads and needed to be oriented. But when we came back onto a certain road, he said, "Now we're on John's road again"; he didn't say, "Now we're back on Route 624." One of our interviewers reported becoming lost on his way to an interview. "I pulled into a gas station to make sure I was headed in the right direction. At first, when I asked the lady working there if she knew where the road was, she did not know. But once she asked me the name of who I was looking for, she gladly helped me out" (Wingfield 1994).

A poem by Jeff Daniel Marion (1976) highlights the land-people connection by describing the way directions are likely to be given.

It's just
over the knob
there—
you know the place,
the one

up there next to
Beulah Justice,
your mother's second cousin
on her daddy's side.
Or
if you go in by
the back road
it's the farm across the way
from Jesse's old barn
that burned down
last June
with them two fine mules
of his.
Why hell, son,
you can't miss it.

USING THE PLACE NAMES

> *Place names, linked with landscape features, encode the shared past, distinguishing members of one group from another. . . . Places and their names are sources of identity and security.*
>
> —Hufford 1987:21–22

> *Local landmarks have been indelibly marked with the names of the families who first came to, and continue to live in the county, and what they have done there.*
>
> —Delicate 1994:5

As people identify themselves as from "Meadow Creek" and their neighbors as from "up Silver Creek" and gaze upon "Archie's Knob," they daily make a connection between the present and the past of the county. Settlements and landforms are named for people who were a part of the county's history. "My great-great-great-grandfather received a grant from the king of England just before the Revolutionary War started. His name was David Jones and David's Creek is named for him."

An analysis of every word of each interview showed that a resident might use as many as forty-seven different words for places in an interview. Not only do the residents know these place names, but they know the history behind them. Here, place names symbolize the genealogical, the geological, and even the botanical landscapes, as can be seen from names such as Dick's Creek, Level Green, and Twin Oaks.

THE LINK BETWEEN NATURE AND CULTURE

Environmental research—especially research done for environmental impact assessment—often makes a distinction between people concerns and environment concerns. This division coincides with social impact assessment and environmental impact assessment. This dichotomy between culture and nature is a long-standing one. But in-depth ethnographic study reaches the conclusion that in these valleys, the culture and the natural environment are inextricably bound together.

The link between the residents' identities and the nature that surrounds them is manifested in multiple, complex ways that we can only list here. That culture and nature are bound together is signified by the residents' emphasis on their perceptions of the environment's beauty; the residents' orienting themselves by the geological markers in their environment; the part nature plays in the history, folklore, and stories of the culture; the uses the culture has made of nature; the cultural knowledge of nature that the people carry; and the land-based connections between people. These elements, together with the long genealogical history on the same land that many of the culture-bearers carry, help create the residents' identities.

CULTURALIZING NATURE

The undivided character of nature and culture—the way one surrounds, penetrates, and finally becomes the other—can be appreciated by examining the major role nature plays in the culture. Nature is a part of the history, the folklore, and the stories. Knowledge of nature is passed down from generation to generation. Nature is used, nurtured, admired, feared, and kept at bay. The length of time residents spend talking about nature and the detail they use in their talk symbolize its significance in their lives.

A computer-aided analysis of all the words in each interview from one county showed the words that had both depth (being used frequently) and breadth (being used in many interviews). These words met two tests: They were the most frequently occurring words in 16 to 100 percent of the interviews *and* they occurred at least once in 75 to 100 percent of the interviews. (Often-used words such as *a, and, be,* and *from* were eliminated from the analysis.) The fifty words that met these two criteria display the many-sided mix of culture and nature. *Home, farm, road, school, county, place, family, people, live*—signs of human habitation—take their turn with natural labels such as *mountain* and *creek* and with nature bent to human use—*land, property, hunt.*

The importance of work is denoted by the presence of *work, worked,* and *working* on the list.

The importance of what is seen is shown by the presence in the most-used words list of *see/seen/saw, beautiful,* and *pretty.* Prepositions that denote directions were used frequently: *around, at, back, out, over,* and *up.*

Some words give evidence of the importance of history—*old* and *year(s)*—and concern for *where* and *time(s) when* events occurred.

Omissions from the most frequently used list are instructive as well. *Beautiful* is on the list; *ugly* is not. *Old* is on the list; *new* is not. *Good* is on the list; *bad* is not. *More* is on the list; *less* is not. Both *big* and *little* are on the list. Economically based words—*money, cash, dollars, pay*—are not on the list of frequently used words.

TAMING THE VALLEYS, REVERING THE MOUNTAINS

> *Taming the valleys: "To keep it clean and habitable, it takes some work."*
>
> *Revering the mountains: "I can see that God's hand sort of shaped that mountain."*

It is possible to take photographs in these valleys that show no trees that human hands have purposely planted, no fences, no cleared pastures. But to do that, the photographer must move the camera's eye up near the horizon. A more honest photo shows nature *and* the signs of culture—a culture that has been here since the 1700s.

When the ancestors of the current residents came to these valleys, the land was verdant, as it is now, but not cleared pastures and fields. Climax forests covered this Ridge and Valley area of Virginia in prehistoric and historic times.

The "old people" who are the ancestors of the current residents carved culture out of this wilderness, and their descendants are still maintaining the carvings. The cultural carvings are in the valleys; the mountain ridges contain natural wildness. The culture values both keeping the wild areas wild and maintaining the rural domesticity of the valleys. Residents cut down trees in the tamed valleys to get a better view of the wild mountains. "Oh, the mountains! It's not part of my land, but I back up to what's called Cap Mountain and Cap Mountain is sort of a horseshoe shape mountain. The Appalachian Trail runs right along the top of it and out my back door. I cut down a bunch of trees so I could look at it. And you know, I can stand there and I can see that God's hand sort of shaped that mountain."

It is obvious that the residents care about and know about nature. All the talk of the flora, the fauna, the weather, the water, the woods, and the natural formations that we heard provides ample evidence. But in the valleys there is also a culture laid onto this nature. Fields and pastures have been cleared, wood has been cut for firewood, ponds have been built, streams have been stocked with fish, yards have been mowed, lanes have been paved, Japanese gardens have been built, and deer and bear have lent their heads to hang on walls. This culture knows and admires nature, but in the valleys there is also a tension between the two.

In the valleys, culture keeps nature at bay. Fences have to be rebuilt when "it rains hard and little flash floods take them out. . . . Poor Sam; it keeps him busy building fence." The deer, lovely as they are to see, threaten the crops and the gardens. Residents devise ways to keep them out. A resident who lives in the wildest of the tame areas showed us a small area beside his house, fenced with a split rail fence, where an almond bush and some other domesticated plants grow—where he tries to keep the deer out. He has built small wire fences around wild plants—berry bushes and ginseng—that he wants to preserve and use.

One resident observed the cultural trait of wanting things to "look nice" and described it this way: "Everybody takes pride in their farms and keeps them looking nice. You very rarely see a grown up thing unless somebody has just died and they haven't settled up their estate, something like that, but most of them are just as clear as you keep your yard."

Brush is a symbol of nature's attempt to come back where it should not be: "There were briars up to here," a resident says to describe his place before he moved in and started mowing. "You used to be able to see over here, but the people who bought that have just let the trees grow up," says a resident of his new neighbors. "So it's sad to see it keep growing up," says another resident of another place. The coming of snakes is a metaphor for what happens when land that has been tamed is allowed to "grow up" or "grow over." Residents explain that snakes come and live in the briars.

USING METAPHORS TO PORTRAY THE BOND TO THE LAND

Anthropologists recognize that a reliable tool for understanding the relationship between people and their culture is finding the metaphors people use. That's because the use of metaphor is itself a powerful way to create identities for ourselves: "Metaphors move us, and their aptness lies in their power to change our moods, our sense of situation" (Fernandez 1974:129).

The metaphors that the research team gleaned from the interviews of residents were of two types: One likened the land to a family member; the other gave the land a religious or spiritual essence. "It's more than just the land; it's our legacy. It's our heritage." "[The land] is like another member of their family. It's almost as important to them as one of their children." "To me this family thinks more of their heritage, their ancestors, and since the farm has been in the family for so long they love it. You know, it's more than just a farm."

Residents described their area as "just a paradise," "the garden of heaven," "God's country," and "heaven" itself. "My husband and I sit in the swing and my sister and her husband do, too, and we'll sit up there on a Saturday night and my husband'll say, 'it may not be heaven but it's close.'" The use of a religious idiom also came into play when residents told us how they acquired their land. Newcomers said, "So [finding this place] was just—it was just an answered prayer . . . and this was just meant to be our home. That's all there is to it." "I would say God probably told us [about this place] because a rainbow came out when we were looking at it."

When we asked, "Where would you go if you had to leave this county," residents answered, "I hope it will be heaven." "I want to go to heaven. That's where I want to go." "I think that the only place that I could go that would be nicer than this would be heaven."

EPILOGUE

As other counties that lie in the path of alternative routes for the power line called on us, study of cultural attachment to land expanded to include eleven semesters, more than 100 undergraduate students in four different courses, and 223 residents of five counties. It produced four technical reports, an honors thesis, and numerous student and faculty presentations and performances on campus, for local historical societies, and at meetings of the Appalachian Studies Conference, the Southern Anthropological Society, and the American Anthropological Association. In the most recent phase of presenting project findings, I was called as an expert witness to the state government body that regulates utilities. How empowering for the citizens was this project? It certainly demonstrated to the culture-bearers that others valued and were interested in their cultures, and it chipped away at the accretions of years of stereotyping. Was it empowering in the sense of making a difference in the decision-making process of a government regulatory body? On that point, the jury is still out (see also Wagner and Hedrick 2001).

Notes

1. The original Radford University Cultural Heritage Research Team collected most of the data and performed the analyses reported here. They are Shannon T. Scott, Megan Scanlon, Stacy L. Viers, Jean A. Kappes, and Melinda Bollar Wagner, with the assistance of Allyn Beth Motley and Lola Coleman. The original research has been supplemented by subsequent interviews and analysis provided by members of Appalachian cultures classes in fall 1994, fall 1995, and fall 1996, Practicum in Anthropology in spring 1995 and spring 1996, and Kristen Hedrick's final honors project in anthropology in spring 1997.

2. Anthropologist Keith Basso (1996:156) says about Native American people, "Much has been made of late, inside and outside of academic anthropology, of the 'sacredness' of American Indian lands, the 'spiritual' nature of human relationships with them, and how, given both, Indian people are able to live in a perpetual state of 'harmony with nature.' At some vague and general level, I suppose this may be true. I also believe . . . that matters are much more complex." Basso goes on to give a reason for his caution: "If it is true—and it is—that old stereotypes of 'Indians' are constantly being replaced by new ones, it seems only prudent to eschew them altogether, or at least to qualify them in careful, informed, and fully local ways." This cautionary tale could be applied to the Appalachian region as well. The hard, violent, moonshining hillbilly image is sometimes replaced by one that is soft, romanticized, and close to nature.

References Cited

Allen, Barbara. 1990. "The Genealogical Landscape and the Southern Sense of Place." In *Sense of Place*. Ed. Barbara Allen and Thomas J. Schlereth. 152–63. Lexington: University Press of Kentucky.

Basso, Keith H. 1996. *Wisdom Sits in Places: Landscape and Language among the Western Apache.* Albuquerque: University of New Mexico Press.

Cohen, Eric. 1976. "Environmental Orientations: A Multidimensional Approach to Social Ecology." *Current Anthropology* 17(1): 49–71.

Delicate, Jane P. 1994. "Cultural Attachment to Land Study." Paper for Anthropology 411: Appalachian Cultures, Radford University, Radford, Va.

Eller, Ronald D. 1979. "Land and Family: An Historical View of Preindustrial Appalachia." *Appalachian Journal* 6(2): 83–109.

Fernandez, James W. 1974. "The Mission of Metaphor in Expressive Culture." *Current Anthropology* 15:119–45.

Foster, Stephen William. 1988. *The Past Is Another Country: Representation, Historical Consciousness, and Resistance in the Blue Ridge.* Berkeley: University of California Press.

Hedrick, Kristen. 1997. "Cultural Attachment to Land." Honors thesis, Department of Anthropology, Radford University, Radford, Va.

Hicks, George L. 1976. *Appalachian Valley.* New York: Holt, Rinehart, & Winston.

Hufford, Mary T. 1987. "Telling the Landscape: Folklife Expressions and Sense of Place." In *Pinelands Folklife.* Ed. Rita Zorn Moonsammy, Rita Zorn, David S. Cohen, and Lorraine E. Williams. 13–42. New Brunswick, N.J.: Rutgers University Press.

Low, Setha. 1994. "Cultural Conservation of Place." In *Conserving Culture.* Ed. Mary Hufford. 66–77. Urbana: University of Illinois Press.

Manzo, Joseph, and Michael Nagy. 1979. "Images of the United States: The View from Southern West Virginia." Paper presented at the Appalachian Studies Conference, Jackson's Mill, W.Va., March 16–18.

Marion, Jeff Daniel. 1976. "In a Southerly Direction." In *Out in the Country Back Home.* Winston-Salem, N.C.: The Jackpine Press.

Neihardt, John G. 1961. *Black Elk Speaks.* Lincoln: University of Nebraska Press.

Plaut, Tom. 1979. "The Meaning of Land and the Political Process." Paper presented at the Appalachian Studies Conference, Jackson's Mill, W.Va., March 16–18.

Relph, Edward C. 1976. *Place and Placelessness.* London: Pion.

Ryden, Kent C. 1993. *Mapping the Invisible Landscape: Folklore, Writing, and the Sense of Place.* Iowa City: University of Iowa Press.

Usack, Lin. 1994. "Cultural Attachment to Land Study." Paper for Anthropology 411: Appalachian Cultures, Radford University, Radford, Va.

Wagner, Melinda Bollar, with the assistance of Anthropology 411 Appalachian Cultures Class. 1996. "Preliminary Report of an Ethnographic Study Documenting Certain Intangible Elements of Cultural Heritage, Folklife, and Living Culture." Appalachian Regional Studies Center and Department of Sociology and Anthropology, Radford University, Radford, Va.

Wagner, Melinda Bollar, and Kristen L. Hedrick. 2001. "'You Have a Culture to Preserve Here, but We Have a Power Line to Stop': University/Community Study of Cultural Attachment to Place in Proposed Powerline Corridors." *Practicing Anthropology* 23 (Spring): 10–14.

Wagner, Melinda Bollar, Shannon T. Scott, Megan Scanlon, Stacy L. Viers, and Jean A. Kappes, with the assistance of Allyn Beth Motley and Lola Coleman. 1995a. "It May Not Be Heaven, but It's Close." Research report, Appalachian Regional Studies Center and Department of Sociology and Anthropology, Radford University, Radford, Va.

———. 1995b. "Position Paper to Accompany Documentation of Certain Intangible Elements of Cultural Heritage, Folklife, and Living Culture: Cultural Attachment to Land." Research report, Appalachian Regional Studies Center and Department of Sociology and Anthropology, Radford University, Radford, Va.

Wagner, Melinda Bollar, Shannon T. Scott, and Danny Wolfe. 1997. "Drawing the Line between People and Power: Taking the Classroom to the Community." In *Practicing Anthropology in the South.* Ed. James M. Wallace. 110–18. Athens: University of Georgia Press.

Wingfield, Kevin. 1994. "Cultural Attachment to Land Study." Paper for Anthropology 411: Appalachian Cultures, Radford University, Radford, Va.

PART 3 Conservation for the Future

The first section of this book presented four accounts of human presence and actions in Appalachian localities to suggest how a comprehensive picture of regional environmental and cultural history might be constructed through collaboration of the multiple cultural science disciplines and their varied research methods. The second section turned from past to present and brought ethnographic insight to bear on the single theme of attachment to place. These final chapters present applications, case studies in which knowledge about the past or present has become a guide for action. The actors are professionals in cultural resource management and planning, educators, and citizen activists committed to seeking sustainable futures for their communities.

Doris Lukas Link, David Brady, and Nancy Kate Givens team to describe their individual roles as community leaders in grassroots opposition to unwanted intrusion of a high-voltage electric power transmission line into the Clover Hollow and Plow Screw communities in Giles County, Virginia. Through the late 1990s, they became informed about federal and state environmental impact assessment procedures and took advantage of the opportunities for public participation. Aware of the work that Melinda Wagner had done earlier in Craig County, they facilitated research of Radford University anthropologists to document attachment to place in their communities, and they conducted their own research to prepare and submit a rural historic district nomination to the National Register of Historic Places.

Gerald Schroedl describes collaborative archaeological excavations at the eighteenth-century lower Cherokee town of Chattooga in the Sumter National Forest. Such research provides the information Forest Service natural and cultural resource managers need, but the Chattooga project also offered outreach to educators in an innovative field school that will yield long-term as well as short-term benefits for the Forest Service. In the short term, the Forest Service stretched the funds invested in research by operating this project under the "Windows in Time" program, which encourages participation of unpaid citizen volunteers. In this case the volunteers were K–12 teachers. As they share with students their enhanced understanding and appreciation of archaeology and Cherokee heritage in South Carolina, they are building multicultural awareness and citizen support in the next generation for cultural resource management on public lands.

The final chapters present two examples of community planning in Tennessee. With the prospect of the Big South Fork National River and Recreation Area turning the Victorian village of Rugby into a gateway community, citizens chose to work with professional planners to create a master plan that would control the pace and direction of development. The alternative means of preservation would have been removing residents and absorbing Rugby into the federal area to become another architectural museum like Cades Cove. As would be expected in a region that has been reluctant to embrace planning and zoning authority, there was conflict and debate during the eighteen-month planning process. The award-winning master plan reflected historical precedent, however. Careful siting and layout of the village in its original 1880 plan offered a clear blueprint, one remarkably compatible with late twentieth-century goals of cultural and natural resource conservation and sustainable development. In chapter 10, Benita Howell and Susan Neff describe the British and American ideals of nature, landscape design, and social betterment that found concrete expression in Rugby's original town plan, especially in the domestic landscapes and in the greenbelt and trail system that surrounded the town.

Whereas Big South Fork tourism is still in an incipient phase, Pittman Center near Great Smoky Mountains National Park has seen Gatlinburg, then Pigeon Forge, and most recently Townsend succumb to rapid growth of tourist-related businesses. The East Tennessee Design Center through its FutureScapes program offered Pittman Center citizens an opportunity to deliberate together on many of the issues entailed in planning for sustainable development. Annette Anderson, who was director of the East Tennessee Design Center at that time, discusses the successes and failures of FutureScapes in Pittman Center.

External pressures of recreation and tourism development pushed both Rugby and Pittman Center into community planning; fortunately, neither community had to finance planning activities from its own resources alone. Rugby's planning was financed by the U.S. Army Corps of Engineers as part of its responsibility to mitigate potential adverse impacts of the new recreation area. FutureScapes was funded by multiple foundations and agencies interested in promoting planning for sustainable development in east Tennessee. These projects offer inspiration and models for other Appalachian communities, but they pose challenges as well. Small rural communities in picturesque settings are most threatened by undesirable impacts from the outdoor recreation and tourism industry that is flourishing, with encouragement from state governments, in Appalachia's postindustrial economy. These communities are least able to finance ambitious planning projects. Aside from the special circumstances that draw federal agencies into local initiatives or such high-profile pilot projects as FutureScapes, who will help the legions of rural counties and small towns in Appalachia take control of their futures through effective planning? Can we ask the poorest communities to choose sustainable development over alternatives that offer greater economic rewards in the short run? Anderson concludes her chapter and this volume by raising the challenging questions of equity and social justice that must be answered in the twenty-first century.

8 Defending the Community: Citizen Involvement in Impact Assessment and Cultural Heritage Conservation

DORIS LUCAS LINK, DAVID BRADY,
AND NANCY KATE GIVENS

Editor's Note: Since 1993, citizens of Craig and Giles counties in southwestern Virginia have been engaged in protesting a proposal by American Electric Power Company (AEP, formerly Appalachian Power Company) to build a 765,000-volt power line from Wyoming, West Virginia, to Cloverdale, Virginia. Because proposed power line corridors traversed extensive tracts of George Washington and Jefferson National Forests, the U.S. Department of Agriculture (USDA) Forest Service became lead agency for coordinating environmental impact assessment (EIA) for the proposed power line. In a potentially precedent-setting decision, the EIA coordinator was persuaded to include a study of cultural attachment to place in the impact research. The contractor for this research was a consulting firm experienced in social impact assessment in the western United States. Not only did this firm lack prior experience in the Appalachian region, but their personnel lacked expertise in ethnographic methods suitable to the study of cultural attachment to place. Cultural attachment is an intangible phenomenon of attitudes, values, and meaning as well as a reflection of historical particulars. Rather than pursuing an emic method of the kind Melinda Wagner describes in chapter 7, the contractors sought to minimize face-to-face interaction with citizens by using "remote sensing" techniques to delineate communities within the study area and gauge each community's degree of place attachment. The logic of impact assessment entails quantification and comparison of severity of impact, but on what basis can researchers assert that one community has more of an intangible quality than another community does? An unfortunate consequence of this logic is that it encourages NIMBY-ism (not in my backyard—but maybe in yours) as the power company returns with a new corridor proposal to replace one deemed unacceptable. Therefore, the same threat loomed over Craig County, then Giles County, and most recently Bland County.

This chapter is a set of three essays by community activists in the Giles County struggle against the power transmission line. First, Doris Link introduces her home community of Plow Screw with an evocative essay that also describes some of the ways in which she and other citizens took on the challenge of fighting the power line and contesting bureaucratic research findings that threatened their future. Then David Brady explains how the two closely linked communities of Clover Hollow and Plow Screw mobilized to make effective use of environmental impact assessment procedures that set aside time for public review and comment on the Draft Environmental Impact Statement (DEIS). I became a *pro bono* consultant to the community in this effort, working with them to obtain information about the contract firm's research procedures and answering questions that arose as they prepared their written comments on the DEIS. The prospect that the Forest Service might adopt this flawed method for studying cultural intangibles in future environmental impact assessment compelled me to file my own comment on this portion of the DEIS on behalf of Appalachian scholars and applied ethnographers. I concluded those comments by noting that in future, the Forest Service should model its conduct of this kind of research on National Park Service standards concerning qualification of applied ethnographers and appropriate research procedures.

Even while the community developed their rejoinder to the contract report's conclusion—that their degree of place attachment was only "medium"—they assisted Melinda Wagner and Radford University students in an alternative ethnographic study to assemble systematic, reliable, quantifiable interview data on cultural intangibles such as place attachment. In addition, Nancy Kate Givens seized this opportunity to amass indisputable evidence of place attachment in the form of the land ownership and genealogical records that place residents and their ancestors in Clover Hollow and Plow Screw over the generations, some families for as long as 200 years. She concludes this chapter with a description of her research and its findings. This became the community's most important strategy because it led to proactive documentation for a National Register Historic District nomination, moving the community beyond crisis mobilization to secure more general and longer-term protection against encroachment from unwanted development.

DORIS LUCAS LINK

When I became involved in the AEP fight in 1993, I never imagined it would take me to college, make an amateur architect of me, send me to the state capitol to speak before the Honorable Judge Howard Anderson in shorts and a T-shirt that stated emphatically "NO POWER LINE!" I performed in a play written by Barbara Carlisle, a Newport resident who works in the Drama Department at Virginia Tech University, and spoke at an Appalachian Studies Conference. To cap it all off, my name is on the AEP enemies list.

I am a sixth-generation descendant of Thomas Lucas, one of the earliest settlers in eastern Giles County, who acquired land there in 1791. My grandson, Adam Jones, is the eighth generation living in this area, which people who care about the history of the place call Plow Screw. When the 911 system went into effect all our roads had to be named, and many of our neighbors didn't want the name Plow Screw on their mail. We had a community meeting and the road was named Rocky Sink after a one-room schoolhouse that once stood there. We came out of this meeting still speaking to each other—a minor miracle.

My mother, my brother, I, and 90 percent of our neighbors have been on this land continuously ever since our ancestor Thomas Lucas bought the land and settled here in 1791. One of the proposed routes of AEP line would cut directly across these lands, dividing property that stretches from the top of John's Creek Mountain all the way to Sinking Creek. Although the land was inherited by several children, it is still being farmed and worked. All of my father's people are buried in the Lucas Cemetery, which is in the path of this monster line. My people held onto their land through the Great Depression. We haven't sold timber from the mountains on our acreage, and because we kept the forest unfragmented, we have a rare species of bat and some rare birds according to our neighbor Dave Brady. Our forested land is bounded on the north by the Jefferson National Forest, through which the AEP Matt Funk line stretches. I feel that the encroachment of this line caused the whippoorwills that I love to hear to move away. The only way I can hear one now is on CD-ROM. Tears come to my eyes when I think of it.

I want to tell you a bit about life as I live it, a way of life threatened like the whippoorwills. I see the sun rise over mountains to the east from my kitchen window, the view unobstructed by power lines. When I work in the vegetable garden, I can listen to the birds singing, the bobwhites calling (three of my neighbors raise them to replenish the area). The soil feels so good in my hands and the smell of the earth in spring is wonderful. It stirs something in the soul. Our garden provides us potatoes and onions for the winter. I can beans, corn, and tomatoes and make jams and jellies. It's best to eat fresh from the garden, though. It's good to know we can provide for ourselves with the Lord's blessing and not be dependent on anyone. Too bad we're so dependent on electricity.

The water we drink is cool, sweet, and pure and comes bubbling out of the mountains for us to enjoy. I'm thankful every day for such a blessing. The trees on these mountains are threatened by acid rain. I've been told that AEP coal emissions are one of the worst sources of pollution in the United States.

In our part of the world, we like to sit on our porches in the summertime. Most everyone has a porch swing. We watch the clouds and birds. Have you watched a mother cardinal teach her young to fly, or a beautiful green chrysalis with a necklace of gold beads change into a monarch butterfly? Have you had a hummingbird eat from your hand? Have you eaten a wild white strawberry or hunted the wild mushrooms in spring? They're all here for us to enjoy, but the noise and visual impact of the power line would destroy all of it.

I love to walk through the woods in spring, see and smell the tiny pink flower of the trailing arbutus, see the Dutchman's britches, jack-in-the-pulpit, and wild orchids and pick wild greens. My mother taught me to recognize ladyfinger, lamb's quarter, chickweed, crow's foot, poke, and wild beets. She isn't able to go anymore, and I miss those days.

In autumn the mountains are spectacular. Once my husband and I climbed to the top of John's Creek Mountain. Below us lay the Big Ridge in Clover Hollow. It looked like a beautiful patchwork quilt, with all the leaves of different colors. That's another thing linking me to the past: my love of quilting. My mother pieced quilts when I was a child, and I have two quilts my grandmother pieced. I feel very close to her when I look at them. Now I'm teaching my granddaughter Emily to quilt, and she loves it.

I belong to the Loosely Woven Quilt Group in Newport. Our group has provided two quilts to Citizens Organized to Protect the Environment, a local organization that is fighting the power line. We were featured in the *Roanoke Times* recently, shown working on a variation of "Log Cabin" that was raffled off at the Eastern Elementary School Arts Festival to benefit their arts program. We kept adding blocks until the quilt was wider than our quilt frames. Luckily, my husband had made an extension for my frame, so we used it. We made a sampler quilt to raise funds for the preservation of the 1916 covered bridge on Sinking Creek. We have three covered bridges in the proposed Greater Newport Rural Historic District (GNRHD). We realized $1,000 from this quilt. The folks who purchased it gave us visitation rights. They're really nice people, even though they are "brought-ins." Our next project is a paper-pieced stained-glass window quilt to donate to First Christian Church as a fundraiser. The congregation is purchasing a wooded area back of the church to keep it from being gobbled up by developers. We hope to have a hiking trail through it and a picnic shelter for the community to enjoy.

The GNRHD nomination process is what brought about my experience as an amateur architectural historian (figure 8.1). Some of us took a short training session, created forms for submitting information about properties, and

Figure 8.1. Moses Atkins house, built in 1831. Greater Newport Rural Historic District, Giles County, Virginia. Photo by Nancy Kate Givens.

spent countless hours out in the community, looking at houses and visiting folks. We were able to smooth the way for Dr. Wagner and her anthropology students by setting up interviews between the old-timers and the students. It's been a wonderful, mutually beneficial experience. Our efforts cost a great deal in time and some funds, but they were well worth it if Historic District status helps us hold on to the rural and scenic beauty of our place.

The love of simple things makes our lives in Plow Screw so good. Why should all this be taken away so that AEP can make more money? We don't have much material wealth, but we do have a way of life worth fighting for. We have clean air, sweet water, and the stars at night (people who live in towns and cities can't see the stars). We have our mountains and our land. Like the Native Americans, I believe there is something spiritual here, and every so often it makes itself felt. We must not keep paving, pushing, bulldozing, and blasting until it's gone forever. Even though I have one toe in the electronic age, my heart and the rest of me hate to see our way of life disappear.

When our fight against the power line started, I was out in the community collecting money, I think for the historic work. An old-timer said to me, "Little girl, there's no use to fight AEP, they're too big." But I say, especially to young people, that our way of life is worth fighting for. At least I can tell my grandchildren and great-grandchildren I did all I could. Too bad the battle has to be fought over and over. By the way, the gentleman gave me $10.

DAVID BRADY

Rural communities of southwest Virginia live from year to year with a steady heartbeat attuned to the seasons. From time to time community lands are threatened by the sudden intrusion of outside forces such as highways, power lines, and other acts of seizure by eminent domain. In such times, the community can survive or be destroyed by the taking or by the struggle itself (see McGuire 1981, 1982). Since 1991, the citizens of Clover Hollow and Plow Screw have faced such a struggle with AEP over siting of the largest power line project in the United States. In assessing the environmental impact of routing this line through the National Forest, cultural attachment to land emerged as an ethnographic tool that might help community activists defend the community by recognizing its inherent qualities.

Clover Hollow is a small Appalachian farming community of about three hundred people surrounded by three mountains and the National Forest in Giles County, Virginia. It actually consists of two conjoined communities: Clover Hollow, in the valley and on the slopes of John's Creek Mountain and Clover Hollow Mountain, and Plow Screw, primarily the descendants of two families (Links and Lucases) living on the shoulder of Salt Pond Mountain. The Clover Hollow–Plow Screw area comprises about ten square miles, and about 70 percent of the land is still in the hands of the descendants of five families who settled here between the 1790s and 1860s.

In 1991 the Appalachian Power Company, now AEP, filed for permits to build a 765,000-volt power line from Wyoming, West Virginia to Cloverdale, Virginia. One of the proposed alternative routes would bisect the north end of Clover Hollow. Citizens of Clover Hollow and the Sinking Creek Valley in Giles and Craig counties joined in opposition to the project.

A long and contentious fight with AEP in state and federal proceedings to determine potential environmental impacts of the project ensued. The U.S. Forest Service, designated the lead agency for environmental assessment, responded to concerns that were raised about sociocultural impacts of power line intrusion by including a novel study of cultural attachment to place in the research leading to a Draft Environmental Impact Statement (DEIS) for the project. This work began in the Peter's Mountain area but eventually expanded to survey seven cultural attachment areas in the power line study area. We hoped that expanding impact studies to consider cultural intangibles such as place attachment would give communities new tools to defend against projects such as the power line.

In the summer of 1995, a representative of the consulting firm that was under contract with the Forest Service to conduct the place attachment study contacted me. We arranged a meeting with several rural communities surrounding Newport, including those of Clover Hollow and Plow Screw. The meeting lasted about two hours. Many of us left thinking that it was a good introduction for us to the consultant and the research that would be done. In 1996 we learned that this meeting *was* our participation in the study.

The Forest Service issued its DEIS in the summer of 1996 recommending No Action; that is, none of the crossings of the National Forest in the proposed power line corridors would be acceptable (including those that affected Clover Hollow and Plow Screw). When we carefully reviewed the federal documents (U.S. Forest Service 1996), however, the Forest Service seemed weakest in its defense of the route affecting Clover Hollow and Plow Screw. The cultural attachment study concluded that Clover Hollow exhibited only "medium" attachment to place and would suffer no significant cultural impacts if crossed by the power line. We began mobilizing to contest those findings.

In mid-July, the community (Clover Hollow and Plow Screw) met at Marty Farrier's farm at the head of the Hollow (figure 8.2) and decided on a twofold course of action. First, we resolved to meet with the forest supervisor as a community, supporting his decision but requesting that he revisit the issue of attachment to place in Clover Hollow. Second, we consulted with Dr. Melinda Wagner, who had been conducting ethnographic interviews with our Craig County neighbors in the Sinking Creek Valley under the power line's preferred corridor. We asked that she initiate similar ethnographic studies to document cultural intangibles in Clover Hollow. Thus we initiated our own process to assess attachment to land in Clover Hollow and Plow Screw. We knew that Dr. Wagner's methods were respected as valid within the anthropological community. We hoped that the evidence Dr. Wagner developed might be used to refute the consulting firm's conclusions about Clover Hollow.

On August 12, 1996, about fifty members of the community met with USFS Supervisor Damon at a public meeting in Blacksburg. We presented a letter signed by nearly every resident of Clover Hollow, children as well as adults,[1] serving notice that we would challenge the substance of the Cultural Attachment Study regarding Clover Hollow and Plow Screw even though we supported his "No Action" decision.

We had a number of questions about the Forest Service process that as citizens we felt inadequate to address. Dr. Wagner referred us to Dr. Benita How-

Figure 8.2. Martin Farrier house, built 1902. Greater Newport Rural Historic District, Giles County, Virginia. Photo by Nancy Kate Givens.

ell, who agreed to consult *pro bono* as we prepared our response to the DEIS. Her assistance enabled citizens to better understand what the consultants had done and how best to focus citizen response. Extensive questioning of the USFS via Freedom of Information Act requests revealed serious shortcomings in the analysis in terms of methods and citizens' due process.

Volumes 3 and 4 of the DEIS included maps of the Clover Hollow Cultural Attachment Area that did not agree with one another.[2] When residents requested an explanation, the consultants issued, via a letter from the Forest Service Environmental Impact Statement (EIS) manager, a third definition of the study area that citizens were to use (Bergmann 1996). They were unconcerned that neither the maps nor their definition resembled Clover Hollow as the people of Clover Hollow cognitively understand it. The contract researchers had imposed boundaries on our community rather than solicit information about community boundaries from us. In fact, Plow Screw never was identified as a distinct community, even though many Plow Screw residents, including the late Ira Price, spoke eloquently in the August 1995 meeting. Parts of Givens family farms, part of Clover Hollow for many generations, were left out of the Cultural Attachment Area, and places that no one from these parts would ever consider part of Clover Hollow were included. Roads were incorrectly named. The study had been conducted without appropriate legal notice (a major legal shortcoming) and possibly in violation of Forest Service Regulations. These constituted the major challenges citizens themselves could raise in the ninety days in which we were allowed to comment on the DEIS.

Dr. Howell's response to the DEIS raised other issues: the lack of professional review of the research design, inappropriate assumptions about place attachment and failure to use an emic (or community residents') perspective in the research, and inappropriate and unethical efforts to conduct the research surreptitiously (Howell 1996, 1999). Some of the issues raised might ultimately provide grounds for administrative or legal challenge should the USFS attempt to approve the route connecting USFS corridors through Clover Hollow. This critique served the communities by almost ensuring the revisiting of the cultural attachment issue relating to Clover Hollow and Plow Screw in any subsequent EIS proceedings or in administrative or legal appeals that may emerge from the process.

Ethnographic studies began in the fall of 1996 with Dr. Wagner's Radford University students interviewing about thirty Clover Hollow residents ranging from first- to ninth-generation families. Studies were conducted over a period of three years, using the same methods used earlier in Craig County (described in chapter 7 of this volume). Dr. Wagner and her class completed their initial report in time for it to be included in the community response to the DEIS. These studies helped the community identify and assess key intangible dimensions of attachment to land in Clover Hollow and Plow Screw and articulate the issue of attachment to decision-makers at the state and federal level.

In addition to enabling the community to respond to AEP proposals, the ethnographic study opened doors to Nancy Kate Givens, our community historian. She swiftly completed her genealogical survey of Clover Hollow and Plow Screw and assembled land ownership records that contributed to our proactive strategy of community preservation: seeking National Register designation as a Rural Historic District. Mr. Paul Capp, a historic preservationist retained by the Virginia Department of Historic Resources (Virginia DHR), used this information while preparing the Department of Interior Nomination Study for the GNRHD. The Virginia DHR approved the nomination for Historic District designation in March 2000, and the National Park Service listed the GNRHD on the National Register of Historic Places on December 12, 2000. This translation of ethnographic research on cultural intangibles into substantive data supporting the historic district nomination ultimately gave Clover Hollow and Plow Screw standing before the Virginia State Corporation Commission, which by law and its own regulations recognizes cultural resource preservation issues.

Clearly, AEP does not want the cultural attachment issue to have any standing before state or federal agencies because it might lead to new restrictions to routing future power lines. AEP brought a later routing proposal for the power line to the Virginia State Corporation Commission (SCC) in 1997. At that time the company had access to all of the prior research and comment on the cultural attachment issue, but they failed to notify the commission that attachment to place was a potential source of negative cultural impact. AEP's failure even to acknowledge the issue in a forthright manner before the commission laid them open to legal challenges ranging from due process violations to bias in their routing procedures. Early in hearings before the SCC, the Greater Newport Rural Historic District Committee (Greater Newport) raised the cultural attachment issue and these challenges. We filed a motion to dismiss the case.[3] The motion failed, but the state's examiner later issued rulings that provide redress to many of the motion's issues, including the substantial additional due process that the Greater Newport committee had sought.

Later in the evidentiary hearings, materials derived from the ethnographic study and data assembled by Ms. Givens enabled Clover Hollow power line opponents to develop tangible specifics of the damage the proposed line route would cause in bisecting the community. In testimony filed before the Virginia SCC, community historian Nancy Kate Givens addressed these impacts on Clover Hollow and Plow Screw (from east to west):[4]

—Splitting the Bob and Eunice Sexton Family Farm in half. This farm was acquired by Eunice and Bob Sexton and sister Maggie Cumbee in 1960. Eunice's family did not own land in Clover Hollow until she was able to purchase this farm, the very land her family has worked as tenant farmers and day laborers for several generations.

—Cutting a large corner from the Mark Givens Family Farm, taking in some of the most desirable pasture acreage of this 614-acre farm. The Givens family have lived on and farmed this land continuously for 132 years and six generations; three generations currently live on the farm.

—Splitting the 532-acre Farrier Family Farm in half. This farm has been lived on and farmed continuously by Farriers for 110 years. Three generations currently live on the farm, including fifth generation family members.

—Cutting the corner of the Betsey and J. C. Link Farm (103.75 acres). Seventh-generation Barry Link had tentative plans to build on this land, currently farmed by Marty Farrier.

—Splitting the Calvin Lucas Farm (73 acres) and portions of the Dale and Shannon Lucas Farms (23.75 acres). Descendants of Thomas Lucas have lived on and farmed these lands continuously for 176 years. Cal, Dale and Shannon are sixth-generation direct descendants of Thomas Lucas. This segment divides Calvin Lucas land from brothers Dale and Shannon Lucas.

—Covering three-quarters of the 26.25 acres belonging to James Barry Link, son of Betsey and J. C. Link. Barry is a seventh-generation lineal descendant of Gaspar Link, the Hessian soldier who held the original land grant on Salt Pond Mountain, and of Thomas Lucas.

—Passing directly over Jerry Harvey's dwelling and the Saunders Family Cemetery, where Link kin are buried.

—Passing directly over Allan and Eleanor Link Farm (33.25 acres). This farm has been lived on and actively farmed by the Link family for four generations. Allan is a sixth-generation descendant of Gaspar Link.

—Cutting a wide swath through the entire length of the Virginia and Henry Kauffelt Farm (153 acres), which was lived on and farmed by the descendants of Thomas Lucas for 150 years. Virginia is a sixth-generation direct lineal descendant of Thomas Lucas.

In the May 2000 Virginia SCC evidentiary hearings on the power line project, issues that had standing before the commission were addressed; assertions of damage to tangible cultural resources (farms owned and worked by the same families for generations) were admitted into the record of the case unchallenged. On the other hand, AEP challenged the methods used in ethnographic interviews on cultural attachment to place. On May 31, 2001, the Virginia SCC issued a final order in the AEP power line case, dismissing AEP's proposed project that would affect Clover Hollow and Plow Screw. This precedent-setting order also specifically validated findings of ethnographic research used in the case and established cultural attachment to land as an issue with standing before the commission. This ruling probably will set a precedent in determining the role that attachment to land can play in future eminent domain cases elsewhere in Appalachia.

Clover Hollow and Plow Screw's experiences demonstrate the value of citizen participation in environmental assessments. Active participation by communities at risk, especially proactive strategies, will be necessary in the future to ensure that consideration of cultural intangibles such as attachment to land can produce tangible protection for communities.

NANCY KATE GIVENS

Let me tell you the story of ten families and their attachment to the land of their grandfathers to great-great-great-grandfathers, two hundred years in the history of Clover Hollow land and people. My search for confirmation of a water right turned into a two-year search to establish connections between people and land for the Clover Hollow–Plow Screw community, an inaccessible mountain area northeast of Rt. 460 in Giles County, Virginia.

Almost 60 percent (72 out of 124) of the households of this community are descendants of the earliest settlers to purchase land here, the Farriers and Givenses, who bought land here in the 1880s, or the Shraders, who purchased more than 200 acres in the 1940s. Of 6,628 acres of land in the area, 4,692 acres (71 percent) is still owned by these same families.

My role in our community's fight to keep the 765,000-volt power line away was to take an interest that I have had since childhood and find concrete numbers to show that this community and its land are one and the same. My interest in local history was sparked by an overturned tombstone lying just outside one of our cultivated fields. All my father could tell me was that it belonged to the people who owned this land before we did. That did not tell me who they were, how they acquired the land, what happened to them, or whether they have any relatives living in the community today.

Just before I retired from teaching I had reason to look at the deeds surrounding my property to check on a water right. I did not find evidence of the oral agreement that I had heard all my life. What I did find was a court-ordered division of the estate of the people named on the tombstone. This made me more curious than ever about the previous owners of my land. I had just begun to trace the lines of ownership and put together some genealogy when the threat of this power line appeared.

As a teenager just ready for college I witnessed the frustration and defeat that my father, my cousin, and a close neighbor experienced in the 1950s when the Appalachian Power Company forced the Matt Funk line over our land and planned to set a tower next to our spring. They had been helpless in finding resources to fight the utilities giant.

Next came the DEIS cultural attachment report, saying that our community had only "medium cultural attachment." What in the world was cultural attachment, and how was it proved or disproved? How did the contract firm determine that this area had only medium cultural attachment when their representative was here for only a few hours and spoke with so few of our citizens? What could we do to prove that the people whose ancestors had been here forever were really one with the land? Enter Dr. Wagner and her Appalachian Studies 411 class and I realized that the research I was doing could help.

Thus my research began in earnest. For the past sixty years I have listened to various community members discuss how certain families were related and how so-and-so came to have such-and-such tract of land. I concentrated my efforts on gathering the facts to prove that most of our lands were still in the hands of the descendants of the original settlers.

I talked with anyone who could give me any information on the genealogy of the citizens of the community and located several family histories already in print. Several of the families are in the process of documenting their family history and were quite helpful in establishing boundaries and sharing genealogy.

Taking what little information I had about my own land, I began searching the land records and deeds in the Giles County Clerk's Office. When I found the survey books of the original grants and inclusive surveys for Giles County, I was able to put together a sketchy picture locating many of the early settlers' land holdings. I have no surveying knowledge, so my map was put together by simply tracing the plats from the survey books and fitting these tracings together—hours and hours of work, but I found it fascinating.

Wills and marriage records of the nineteenth century added much-needed genealogical information and gave insight as to how and why some of the land had changed hands as it did. Census records from 1850 onward list the individual names in each household. From these I was able to trace many of the families back to the early settlers.

Giles did not become a county until 1805, so any records of land grants or transfers that took place before that time were in the Montgomery or Botetourt County Clerk offices. Once I had most of the names of the men who received the grants, I used the Library of Virginia Digital Collections Web site <http://www.lva.lib.va.us/dlp/index.htm> to confirm the surveys I had found in Giles, Montgomery, and Botetourt counties. I found some additional ones that were not in the county records.

In 1998 I found a computer program called Deedmapper to plot the old deeds. It helped tremendously in putting together the bits and pieces I have gathered. There are many problems with the calls on these old deeds, and it takes a tremendous amount of time to get them in the proper place.

As my research on the Land Grants in Clover Hollow has progressed, I have learned that the early settlers found the land by two entrances. The Lafons and others came up the James River, up Craig's Creek, over the mountains, and into the northeastern end of Clover Hollow. We can trace John Lafon's father-in-law's land holdings from the James River to Craig's Creek and finally into Clover Hollow. John Lafon raised a family of twelve children in Clover Hollow. Most of these children married within the community and raised their families here. John acquired almost 1,000 acres on the eastern end of John's Creek Mountain and Clover Bottom before he was killed by a falling tree in 1840.

The Price and Harless families had settled on the New River at what is now Price's Fork. It is reasonable to assume that they traveled New River to Spruce

Run and found the lands on Sinking Creek and the dry branch of Sinking Creek suitable for settlement.

David Price Jr. acquired about 600 acres, and his son added another 200 acres to this tract adjoining John Lafon. Today approximately 500 acres of this tract is owned by a Givens descendant.

On the northern side of Clover Hollow Mountain, Martin Harless and his sons acquired numerous land grants. The Harless offspring married Lafons, Lucases, Prices, and Martins and left their mark on the community. With the exception of Ferdinand, however, they soon ventured further west.

On the western end of John's Creek Mountain, Thomas and Hannah Lucas settled. Family researchers have not established whether he was a son or grandson of Parker or Charles Lucas, both of whom owned land on New River at the time of the Revolution. Hannah was the granddaughter of David Price Sr.

Thomas acquired 780 acres on the southern slope of John's Creek Mountain, and 90 percent of this land is still in the hands of the descendants of Thomas Lucas and John Lafon. Thomas's daughter Peggey married John's son Zachrus, and Thomas's son Isaac married John's daughter Eliza. The descendants of these two unions are the present-day citizens of Plow Screw. Throughout the decades other intermarriages have occurred, so that many of these residents are related in numerous ways. Letting people know exactly how long and how many generations their family lived here has been one of the pleasant outcomes of this research. They knew they had been here forever, but no one had presented that as something to brag about.

Thomas and his direct descendants found various and unique ways of transferring the ownership of this land to the next generation, including wills, sales, deeds of gift not to be recorded until after the death of the grantor, and right of survivorship spanning two or more generations. Most of the residents of the Plow Screw section can trace their ancestors to Thomas Lucas. Because he married Hannah Hale, granddaughter of David Price Sr., they are connected to the Price family as well.

To the west of Thomas Lucas on the southern slopes of John's Creek and Salt Pond Mountains were the grants acquired by Gasper Link. The researchers for the Link family have done a thorough investigation of his land and descendants. Many of the people in the Plow Screw section can trace their ancestors to Gasper. The Links married the Lafons, Prices, Lucases, and Harlesses.

Two other large landholders in Clover Hollow in the early 1800s were John Fisher and David Price Jr. John Fisher made his way here from Pennsylvania. He and his son John Fisher Jr. acquired about 900 acres. There are several descendants of John Fisher and David Price Jr. in the community today.

For approximately the first half century that this area was settled, there were six large landowners, each controlling 600 to 1,500 acres: John Lafon, Ferdinand Harless, John Fisher, David Price Jr., Thomas Lucas, and Gaspar Link. Numerous other people received grants or bought tracts of land here. They either soon sold out or married into one or more of these six families. Several people living here, including Doris Link's children and grandchildren, can trace a line of ancestors to all six of these landowners.

In the 1840s several new names appeared on the land books for Clover Hollow. Jake Sibold, Michael Surface, and Samuel Kinzie, who were connected by marriage at the time, purchased land in Clover Hollow. Michael Surface acquired more than 1,500 acres and raised a large family, but I have found no descendants. Jake Sibold acquired almost 1,000 acres in Clover Hollow and over Clover Hollow Mountain. Only one family relative remains in Clover Hollow today. Samuel Kinzie acquired more than 500 acres. One family related to him remains just outside the area of study. In the late 1850s and early 1860s there must have been some incentive to claim all the mountainous land available. I have found numerous inclusive surveys in which large tracts were taken to "quiet and perfect his deed." These were the surveys I used to complete my first Early Settlers Map.

I have not done much research on the Civil War period in Clover Hollow, but I do know that much of the land changed hands soon after the war ended. Beginning about 1880, two prominent families from the Sinking Creek Valley began buying all available land in the hollow. A. J. Farrier and the descendants of Isaiah Givens owned more than 95 percent of all the land in the Clover Hollow section by 1920. James Stafford Givens and his sons, Floyd H., Cale, and Monroe, purchased large tracts of land. Isaiah Givens's granddaughters married Adam Sarver, A. L. Caldwell, and George Lucas, who bought other large tracts of land. In the 1940s Johnson Shrader and two of his sons purchased one of the Givens farms; with the exception of eleven acres it is still in the hands of their descendants.

Today 71 percent of the land in the Clover Hollow–Plow Screw community is owned by descendants of four early settlers (Gaspar Link, Thomas Lucas, John Lafon, and David Price), the 1880s settlers Isaiah Givens and A. J. Farrier, and the 1940s settler Johnson Shrader. A shift in ownership seems to occur about every fifty years, leaving some who are really a part of the land here in our community. Those who have stayed have a oneness with the land that is difficult to explain. No family here lives exclusively on the income from the land they farm. Several farm full time, but they or their spouses also hold jobs other than farming. They live on the land of their ancestors and hold other jobs to keep the land and its legacy in the family.

We are a small mountain community with many of the same values our ancestors had 50, 100, or 200 years ago, here in the same place. The older ones speak of the hard times with a sense of reverence for the land that has provided for them as they have cared for it.

Notes

1. Only two residents who could be reached declined to sign the letter. They no longer live in Clover Hollow.

2. The discrepant maps are figure 3.15-1, "Areas of Cultural Attachment," in DEIS Volume III Appendix M and Map 3 in DEIS Volume IV.

3. Greater Newport Rural Historic District Committee filed a Motion to Dismiss or Indefinitely Suspend Proceeding in Virginia State Corporation Commission Case PUE970766, May 19, 1998.

4. It is worth noting that during the evidentiary hearings on AEP's power line application in May 2000, AEP and the commission staff accepted without comment or rebuttal this testimony elaborating damage of the proposed line to the communities of Clover Hollow and Plow Screw.

References Cited

Bergmann, Frank. 1996. Letter from Frank Bergmann, USFS EIS project coordinator, to David Brady, August 22, 1996.

Howell, Benita J. 1996. "Response to DEIS for the APCo 765kV Transmission Line: Comments on Methodology for Cultural Attachment Study." Manuscript submitted to Frank Bergmann, USFS, September 30.

———. 1999. "Contesting Bureaucratic Impact Assessment: The Need for Community-Based Research." Paper presented at the Appalachian Studies Conference, Abingdon, Va., March 19.

McGuire, Patrick. 1981. "Power through the People: A Case Study of the Imposition of a 765kV Line in a Rural New York Community." *Small City and Regional Community* 3:219–31.

———. 1982. "The Damage Done: A Longitudinal Study of the Effects of High Voltage Powerline Construction on the Social Structure and Relations of a Rural Community." *Small City and Regional Community* 4:379–90.

U.S. Forest Service. 1996. *Draft Environmental Impact Statement, APCo Wyoming to Cloverdale 765kV Transmission Line.* 5 vols. Roanoke, Va.: George Washington and Jefferson National Forests.

9 The Complementary Roles of Research, Cultural Resource Management, and Public Outreach in the Chattooga Archaeological Project

GERALD F. SCHROEDL

Chattooga is an eighteenth-century Cherokee Lower town located in Oconee County, South Carolina where archaeological studies were conducted from 1989 through 1994 by the University of Tennessee. The site is in the Sumter National Forest and is included in the Chattooga Wild and Scenic River Area. Cherokee settlements were located in the Appalachian Summit area of North Carolina, Georgia, South Carolina, and Tennessee. Geographically these constituted the Lower, Valley, Middle, Out, and Overhill Towns, consisting of about sixty semiautonomous villages, each with a population of 100 to 400 (Gilbert 1943; Gearing 1962; Goodwin 1977). The Cherokee became intimately entangled with Europeans, particularly the French and the British, as they colonized and competed for control of the Southeast during the eighteenth century. The Lower towns were the first to feel the impact of sustained contact as the British penetrated the interior from their base established at Charleston in 1670 (Corkran 1962; Crane 1929; Hatley 1993). Varnard's 1721 census suggests that Chattooga was a small village with no more than about 100 people (Fernow 1890). The town's absence from ethnohistorical accounts and maps suggests its abandonment no later than about 1740 (Schroedl and Riggs 1989). Smallpox epidemics, intermittent conflicts with other Native Americans and European colonizers, and changes in social and economic institutions surely contributed to its demise just as the same conditions subsequently led to the destruction of all the Lower towns and eventually all the Cherokee villages of the Appalachian Summit. Early in the nineteenth century this culminated in the removal of most Cherokee people to Indian Territory in Oklahoma (Brown 1938; Mooney 1890). Significantly, small numbers of Cherokee evaded removal and formed the nucleus of the Eastern Band now living on the Qualla Boundary in western North Carolina (Finger 1984; King 1979).

The Chattooga Project was organized to accomplish archaeological research, public outreach, and cultural resource management goals pertaining to historic Cherokee settlement in the Appalachian Summit. To achieve these goals two cooperative funding arrangements, Challenge Cost Share and Passport in Time, were implemented between the University of Tennessee and the U.S. Forest Service. Both are components of the Forest Service's Windows on the Past nationwide initiative developed in response to public interest in cultural resource interpretation and education (Haas 1995:45; Osborn 1991, 1994a, 1994b). These programs supplement the broader responsibilities of the Forest Service to locate and manage archaeological resources in the nation's national forests. The primary funding mechanism for the Chattooga investigations was a series of annually renewed matching or cost-sharing grants in which Forest Service funds were matched against direct (actual dollars) and indirect (time, equipment, and facilities) resources provided by the university. Separate research contracts were negotiated for Passport in Time (PIT) projects conducted in 1991, 1992, and 1993. Fieldwork carried out under the provisions of both arrangements was conducted concurrently during each six-week field season.

RESEARCH GOALS

Various researchers, beginning with Cyrus Thomas (1890), have focused attention on culture patterning in the Cherokee ethnohistorical and archaeological records. These investigations have centered on three questions: the origins and antiquity of the Cherokee, description of eighteenth-century Cherokee culture, and identification of patterns of Cherokee culture change resulting from European and American contact (Coe 1961; Dickens 1976, 1979, 1986; Schroedl 1986a, 1986b) The Chattooga site was particularly well suited for addressing these questions, and therefore pertinent to the long-term study of eighteenth-century Cherokee culture, because the site was well preserved and well protected from vandalism and development by virtue of its inclusion in the Chattooga Wild and Scenic River Area.

The Chattooga research was of further importance to the study of Cherokee culture because investigations at other Cherokee Lower towns generally have been too limited or cursory to unambiguously define Cherokee artifact assemblage patterning (Harmon 1986). The kinds of European trade goods and their frequencies at Chattooga were expected to reflect initial trade with the English coming from Charleston in the late seventeenth century. Of further importance is that artifact assemblages of the English Contact period (1670–

1745), so well represented at Chattooga, are absent or difficult to identify among abundant remains of Colonial period (1746–75) and later occupations at most other excavated Cherokee sites (Schroedl 1994). Thus Chattooga offered the opportunity to study a period of contact poorly known from other sites. The possibility also existed that architectural and ceramic artifact data might represent Cherokee occupation predating the initiation of English trade. Studies of trade goods in conjunction with analysis of ceramic and lithic artifacts would contribute to an assessment of the kind and degree of material culture change in the late seventeenth and early eighteen centuries. At no other single Cherokee site had researchers had the opportunity to describe the transition from the period of absence of trade goods before 1670 to a period of abundance after this date. Nor had archaeologists unambiguously described the initial impact of such contact.

Patterns of public and domestic structures and settlement and village organization of the Middle and Valley towns in western North Carolina had been described well (Dickens 1976, 1978; Keel 1976). There were fuller descriptions for the Overhill towns in eastern Tennessee (Schroedl 1986b, 1989), but the Lower towns had not yet been described adequately. In fact, only at Toxaway (Combes 1972; Harmon 1986) had Cherokee domestic structure patterns been mapped, and these were clearly middle rather than early eighteenth-century examples. The use of controlled surface collections and geophysical prospecting to define occupational patterning had not been previously attempted at any Cherokee site; the topography, sediments, and accessibility of the Chattooga site were ideal for using these techniques. It was anticipated that test excavations and small block excavations would reveal public and domestic structures comparable to those recorded in the Overhill towns.

Studies of the Chattooga ceramics were especially important in regard to these questions. Analyzing pottery excavated at Tugalo, Chauga, and Estatoe in the 1950s and 1960s, David Hally (1986) defined two ceramic phases for the Cherokee Lower towns. He proposed the Tugalo phase to describe pre-eighteenth-century Lower town Cherokee ceramics, and he used the Estatoe phase to describe eighteenth-century Lower town Cherokee ceramic variability. The ceramics from both phases are very similar and are characterized by the predominance of complicated stamping in a variety of motifs. The most important difference between the two phases is the near absence of check stamping in the earlier Tugalo phase. The sherd sample from Chattooga would help improve the Tugalo and Estatoe phase descriptions and further the identification of Lower town ceramic variability.

Overall, archaeological and ethnohistorical studies of Chattooga were considered important for further describing regional variability in eighteenth-century Cherokee culture, comparable to data available for the Middle, Valley, and especially Overhill towns. It was essential to integrate the Chattooga data appropriately with analyzed materials from other excavated Lower towns. Research at Chattooga was perhaps most significant for defining initial Cherokee response to sustained European contact for which data had not been previously obtained.

CULTURAL RESOURCE MANAGEMENT

Federal laws, particularly the National Historic Preservation Act (NHPA), the Archaeological Resources Protection Act (ARPA), and the Native American Graves Protection and Repatriation Act (NAGPRA), compel federal agencies to identify cultural resources; assess their integrity, significance, and research potential; and manage, preserve, and protect archaeological sites on federal lands for the benefit of the American people. To meet these goals, federal agencies, especially those with land management responsibilities such as the Bureau of Land Management and the U.S. Forest Service, have established large cultural resources programs. Much of the archaeological research essential to agencies meeting their management needs is conducted by archaeologists they employ, but agencies often procure the information they need by establishing cooperative programs or contractual agreements with archaeologists from cultural resource consulting companies or public research institutions.

Because the Chattooga site is situated in the Chattooga Wild and Scenic River Area, the Forest Service has additional responsibilities respecting the preservation and protection of individual species and their habitats, water quality, and integrity of watersheds while maintaining a suitable level of public access to the area. Public access also entails providing appropriate interpretive information, including historical markers, plaques, signs, brochures, booklets, and public lectures. The descendants of the people who once lived at Chattooga are the Cherokee people of North Carolina and Oklahoma. There is an obligation to provide the Cherokee people information about the site that they might use to expand the understanding of their cultural heritage and to include them in the site's management and interpretation.

The Chattooga archaeological investigations were developed and carried out in the context of the Forest Service's cultural resource management responsibilities. Three broad fieldwork strategies were established: The investigations must be as minimally destructive to the site deposits as possible, the fieldwork must cover the entire area where we might reasonably expect to find Cherokee archaeological materials, and areas disturbed by archaeological work must be properly restored in appearance. To address these concerns, recovery procedures at Chattooga included controlled surface collections, geophysical prospecting, soil geochemical techniques, and shallow excavations of plow-disturbed sediments in individual test pits and larger block excavations.

To make controlled surface collections, the entire site was gridded into 50-meter squares that were designated mapping sections (Schroedl 1994). The site occupies about 32 hectares and included 132 mapping sections. Areas arbitrarily defined by the site grid or by patterns of vegetation and topography were examined. Each field season the largest possible contiguous areas that could reasonably be examined in six weeks were plowed, disked, and reseeded with cover crops suitable for wildlife forage. Each section was divided into 10-meter squares, and all modified and unmodified rocks and modern farming and recreational debris were collected according to these units. Point plot proveniences were obtained for all other individual artifacts, primarily pottery sherds, stone tools, and eighteenth-century trade goods such as fragments of brass kettles, gun flints, and kaolin smoking pipes. Collections were completed before the growth of the newly planted cover crop obscured the ground surface. In this fashion about 7.3 hectares, or about 25 percent of the site, was surface collected. Approximately 5,800 artifacts were individually plotted, and more than a metric ton of rocks were recovered.

After the surface collections but before the excavation of any test pits, proton magnetometer and ground-penetrating radar surveys were made over the same selected areas. These are noninvasive geophysical techniques designed to locate buried archaeological objects and features (see Weymouth 1986:311–95 for a description of these techniques). A proton magnetometer does this by measuring anomalies in the earth's magnetic field created by buried features such as pit features, burials, hearths, or any other disturbance. Ground-penetrating radar detects the same disturbances by recording differences in the reflections of electromagnetic radiation (radar) caused by the electrical properties of sediments. At Chattooga, magnetometer and ground-penetrating radar readings generally were made every 2 meters, although 1-meter and 0.5-meter intervals were also used to obtain finer-scale data. Geophysical data were collected from two contiguous areas totaling approximately 1.5 hectares (Cutts 1997; Schroedl 1994). Soil chemistry studies were made in one 50-square-meter area using 5- to 10-gram samples taken with a 1-inch tube-type probe at 1-meter intervals from the base of the plow zone (Myster et al. 1989).

Test pits 1 meter square were excavated at the northwest corner of each 10-meter surface collection unit to determine the accuracy of the surface collection, estimate the kind and density of artifacts at the site, and discover subsurface features such as postholes and pit features representing occupation areas. Test pits were also excavated in areas where surface vegetation prevented making surface collections. A total of 140 test pits were excavated to the base of the plow zone (ca. 30 centimeters deep), and 19 others were dug as deep as 1.4 meters. One-meter pits were combined into contiguous block excavations in three areas to investigate domestic and public architecture (figure 9.1). These excavations uncovered domestic structures in two areas covering 168 square meters and 43 square meters. Over the course of six field seasons, the third and largest excavation at the site (688 square meters) uncovered the townhouse or council house. In a fourth block excavation measuring 2 by 3 meters, artifact samples were obtained from cultural deposits buried as much as 1.2 meters deep. All excavations were backfilled and reseeded at the conclusion of each field season.

The combination of field techniques used at the site defined the spatial occurrence of site occupation and delineated the surface distribution of archaeological components (see Howard 1997). Although materials representing earlier Native American and later Anglo-American site use were identified, more than 90 percent of the artifacts and the patterning they represent are attrib-

Figure 9.1. Passport in Time Volunteers Beginning Excavation of a Cherokee Domestic Structure at Chattooga.

utable to seventeenth- and eighteenth-century Cherokee activities. The fieldwork identified a village plaza and associated townhouse and summer townhouse structures exhibiting multiple building episodes (figure 9.2). Because the final townhouse building had burned and its remains were well preserved, it was possible to record architectural details and patterning in the organization and use of space not previously observed at an eighteenth-century Cherokee site. Information relating to domestic activities included excavations in two structure areas and the identification of as many as seven other house sites from surface collections (Howard 1997). These occurrences were widely but evenly dispersed across the site, showing that almost no area of Chattooga is free of aboriginal occupation. The data demonstrate the spatial and cultural integrity of the site deposits and confirm the significance of the site to the study of Cherokee history and archaeology. Also evident is the potential of the site for the conduct of future research.

Because spatial patterns in the archaeological record are known across almost the entire site, the Forest Service is able to conduct its wildlife management programs with far less damage than had previously occurred at the

Figure 9.2. University of Tennessee Field School Students and Volunteers Beginning to Excavate the Chattooga Townhouse.

site. In fact, the potential for initiating new and improved management programs now exists because archaeological concerns have been taken into account.

PUBLIC OUTREACH AND EDUCATION

Public outreach and education was conducted at several levels of the Chattooga Project, but the foremost of these was the participation of undergraduate and graduate students in fieldwork and laboratory studies. Each field season the core of the work force consisted of undergraduate students, mostly from the University of Tennessee, but students from as near as Clemson University and as far as the University of California also were enrolled in the program. Graduate students from the University of Tennessee supervised the fieldwork. They and undergraduate student volunteers undertook the task of washing, cataloging, and analyzing the recovered artifacts. Some student laboratory workers had participated in the excavations, but just as many others had not been involved in the fieldwork. They took advantage of the opportunity to acquire additional archaeological training by helping with laboratory studies. Several students who were enrolled in field school also worked as volunteers on subsequent excavations at the site, and three of the graduate field assistants received graduate degrees using research materials from Chattooga or other historic Cherokee fieldwork.

Because the Forest Service has procedures that permit members of the general public to work as volunteers on almost the full range of its activities, it was easy to have interested people participate in the Chattooga research, including people not yet twenty-one years old. Except for the Passport in Time program described later in this chapter, however, volunteers were not actively solicited. Nevertheless, as people in the local community and elsewhere heard about the project and expressed their interest and willingness to work, their requests were considered. In consultation with Forest Service archaeologists, three criteria determined their participation: that they understood that hard work was involved and they would be expected to do the same tasks as everyone else, that they participate for a minimum of one week, and that they represented no immediate or future threat to the site. Volunteers included several local avocational archaeologists and several other people who were interested in Cherokee history. An interest in simply being outdoors motivated still others. A second group of volunteers were high school students whose curriculum required their involvement in an extramural activity relating to a career or to environmental issues.

From the project's beginning, Forest Service archaeologists briefed the Eastern Band of Cherokee Indians about the goals and character of the investigations at Chattooga. This included invitations for tribal members and leaders to visit the project, and it also involved discussions about the possibility of including materials from the site in museum exhibits in Cherokee, North Carolina. Direct participation of tribal members in the research took place in 1992 when two Cherokee anthropology students from Western Carolina University worked on the field crew as Forest Service interns. As such they received hourly wages from the Forest Service. Passage of NAGPRA in 1990 and the NHPA Amendments of 1992 had little immediate effect on the Chattooga research because these laws were enacted late in the project's history, and the Chattooga excavations encountered no human burials. Furthermore, even before NAGPRA was passed, the policy of the Forest Service, which the Chattooga project followed, was to leave burials undisturbed.

The Chattooga River Watershed Coalition, an environmental group involving more than twenty business and nonprofit entities and dedicated to the ecological integrity of the Chattooga River drainage, took a special interest in the archaeology of the Chattooga site. They were particularly keen to have information with which to better understand how the historic Cherokee and earlier cultures had used and changed the river valley. They regarded the archaeology of Chattooga as an essential component of the human and ecological history of the river. Local river guides wanted to include Native American cultures in the information they provided to their clients who were interested in the natural and cultural history of the region. Consequently, the guides were eager to learn all they could about the archaeological research at the site. Each field season an evening on-site lecture and open house was held for the guides, and six weekly evening programs were offered as part of the summer recreational activities at Oconee State Park in 1994.

The Forest Service also produced a videotape documentary titled "Cherokee Chattooga Town: A Precious Natural Resource" (20 minutes), which was widely distributed within the Forest Service and made available to public interest groups. Extensive coverage of the Chattooga excavations and laboratory studies is also included in the video "How They Lived" (15 minutes), produced by the University of Tennessee's Frank H. McClung Museum and used primarily in its education programs for middle and high school students. The video is sent to schools in preparation for students making a field trip to the museum.

The primary vehicle for direct public participation in the Chattooga research was the Forest Service's Passport in Time (PIT) program. This public outreach initiative, established in 1988, makes it possible for citizens to take part in a variety of historical and archaeological research projects in the National Forests. Although participants provide valuable assistance with cultural resource projects, the Forest Service regards PIT primarily as a recreational and educational program for the public. The objective of the program is to increase understanding of prehistoric and historic resources and how archaeologists and historians study and care for these resources (Osborn and Peters 1991:4). Among the explicit guidelines for the conduct of PIT projects are the following:

1. There must be a legitimate scientific reason for a project.
2. Each project must feature an educational recreation experience as well as scientific research.
3. Volunteers should be treated as research associates, not as free laborers for F[orest] S[ervice] research interests.
4. A PIT project should not be a site or project for which there is a deadline for producing information; a research interest must drive the investigation of the site.
5. A trained archeologist or historian must be a direct supervisor of all volunteers.
6. A summary should be written, in language for the lay public, of the scientific results of each project. (Osborn and Peters 1991:4–5)

Individual projects are developed through specific forest supervisors and staff archaeologists before being compiled and organized by a central office, the PIT Clearinghouse, which is conducted under contract with Statistical Research Incorporated, a private cultural resource management firm based in Tucson, Arizona. Projects are described and listed for prospective volunteers in the *PIT Traveler,* a newsletter issued twice yearly. The clearinghouse receives and then forwards individual applications to the appropriate forest personnel. Unlike many environmental or ecotourist experiences, the Forest Service charges no fees for joining a PIT project. Through 1998, PIT had provided over 9,000 volunteers archaeological and historical experience on more than 950 projects (Osborn 1998a). The contribution of their work was valued at nearly $4.4 million. The growing popularity of the PIT programs is illustrated, for example, by articles in national magazines such as *Time* (June 2, 1997), *Country Living* (August 1998), and *Family Circle* (August 4, 1998) and by television coverage on ABC's *Good Morning America* (August 7, 1998) (Osborn 1998b).

The initial PIT project at Chattooga in 1991 was coordinated with the program called South Carolina Classroom Archaeology: Summer Institute for Social Studies Teachers (later shortened to Archaeology in the Classroom; Ingram and Judge 1991). This program was begun in 1989 as a cooperative effort funded by the South Carolina Institute of Archaeology and Anthropology and the South Carolina Department of Education, with subsequent funding provided by the South Carolina Humanities Council. The Archaeology in the Classroom program was a three-week intensive program for South Carolina social science teachers to assist and encourage them to present archaeology in the public schools. Two weeks of classroom work were followed by a week of independent study in which teachers produced a teaching module on a specific aspect of South Carolina archaeology.

Seven graduates of this program constituted the first group of PIT volunteers to work at Chattooga (Schroedl et al. 1993). In addition to fulfilling the goals and objectives set forth by the Forest Service for PIT projects, this volunteer experience made it possible for the teachers to amplify their Archaeology in the Classroom training, which previously had included no fieldwork. As a result, they can do an even better job of presenting archaeology to their students. Neither program was "designed to train teachers to conduct excavations with their students" (Ingram and Judge 1991:7). The expectation was that teachers would prepare a classroom module on general archaeology, South Carolina archaeology, or more specifically Cherokee archaeology and history. The week-long PIT session was supervised by two anthropology graduate students, and the participants worked with archaeological field school students, conducting surface collections, excavating test pits, and opening block excavations. Participation included a course syllabus and reading list as well as discussion sessions and more formal presentations on Cherokee archaeology and the specific research objectives of the Chattooga project.

The PIT program in 1992 lasted two weeks. Five of the eleven volunteers were teachers from the first year, and the remaining volunteers were selected through the PIT Clearinghouse. In 1993, nine PIT volunteers, five of whom had been there the previous two years, spent one week at the site. The remaining PIT volunteers were mostly from the Southeast, but several came from as far away as Minnesota to work at Chattooga. Fieldwork activities and supervision followed the pattern established in 1991. The added experience of individuals repeating the program especially contributed to increasing the amount of work devoted to domestic structure areas at Chattooga. Besides their formal participation in the PIT project, several of the volunteers returned to the site to work for as little as a few days to more than two weeks in 1991, 1992, or 1993.

Participant reaction to PIT projects has been overwhelmingly positive (Osborn 1994a, 1994b), and this was the case at Chattooga. More specifically, the teachers who worked there cited personal and professional benefits from their experience, incorporating it into their curriculum units on archaeology, for example, by using overhead transparencies and color slides of the project. Some teachers developed simulated excavations for their classrooms, and one teacher generated a multimedia presentation using text, photographs, newspaper articles, and drawings of the excavations. Probably the most lasting benefit was the knowledge and enthusiasm for archaeology that teachers have passed on to their students. Two teachers (Dabbs and Sheorn 1991), for example, wrote to the Forest Service, "As teachers of gifted and talented middle school students, we have been able to share our love of archaeology with our students by introducing a unit at the seventh grade level. The field experience we have had at Chattooga will add dimension to our study as we take our students through European encounter and the colonial experience. Our primary goal has been to develop in our students a deeper understanding for the role of archaeology in discovering who we are and what has shaped our lives as well as an ethical attitude toward the history that is revealed through archaeology."

Elsewhere, Ingram and Judge (1991:7) reflect on the importance of their Chattooga experience in the context of public school education: "The teachers have a captive audience of students who can be educated about what it means to be responsible citizens and about the importance of preserving and studying our heritage." The PIT volunteers at Chattooga met the guidelines and fulfilled the goals set forth by the Forest Service, and the South Carolina public school teacher participants have used their experience to exceed these expectations.

PUBLIC BENEFITS

Although the research importance of the Chattooga site is clearly demonstrable and should not be underestimated, the importance of the site to the general public and especially to the Cherokee people should not be overlooked. First, most eighteenth-century Cherokee villages located on public lands have been seriously damaged or destroyed by modern agricultural, industrial, or urban development. The major Overhill Cherokee villages on the Little Tennessee River in east Tennessee, for example, are now inundated by the Chilhowee and Tellico Dam Reservoirs. The towns on the Lower Hiwassee River have been destroyed or are seriously threatened. In western North Carolina, the few remaining Cherokee Middle and Valley towns are on private land and are affected by continuing agricultural use and the threat of looting. Most of the Cherokee Lower towns were destroyed by reservoir construction or, like Tomassee, are unprotected from damage. The Chattooga site is one of the few remaining eighteenth-century villages that is held in public trust by a federal agency. Because of its location in the Chattooga Wild and Scenic River corridor, though readily accessible, it is well protected and well preserved.

The general public and the Cherokee people have access to very few village sites of the eighteenth century, and there is almost no on-site interpretation of eighteenth-century Cherokee towns. The Sequoyah Museum, near Vonore, Tennessee, interprets the Overhill towns excavated on the lower Little Tennessee River. The Red Clay site, near Cleveland, Tennessee, and the Vann House and New Echota, both near Chatsworth, Georgia, provide interpretations of nineteenth-century Cherokee culture. There are no similar historic sites in western North Carolina, even on the Qualla Boundary, that are accessible by the public. Although the Cherokee have recently acquired the large and important Kituwah site near Bryson City, North Carolina, the nature and character of future public access to this town are undetermined at present (Riggs et al. 1998). It may not be possible or practical to provide facilities at Chattooga like those found at Red Clay or New Echota, but maintaining access to the site and providing interpretive signs or displays would make possible public visitation to at least one eighteenth-century Cherokee village (Schroedl 1993). The North Carolina Arts Commission and Eastern Band of Cherokee Indians Tribal Council are developing a heritage trail that would include important sites and places in Cherokee culture open for public visitation (Townsend and Wilkerson 1998). Currently, only sites in western North Carolina and eastern Tennessee are being considered. Whether included as one of these sites or not, further on-site public interpretation of Chattooga would provide both Indian and non-Indian people a rare tangible linkage to early colonial history.

CONCLUSION

The primary objective of the Chattooga Archaeological Project has been to conduct historical and anthropological research on Cherokee culture of the eighteenth century. The project was accomplished in the context of programs and policies implemented by the Forest Service, which recognizes and supports the proposition that resource interpretation and management are derived from sound research. Sound research occurs in the context of a conservation ethic that regards archaeological resources as components of the natural and cultural environment. Public approval and support for such a position are founded in public involvement, passively through recreational activities such as camping, hiking, and visits to cultural sites or more actively as on-site volunteers working with foresters, recreational specialists, or archaeologists.

Archaeological studies at Chattooga were successful because of the complementary roles played by research, cultural resource management, and public outreach. The archaeological research addressed questions about the nature of Cherokee settlements and Cherokee cultural change. These data have added important new comparative information to the understanding of the Cherokee Lower towns and to the broader interests in Cherokee culture of the Appalachian Summit. The investigations, at the same time, were designed to provide the Forest Service with information on the distribution and integrity of the Chattooga archaeological deposits so that they could ensure proper site preservation and protection. Not only was this accomplished, but the Chattooga work and the relationship that was established with professional archaeologists from an academic setting has assisted Forest Service archaeologists in accomplishing their obligations at other sites. This has helped raise the consciousness of other environmental personnel within the Forest Service to cultural resource issues. Because concerned and interested citizens, through the PIT program, participated in the research, more was accomplished at the site than could have been done with traditional undergraduate field school students alone. The PIT volunteers had the opportunity to be active members of a research team and in so doing were confronted with the same questions, problems, and concerns as the professional archaeological community. Because the focus of the Chattooga PIT program was South Carolina public school teachers, heritage education in the state has been greatly enhanced. The Chattooga project could have succeeded on the merits of research alone, but ultimately its success was realized in responding to the mutual needs of research, management, and public outreach.

Note

I thank first Benita J. Howell for asking me to contribute this chapter. I am grateful to Forest Service archaeologists Robert Morgan and James F. Bates for their efforts in securing and administering project funding and in arranging for logistical support by the Forest Service. I also thank Dr. Kent Schneider, southeastern regional archaeologist with the Forest Service, for his assistance on behalf of the project. At the University of Tennessee campus, administrators Clif Woods and Sheadrick Tillman secured project matching funds. I thank Jill Osborn, national coordinator of the Passport in Time program, for her encouragement and assistance with this essay. Christopher Judge graciously provided information about the South Carolina Classroom Archaeology Summer Institute for Social Studies Teachers, as did the South Carolina Institute of Archaeology and Anthropology. I appreciate the efforts of the many undergraduate and graduate students and volunteers who conducted the fieldwork at Chattooga. The South Carolina public school teachers who participated in the Passport in Time programs deserve special recognition, particularly Gail Ingram, Helen Sheorn, and Carlene Miller.

References Cited

Brown, John P. 1938. *Old Frontiers: The Story of the Cherokee Indians from Earliest Times to the Removal to the West, 1838*. Kingsport, Tenn.: Southern Publishers.

Coe, Joffre. 1961. "Cherokee Archaeology." In *Symposium on Cherokee and Iroquois Culture*. Ed. W. Fenton and J. Gulick. 53–60. Washington, D.C.: Bureau of American Ethnology Bulletin 180.

Combes, John. 1972. "Comments on House Structures from Lower Cherokee Towns." *Southeastern Archaeological Conference Bulletin* 15:62–63.

Corkran, David. 1962. *The Cherokee Frontier: Conflict and Survival, 1740–1762*. Norman: University of Oklahoma Press.

Crane, Verner. 1929. *The Southern Frontier, 1670–1732*. Durham, N.C.: Duke University Press.

Cutts, Russell. 1997. "Archaegeophysical Detection and Mapping of 18th Century Cherokee Village Patterning at the Chattooga Town Historic Site (38OC18), South Carolina." Master's thesis, Department of Anthropology, University of Georgia at Athens.

Dabbs, Kate, and Helen Sheorn. 1991. Letter to Dr. Kent Schneider, June 27.

Dickens, Roy S. 1976. *Cherokee Prehistory: The Pisgah Phase in the Appalachian Summit Region*. Knoxville: University of Tennessee Press.

———. 1978. "Mississippian Settlement Patterns in the Appalachian Summit Area: The Pisgah and Qualla Phases." In *Mississippian Settlement Patterns*. Ed. B. D. Smith. 115–39. New York: Academic Press.

———. 1979. "The Origins and Development of Cherokee Culture." In *The Cherokee Nation: A Troubled History*. Ed. D. King. 3–32. Knoxville: University of Tennessee Press.

———. 1986. "An Evolutionary-Ecological Interpretation of Cherokee Development." In *The Conference on Cherokee Prehistory*. Comp. D. G. Moore. 81–94. Swannanoa, N.C.: Warren Wilson College.

Fernow, Berthold. 1890. *Ohio Valley in Colonial Days*. Albany, N.Y.: Joel Munsell's Sons.

Finger, John R. 1984. *The Eastern Band of Cherokees, 1819–1900*. Knoxville: University of Tennessee Press.

Gearing, Fredrick. 1962. *Priests and Warriors: Social Structures for Cherokee Politics in the 18th Century*. American Anthropological Association Memoir 93. Washington, D.C.

Gilbert, William H. 1943. *The Eastern Cherokee*. Bureau of American Ethnology Bulletin 133. Washington, D.C.: Smithsonian Institution.

Goodwin, Gary C. 1977. *Cherokees in Transition: A Study of Changing Culture and Environment prior to 1775*. Research Paper 181, Department of Geography, University of Chicago.

Haas, Daniel. 1995. "Education and Public Outreach in Federal Programs." *CRM* 18(3): 43–48.

Hally, David J. 1986. "The Cherokee Archaeology of Georgia." In *The Conference on Cherokee Prehistory*. Comp. D. G. Moore. 95–121. Swannanoa, N.C.: Warren Wilson College.

Harmon, Michael. 1986. *Eighteenth-Century Lower Cherokee Adaptation and Use of European Material Culture*. Volumes in Historical Archaeology 2. Columbia: University of South Carolina Institute of Archaeology and Anthropology.

Hatley, Tom. 1993. *The Dividing Paths: Cherokees and South Carolinians through the Era of Revolution*. New York: Oxford University Press.

Howard, A. Eric. 1997. "An Intrasite Spatial Analysis of Surface Collections at Chattooga: A Lower Town Cherokee Village." Master's thesis, Department of Anthropology, University of Tennessee.

Ingram, Gail, and Christopher Judge. 1991. "Passports in Time at the Chattooga Town

Archaeological Project." *Features and Profiles* (Newsletter of the Archeological Society of South Carolina), September/October: 6–7.

Keel, Bennie C. 1976. *Cherokee Archaeology: A Study of the Appalachian Summit.* Knoxville: University of Tennessee Press.

King, Duane H. 1979. "The Origin of the Eastern Cherokees as a Social and Political Entity." In *The Cherokee Nation: A Troubled History.* Ed. D. King. 164–80. Knoxville: University of Tennessee Press.

Mooney, James. 1900. *Myths of the Cherokee.* Nineteenth Annual Report of the Bureau of American Ethnology. Washington, D.C.: Smithsonian Institution.

Myster, James E., Gerald F. Schroedl, and Michael E. Timpson. 1989. "Soil Chemistry Research at Chattooga (38OC18), Oconee County, South Carolina." Paper presented at the 46th Southeastern Archaeological Conference, Tampa, Fla.

Osborn, Jill A. 1991. "Passport in Time Philosophy and Guidelines." Paper circulated by the USDA Forest Service, Washington, D.C.

———. 1994a. "Engaging the Public." *CRM* 17(6): 15.

———. 1994b. "Passport in Time." *CRM* 17(6): 16.

———. 1998a. "Notes on PIT Statistics Reported by SRI, August 17, 1998." Internal report prepared by the USDA Forest Service, Boise, Idaho.

———. 1998b. "Passport in Time and Heritage Expeditions, August 18, 1998." Internal report prepared by the USDA Forest Service, Boise, Idaho.

Osborn, Jill A., and Gordon Peters. 1991. "Passport in Time." *Federal Archeology Report* 4(3): 1, 4–6, 30.

Riggs, Brett H., M. Scott Shumate, Patti Evans-Shumate, and Brad Bowden. 1998. "An Archaeological Survey of the Ferguson Farm, Swain County, North Carolina." Report submitted to the Office of Cultural Resources, Eastern Band of Cherokee Indians.

Schroedl, Gerald F. 1986a. "Toward an Explanation of Cherokee Origins in East Tennessee." In *Proceedings of the Conference on Cherokee Prehistory.* Comp. D. G. Moore. 122–38. Swannanoa, N.C.: Warren Wilson College.

———. 1986b. "Overhill Cherokee Archaeology from the Perspective of Chota-Tanasee." In *Overhill Cherokee Archaeology at Chota-Tanasee.* Ed. G. F. Schroedl. 531–49. Report of Investigations 38. Department of Anthropology, University of Tennessee at Knoxville.

———. 1989. "Overhill Cherokee Household and Village Patterns in the Eighteenth Century." In *Households and Communities: Proceedings of the 21st Annual Chacmool Conference.* Ed. S. MacEachern, D. Archer, and R. Garvin. 350–60. Calgary, Alberta: Archaeological Association of the University of Calgary.

———. 1993. "Text and Suggested Figures for an Interpretive Sign at the Chattooga Town Archaeological Site." Report submitted to the USDA Forest Service, Columbia, S.C.

———. 1994. "A Summary of Archeological Studies Conducted at the Chattooga Site, Oconee County, South Carolina, 1989–1994." Report submitted to the USDA Forest Service, Francis Marion and Sumter National Forests. Columbia, S.C.

Schroedl, Gerald F., and Brett H. Riggs. 1989. "Cherokee Lower Town Archaeology at the Chattooga Site (38OC18)." Paper presented at the 46th Southeastern Archaeological Conference, Tampa, Fla.

Schroedl, Gerald F., James F. Bates, and Robert Morgan. 1993. "The Chattooga PIT Project: The Archaeology and Ethnohistory of a Lower Cherokee Town." Paper presented at the 58th annual meeting of the Society for American Archaeology, St. Louis, Mo.

Thomas, Cyrus. 1890. *The Cherokee in Pre-Columbian Times.* New York: N. D. C. Hodges.

Townsend, Russell, and Julie Wilkerson. 1998. "Cherokee Sites Inventory for East Tennessee." Report submitted to the Blue Ridge Heritage Trails Task Force, Cherokee, N.C.

Weymouth, J. M. 1986. "Geophysical Methods of Archaeological Site Surveying." In *Advances in Archaeological Method and Theory,* vol. 9. Ed. M. B. Schiffer. 311–95. Orlando, Fla.: Academic Press.

10 Victorian Environmental Planning in Rugby, Tennessee: A Blueprint for the Future

BENITA J. HOWELL AND SUSAN E. NEFF

Tucked away near the southern end of the Big South Fork National River and Recreation Area in Morgan County, Tennessee, the village of Rugby owes its existence to a colonization scheme jointly sponsored by Boston industrialists and English social reformer Thomas Hughes. Rugby attracted English gentry and Americans, summer people and permanent residents, by offering the amenities of cultivated urban life in a healthful, rustic setting. The town plan formulated between 1878 and 1880 reveals an environmental awareness that resonates remarkably with late twentieth-century concerns for sustainable development and spirit of place. In many respects, Rugby's original plan continues to offer a solid framework for meshing tourism with environmentally sensitive development. This chapter has two purposes: to explore the conceptual background of Rugby's plan, especially its integration of built features into the natural environment, and to describe how Historic Rugby, Inc., the nonprofit organization that now manages several original structures in the village as a heritage tourism site, is continuing to implement the original blueprint through natural conservation measures and landscape restoration as well as historic preservation.

ORIGINS OF THE RUGBY COLONY

Opening ceremonies for the Rugby colony took place on October 5, 1880, to great fanfare from the press in England and the northeastern United States. Thomas Hughes, colony founder and president of the Board of Aid to Land Ownership, had traveled from England to deliver the inaugural address. In addition to being the popular author of *Tom Brown's School Days,* Hughes was an illustrious social reformer and Christian Socialist who had championed the trade union movement in its infancy (Mack and Armytage 1952; Worth 1984). Hughes countered Chartist agitation and the threat of revolution in the 1840s by arguing that England should support both intellectual and moral education for the working class, encourage cooperation to restrain the excesses of capitalism, and treat all people according to individual merit. Such reforms would encourage English workers to become patriotic citizens who shunned class conflict. Hughes was active in cooperative societies and had been the most influential political ally to trade unions during the 1850s, but by the time he became principal of the London Working Men's College in 1872 after losing his seat in Parliament, the labor movement had found its own leaders whose radical, secular views Hughes could not support.

Thus Hughes turned to the cause of English emigration. He had long been concerned that the rising generation of public school men were having difficulty entering the genteel professions open to them, and he despaired that social conventions in England would ever permit them to take up commerce or trades without stigma. Emigration seemed to offer the best opportunity for these men to put their talents and energies to use. During his first visit to America in 1870, Hughes may have encountered members of the Boston Board of Aid, who after the financial panic of 1873 began planning a resettlement colony for American industrial workers on the Cumberland Plateau. Their leader, Franklin W. Smith, was convinced that the economic depression and layoffs of industrial workers should be resolved by returning surplus workers from the cities to farming, which he considered to be the foundation of the national economy. In any case, the Boston Board of Aid forged a partnership with Hughes that brought his "noble experiment" in emigration to Morgan County, Tennessee.

TOWN PLANNING WITH AN EYE TOWARD NATURE

Correspondence in the Historic Rugby Archives indicates that before Hughes's involvement, surveyors and architects employed by the Boston Board of Aid had drawn up plans for the town they originally called Plateau (Board of Aid to Land Ownership 1880b). Having already invested considerable effort in locating the site and securing options to buy land, Smith and his associates were having second thoughts about their project as the financial depression of the 1870s abated, so they welcomed Hughes's interest in establishing an American colony and offered their land. Attorney John Boyle came from England, visited and approved the site (Boyle 1878), and negotiated an agreement in which the Bostonians, led by Franklin W. Smith, joined forces with the

English Board of Aid to establish an Anglo-American colony where cultivated people of modest means could establish comfortable homes in a healthful country setting (Board of Aid to Land Ownership 1880a).

As with most such colonies, startup costs mounted, and there was no immediate way to recover the investment. For Rugby, these costs included construction of a seven-mile road from the station at Sedgemoor, where settlers would arrive via the recently completed Cincinnati Southern Railroad. Smith appreciated that the new railroad would bring not only colonists but a steady stream of vacationers to enjoy the mountain vistas and picturesque stream gorges. And just as with today's resort promotions, Smith relied on visitation to sell town lots and farms on the 40,000 acres the board had obtained for resale to colonists. So the site for Rugby, chosen with an eye to health, scenery, and the potential drawing power of the resort hotel to be built there, was a high, cool location along three narrow vestiges of the Cumberland Plateau where the Clear Fork and North White Oak had cut deep ravines.

Surveyor Rufus Cook of West Newton, Massachusetts, laid out winding residential streets, the town center, and Beacon Hill Park, each area suited to its topography and natural setting. Written instructions to land agent and site manager Cyrus Clarke confirm that Smith was concerned about tourism as he tried to resolve delays in land acquisition and speed road construction during the summer of 1880: "The Riseden and Massengale lands will offer many lovely sites close to us and only a pleasant walk from the hotel. Such competition may be very embarrassing—and may influence us to inaction as Mr. Boyle and Mr. Hughes wrote a few weeks ago, until they are secured. They are far more important than any others (i.e., other tracts of land to be purchased) for we open them by our road" (Board of Aid to Land Ownership 1880b).

By the summer of 1880, an advance guard of young men, some of the Tom Browns and Will Wimbles whom Hughes hoped to give a new start in America (Hughes 1881), were at the site. Construction crews were grading the road from the depot and clearing trees to form the main street, Central Avenue. The hotel was under construction, with personal supervision from architect George Franklin Fuller, another resident of West Newton, whose architectural offices were in Pemberton Square, Boston, near the Board of Aid office. Board of Aid correspondence with Cyrus Clarke, Fuller, and Cook (Board of Aid to Land Ownership 1880b) suggests that Smith personally selected the project's technical designers and consulted closely with them throughout most of 1880.

Before sailing for America in the summer of 1880, Hughes was anxious about construction delays and mounting costs. Only when town lots and surrounding farms were sold could the investment be recouped. In late June, Hughes cabled to Smith: "Telegraph Clarke keep expenditure down. Stop paths. Only clear twenty foot street. Hughes" (Board of Aid to Land Ownership 1880b). Yet when Hughes finally arrived in Rugby early in September, he praised all that he saw, especially the paths. In essays dispatched to *The Spectator* in England, he described a ride along the bridle path from the hotel to the Clear Fork and declared, "These gorges of the Clear Fork and White Oak are as fine as any of their size that I know in Scotland" (Hughes 1881:51). Now he decided that grading three miles of trail for less than £100 "even before an acre has been sold" was "a judicious outlay" (Hughes 1881:51). Only the name Plateau displeased him, so the town became Rugby to honor his old public school.

Hughes seems to have had a secondary role at best in the physical design of Rugby; however, Smith's letters and Hughes's more public pronouncements show that both men had absorbed the sensibilities toward nature that philosophers and landscape designers such as John Ruskin, Sir Uvedale Price, William Gilpin, and J. C. Loudon had instilled in England's reading public and later transmitted to American disciples, especially Andrew Jackson Downing (Darley 1975; Simo 1988). They popularized a Picturesque aesthetic that bridged Burke's philosophical divide between sublime, wild nature that was awful to contemplate and the tame, artificial beauty of landscaping for landed estates that Lancelot "Capability" Brown made fashionable in the late eighteenth century (Elliott 1997). Ruskin's concern for fitting buildings harmoniously into their natural surroundings signaled the Victorians' growing eagerness to experience nature, a radical departure from earlier Euro-American attitudes of fearfulness or determination to conquer wilderness. Hughes and his contemporaries, confronted by the urban problems associated with industrialization, embraced rusticity. They believed that life lived closer to nature not only improved physical health but also enhanced human spirituality, morality, and social cooperation.

Rugby's aim was to provide the best of cultivated town life (its fine library, drama group, and cornet band) alongside closeness to nature. In the words of *The Rugby Handbook,* "The walks and drives around Rugby, with the quiet and, to most people, the novel scenes of primeval forest life, touched by distant peeps of mountain ranges, and the near tumbling, or smooth-flowing streams, all give an ever-recreative strength to mind and body" (Board of Aid to Land Ownership 1884).

Hughes's opening day address, later published for wider circulation and for posterity, called attention to the community's natural assets and endorsed provisions for conserving them.

> We have here two beautiful streams which will be a delight for ever to those who dwell here, if they are left free for the use and enjoyment of all. There-

> fore, in laying out the town we have reserved a strip of various widths along the banks, which will remain common property, and along which we hope to see walks and rides carefully laid out, and kept in order by the municipal authorities. We have already, in a rough way, made a beginning by carrying a ride along the banks of the Clear Fork and White Oak Streams. Then there must be reservations for parks, gardens, and recreation grounds. In the present plans, provision has been made for these purposes. There is Beacon Hill, the highest point, from which there is a view of the whole surrounding country such as few towns in the old or new world can boast. This also will be common property, and the English gardens, lawn tennis, and cricket ground. . . . Our wish is to preserve the natural beauties of this place for the people who live and visit here, and make them a constant means of educating the eye and mind. With this example and ideal before their eyes, we may hope that the lots which pass into the hands of private owners will also be handled with an eye to the common good. Private property must be, of course, fenced in, but the fences may surely be made with some regard to others than the owners. It is hoped that the impervious walls and fences, so common in England, may be avoided, and that, in dealing with lawns and trees, we may each of us bear his part in producing a beautiful picture. (Hughes 1881:97–98)

Public access to commons was one of many forms of social cooperation that Hughes envisioned for Rugby, a concept equally familiar to British and Bostonian members of Hughes's audience. Like English villages, Boston had its Common. America borrowed its interest in urban public parks from Victorian England. Frederick Law Olmsted, the father of professional landscape architecture in the United States, drew inspiration for complex systems of winding roads and planted areas from visiting Birkenhead Park near Liverpool (Darley 1975; Zaitevsky 1982). Even earlier, Andrew Jackson Downing had derived principles of harmonious landscape design from J. C. Loudon's publications that presented architectural designs together with examples of landscape design according to the author's Gardenesque aesthetic (Schuyler 1996). Through editing *The Horticulturist* and in book publications, Downing heightened public awareness of landscape aesthetics.

Whereas Downing became an evangelist of British middle-class taste for antebellum Americans, Loudon shared many of Hughes's interests in improving education and conditions of employment as well as housing for the working class. Loudon complained that improvements on Britain's landed estates had ill served workers, whether the designers had used picturesque cottages with fashionably quaint exteriors (but unimproved living space) as landscape features or, following Capability Brown's lead, had demolished whole villages to open unobstructed vistas from the manor house. Based on his extensive professional travels, Loudon concluded that housing quality for workers had actually deteriorated during the 1820s and 1830s, even as agriculture and the landed estates supposedly were being improved (Boniface 1987).

By publishing building plans and aiming to balance practicality and aesthetics in buildings and landscapes, Loudon hoped to encourage estate owners and industrialists to provide good housing and gardens for laborers and access to public parks for all classes. His pattern books included cottages for laborers and villas for the middle class. As reformers more concerned with social life than abstract political philosophies, Loudon and Hughes did not lack models to contemplate. A plethora of nineteenth-century Utopian colonies established by Robert Owen, the Chartists, workers' cooperative societies, and millenarian sects were experimenting with novel human environments and socialist principles (Armytage 1961; Darley 1975). Although Loudon influenced Downing only indirectly through publications, Downing ultimately recruited a young English architect, Calvert Vaux, to design cottages and villas for his landscape settings.

After Downing's untimely death in 1852, Vaux worked with Frederick Law Olmsted, who brought to fruition in Central Park Downing's initial proposals for a vast, multipurpose public park in New York City (Schuyler 1996:202–3). Zaitzevsky (1982:20) asserts that Olmsted's travels to England in 1850 were a formative force in his turning from farming and horticulture to landscape architecture as a career. He was impressed by Birkenhead Park and the fact that "the poorest British peasant is as free to enjoy it in all its parts as the British queen. More than that, the baker of Birkenhead has the pride of an owner in it" (Olmsted 1852:81). But the countryside itself made an indelible impression: "Such a scene I had never looked upon before, and yet it was in all its parts as familiar to me as my native valley. Land of our poets! Home of our fathers! Dear old mother England! It would be strange if I were not affected at meeting thee at last face to face" (Olmsted 1852:99).

Although no evidence clearly places Olmsted in contact with Smith and the architects of Plateau, Olmsted was in Boston beginning his involvement in design of its parks and preparing a plan for the Arnold Arboretum between 1878 and 1880 (Zaitzevsky 1982), the same years when Rugby's plan with its streamside greenbelts was devised. With public reporting and discussion of the various park projects taking shape in Boston, Smith and his associates certainly would have been aware of landscape design issues. Although Rugby's town plan was conceived in Boston, not in England, as the Loudon-Downing-Vaux-Olmsted connection indicates, by the 1870s Americans had so fully embraced English architectural and landscape conventions that Smith and Hughes would have held similar notions about what good town planning should entail.

Travel essays prepared for publication in *The Spectator* have preserved Hughes's first impressions of Rugby and its surroundings. His very first communication from Rugby began by praising "the freshness and delight of this brisk, mountain air. . . . For mere physical enjoyment, I have certainly never felt its equal, and can imagine nothing finer" (Hughes 1895:181). Along with the young men already in the colony by the summer of 1880, Hughes enjoyed the outdoors. He remarked how everyone used verandahs (an "American" architectural feature that Downing had championed) for visiting and conversation. Expeditions on wagon or horseback "with no object in view beyond enjoying one another's company, and possibly lunch or tea at the junction of the two mountain-streams" (Hughes 1895:188) had become another popular pastime. Rugby's critics, and sometimes the Rugbeians themselves, chided the English public school men for their priorities—building bridle paths and tennis courts while essential structures were still lacking—but Hughes himself, who had been more athlete than scholar at Rugby School, applauded their enthusiasm.[1]

One colonist particularly attracted Hughes's notice, however. Amos Hill was an Englishman who had made his own way to America thirty years before Rugby was founded. He was among the Union soldiers who first saw east Tennessee during the Civil War and later returned to settle in this part of the South that was sympathetic to Northerners. It was Hill ("Our Forester" [Hughes 1881:69–77]) who had laid out the bridle paths, a task for which he was suited by virtue of prior experience in the woods of Michigan and a boyhood spent working in the garden of an English estate. He had already established a farm near Rugby and in the spring of 1880 began an English garden for the colony through which less skilled colonists could learn which vegetable, small fruit, and orchard varieties to plant and how to cultivate them. Hughes was impressed with the garden and with Amos Hill, who showed what an admirable man a laborer's son could become, given the right opportunities.

Whereas Hughes and perhaps Smith viewed the colony as a "noble experiment" or benefaction, surely most investors hoped to reap financial rewards from the timber and minerals that the new railroad was opening to exploitation. Between these prospects and tourism, they were not overly concerned about the limited agricultural potential of Plateau soil. Rugby suffered several misfortunes during its first decade, however: drought, followed by a much-publicized outbreak of typhoid fever; fire that destroyed the colony's most viable economic enterprise, the Tabard Inn; and failure of other business ventures to thrive. News of these events discouraged prospective settlers and summer visitors, and the press prematurely announced Rugby's demise, exacerbating the colony's persistent financial difficulties (Stagg 1973; Egerton 1977). The town that once boasted a population of 300 gradually lost most of its residents and was fading into quiet obscurity by the 1890s, with Hughes and other financial backers suffering substantial losses.

Even so, just months before the old Board of Aid management structure was dismantled, Hughes wrote to a friend in Rugby, "I can't help feeling and believing that good seed was sown when Rugby was founded and that someday the reapers . . . will come along with joy, bearing heavy sheaves with them" (Hughes 1891). Ironically, past failure paved the way for Rugby's renaissance. Because the village languished in the 1890s rather than developing as its backers had hoped, the original town plan could be resurrected to guide Rugby's development in the 1990s.

RUGBY IN THE TWENTIETH CENTURY

Rebuilt after the first fire in 1884, Rugby's second Tabard Inn burned in 1900. Although a few colonists and their descendants remained and a handful of newcomers discovered Rugby and acquired the old houses for summer homes, many buildings burned or were razed over the years. The land company that had acquired Board of Aid assets in 1892 drilled some oil and gas wells and permitted extensive timber cutting on land surrounding the town. Only the occasional published reminiscence and an abortive effort to create a state park in the 1930s recalled Rugby to the outside world. Then Brian Stagg, a high school student in nearby Deer Lodge, became intrigued with Rugby. Passage of the Historic Preservation Act of 1966 legitimated Stagg's aspirations to save Rugby and provided means to do so.

The forerunner of Historic Rugby, Inc., the Rugby Restoration Association, formed in 1966 and achieved National Historic District status for Rugby in 1972, making Rugby eligible for grants-in-aid to rehabilitate original buildings that were still standing. State legislation in 1972 created a Rugby Historic Commission, but its authority and means for acting were not spelled out.

Establishment of the Big South Fork National River and Recreation Area made it imperative that uncertainties about Rugby's future not be left to chance. Without careful planning and regulation of development, Rugby might come to resemble the typical national park gateway more than the unique resource the Rugby Restoration Association hoped to protect. Big South Fork planners initially wanted to include the Rugby Historic District in the recreation area as an architectural history resource similar to Cades Cove in Great Smoky Mountains National Park: a collection of buildings without people. Activists in the

Rugby Restoration Association countered this proposal by arguing that Rugby's significance lay not in the assemblage of Victorian buildings but in the social principles Hughes espoused. Restoration of Historic Rugby ultimately would entail recreating the living community Hughes had envisioned.

In the end, the recreation area boundaries excluded Rugby, but the threat caused the community to formulate a long-term management plan to address the likely impacts of increased tourism. Significantly, the U.S. Army Corps of Engineers, planning agency for Big South Fork, committed itself to do much more than fulfill minimal requirements of the Historic Preservation Act of 1966 when it provided funding and technical support for this planning project. A Nashville consulting firm, Building Conservation Technology, Inc. (BCT), assembled a local steering committee and began the planning process with an eighteen-month series of workshops for local residents and the general public held during 1980 and 1981. A newsletter kept all interested parties informed about findings of historical research and issues being discussed, such as zoning restrictions. The BCT project culminated in 1986 with publication of an award-winning master plan (BCT 1986).

Like the original town plan, Historic Rugby's Master Plan incorporates green space, especially public recreational access to the scenic corridor along Clear Fork and White Oak Creeks. In this respect, Rugby's objectives coincide with the National Park Service mandate for managing the Big South Fork National River and Recreation Area to conserve natural and cultural resources and provide outdoor recreation. Since federal acquisition of land along the stream gorges, recently logged areas have reverted to forest; federal management policy for stream gorge areas will ensure long-term preservation of the original greenbelt on two sides of Rugby.

Rugby is not an incorporated town with zoning authority, so Historic Rugby, Inc. ensures compatible architectural design and land use restrictions through a program of purchasing property inside the historic district and reselling it with restrictive covenants attached. New landowners have begun building in Carpenter Gothic and other Victorian styles on lots in Beacon Hill along streets surveyed in Rugby's original plan but nearly undeveloped until the 1990s. An architectural review board ensures that new construction conforms to design guidelines included in the Master Plan.

Like Loudon in England, Downing, Vaux, and American successors such as Frank J. Scott offered the late nineteenth-century middle class not just architectural plans but also models of "correct" landscape design. To be faithful to its entire design heritage, Rugby must undertake restoration of town landscapes as well as buildings. Accordingly, Neff (1996) completed an additional Master Plan component that provides detailed landscape design guidance for the Rugby Historic District.

Some original landscape elements and plantings still were visible, but the passage of time had obliterated many details; therefore, historical research was a crucial first step toward developing the Landscape Master Plan. Neff combed 1880s newspapers and Rugbeians' letters and memoirs for descriptions of building projects and gardens and references to specific plants. Historical photographs of Rugby hold important clues about landscaping conventions, details of gardening practices, and the plant materials that Rugbeians used during an era of rapid change in available cultivars, technologies, farming methods, and horticultural techniques.

Even before completing the Landscape Master Plan, Neff conducted a workshop for Beacon Hill landowners to encourage and prepare them to incorporate historically appropriate landscaping into new home construction. This presentation included general information about Victorian landscaping and gardening preferences as well as a slide presentation on Rugby's historic landscapes.

The Landscape Master Plan includes detailed site analysis for each historic structure so that small improvements to landscaping and plantings can be implemented gradually. The most ambitious of these projects will be restoration of the grounds, outbuildings, and residence at Uffington House, the home of Thomas Hughes's mother and his niece Emily. Living history interpretation at Uffington House will highlight Emily Hughes's gardening and small stock raising as well as the social and artistic activities her grandmother presided over in the parlor.

Much more than a guide to garden restoration, however, the Landscape Master Plan is a critical tool in the town of Rugby's quest to revive itself as a livable community while increasing tourism to fund historic preservation and restoration efforts. At the community-wide level, Neff's landscape design addresses separation of vehicular and pedestrian traffic, defines commons, and provides buffers between private residential areas and the public areas where tourism is concentrated.

THE FUTURE

Long-term improvements in Rugby are linked to removing the most discordant feature from the present environment, state highway 52. The modern manifestation of Sedgemoor Road–Central Avenue brings not only tourists but also heavy trucks and oil field service equipment roaring through the middle of town. The Tennessee Department of Transportation has begun extensive improvements to highway 52 as part of the Upper Cumberland Development Corridor. Initial funding for a long-sought bypass to reroute the highway south of Rugby was included in the state's 1999–2000 budget. Although the highway project will provide easier access into the area for residents and tourists, Central Avenue itself can become the quiet, shady road it once was, providing vehicular access mostly to Rugby residents. With grant support and private donations, Historic Rugby, Inc. has acquired Allerton Ridge, situated between the bypass corridor and the Historic District. The Landscape Master Plan calls for new access points and parking areas for visitors to Rugby to be built there, outside the central Historic District where visitors now must park. Allerton Ridge also will provide greenbelt buffering between the Historic District and commercial development likely to occur along the new highway corridor.

Because of its history as a planned community and the special circumstances that brought about its 1986 Master Plan, Rugby is better positioned than most communities to hold future generations responsible for continuing to implement the plans this generation has fashioned. Historic Rugby, Inc. has successfully used museum development grants and tourism revenues to spread the costs of historic preservation beyond the small local population. But will Rugby ever become the flourishing community that Thomas Hughes and Franklin Smith aimed to establish? Rugby's greatest future challenge is the same one that the colony's exurbanites faced a century ago: how to build a viable economy and a rich community life while preserving and enjoying the advantages of rusticity.

Notes

Thanks to the staff of Historic Rugby, Inc. for facilitating access to the Rugby Archives and especially to executive director Barbara Stagg for sharing her knowledge of the materials housed there.

1. In the version of these essays published in 1881 to promote the Rugby Colony, Hughes occasionally tempered his enthusiasm. In that version, he has "scarcely ever" felt the equal of Rugby's air (Hughes 1881:36). Omitted entirely from *Rugby, Tennessee* is the essay "The Luxury of Loafing," perhaps because Rugby's detractors commented so often that the young Englishmen were experts in this field and unsuited to the serious work at hand.

References Cited

Armytage, W. H. G. 1961. *Heavens Below: Utopian Experiments in England, 1560–1960.* Toronto: University of Toronto Press.

Board of Aid to Land Ownership. 1880a. *Colonization of the Cumberland Plateau. Bulletin #3.* Boston: Board of Aid to Land Ownership, Rugby Archives.

———. 1880b. Letterbook Containing Correspondence of Franklin W. Smith and Secretary Albert M. Knight. Rugby Archives.

———. 1884. *The Rugby Handbook of the English-American Colony, on the Plateau of the Cumberland Mountains, in East Tennessee.* Reprint, Rugby, Tenn.: Historic Rugby Press, 1996.

Boniface, Priscilla, ed. 1987. *In Search of English Gardens: The Travels of John Claudius Loudon and His Wife Jane.* London: Lennard Publishing.

Boyle, John. 1878. *Letter of John Boyle, Esq., Barrister-at-Law to the Boston Board of Aid to Land Ownership, in Relation to His Visit to the Tennessee Estate.* Boston: Board of Aid to Land Ownership, Rugby Archives.

Building Conservation Technology. 1986. *Master Plan for the Development, Management and Protection of the Rugby Colony Historic Area.* N.p.

Darley, Gillian. 1975. *Villages of Vision.* London: Architectural Press.

Egerton, John. 1977. *Visions of Utopia: Nashoba, Rugby, Ruskin, and the "New Communities" in Tennessee's Past.* Knoxville: University of Tennessee Press.

Elliott, Charles. 1997. "From Canvas to Landscape." *Horticulture* 94(7): 30–35.

Hughes, Thomas. 1881. *Rugby, Tennessee, Being Some Account of the Settlement Founded on the Cumberland Plateau by the Board of Aid to Land Ownership.* London: Macmillan.

———. 1891. Letter to Doctor Kemp, July 18, 1891. Rugby Archives.

———. 1895. *Vacation Rambles.* London: Macmillan.

Mack, Edward, and W. H. G. Armytage. 1952. *Thomas Hughes: The Life of the Author of "Tom Brown's Schooldays."* London: Benn.

Neff, Susan E. 1996. *Landscape Master Plan Prepared for Historic Rugby Inc. Properties, Rugby, Tennessee.* N.p.

Olmsted, Frederick Law. 1852. *Walks and Talks of an American Farmer in England.* New York: Dix, Edwards.

Schuyler, David. 1996. *Apostle of Taste: Andrew Jackson Downing, 1815–1852.* Baltimore: Johns Hopkins University Press.

Simo, Melanie Louise. 1988. *Loudon and the Landscape: From Country Seat to Metropolis, 1783–1843.* New Haven, Conn.: Yale University Press.

Stagg, Brian L. 1973. *The Distant Eden: Tennessee's Rugby Colony.* Knoxville: Paylor Publications.

Worth, George J. 1984. *Thomas Hughes.* Boston: Twayne Publishers.

Zaitzevsky, Cynthia. 1982. *Frederick Law Olmsted and the Boston Park System.* Cambridge, Mass.: Belknap Press.

11 Pittman Center, Tennessee: Planning with Citizens for Sustainable Development

ANNETTE ANDERSON

Pittman Center is one of the smallest incorporated places in the state of Tennessee. For several miles its corporate boundary is the boundary of the Great Smoky Mountains National Park. The Little Pigeon River runs out of the Great Smoky Mountains as pure as any watercourse in the country and tumbles into the town and through it. One writer described the town as "this hollow of an ancient mountain range, Pittman Center's creeks, its meadows, its views of enormous green mountains, are pure, untouched, luminous in their beauty" (Neely 1995). Pittman Center's importance to the region and its environment lies in the fact that it is the least developed gateway to the Great Smoky Mountains National Park and that about seven miles of largely undeveloped frontage along the major highway that connects Interstate 40 with the park run through it.

Its 500 citizens occupy only a small part of their ten-square-mile town. The town was incorporated so that its citizens could have more effective control over its development. Incorporation followed the success of residents in blocking plans by adjacent Gatlinburg to build a water treatment plant on the Little Pigeon River in the area that became the town of Pittman Center. With the assistance of the regional Southern Appalachian Man and the Biosphere organization, the new town soon conducted a residents' opinion survey to determine community attitudes and objectives. As a result of the survey, the town officially adopted a mission statement: "To create and perpetuate a quality living environment and to encourage quality development that supports that end. To encourage development that supports a tourist-oriented economic base that is related to and magnifies our unique relationship to and with the Great Smoky Mountains." Early in its corporate life Pittman Center established a strong planning commission, chaired now by an outspoken architect and politician who is supported by and who in turn supports an equally outspoken and energetic mayor who is the niece of the town's long-time first mayor and local legend.

The town had its origins in the Pittman Center Methodist Mission elementary and high school, clinic, and community center, established in 1920. Citizens retain a high respect for education and an above-average educational level. Pittman Center's citizens are mostly native to the area, most with long family histories in surrounding mountains and the cove in which Pittman Center is located. They share their town now with an increasing number of retirees and other newcomers. The citizens of Pittman Center are clear in their agreement that they want to preserve for their children and successors the qualities of mountain heritage, the character of place, and the kinship and social relationships that they enjoy now.

FUTURESCAPES ENTERS THE SCENE

For a year and a half in 1994 and 1995, environmental planning in Pittman Center was part of the FutureScapes program of the East Tennessee Community Design Center. FutureScapes is a planning program initiated by east Tennessee designers and planners who feel that they have both the time and technology to preserve the distinctively Appalachian character and livability of east Tennessee but that time is running out. As more communities "kill the goose that laid the golden egg" in pursuit of the tourist dollar, opportunities to demonstrate a better way to develop are disappearing rapidly.

The values of the citizens of Pittman Center and the planners and designers who initiated the FutureScapes planning program were compatible; the FutureScapes program was offered to Pittman Center as a partnership between the community and professional designers and planners, not as conventional consulting or technical assistance services. The model for their intended relationship was that described by John Friedmann in *Retracking America* (1973) as a transactive relationship, one that views planning as a series of learning and sharing transactions through which the planners and community leaders recognize that they are equals in knowledge and ignorance, that each brings to the planning process equally valuable perspectives and information, and that they learn equally to produce a plan that is better than either alone might produce. Therefore, the FutureScapes process was intended to address the values of both the citizens of Pittman Center and its planners and designers.

LESSONS ABOUT THE HUMAN DIMENSION OF PLANNING FOR SUSTAINABLE DEVELOPMENT

Six of the many lessons learned from FutureScapes seem especially relevant to planning for sustainable development in other communities.

1. Pittman Center planning demonstrated, as many planners have learned many times, that everything depends on champions: the people in a community who accept personal responsibility for civic improvement and innovation and who are willing to be advocates for change. Pittman Center is fortunate to have three or four persistent and effective community champions. FutureScapes would have been much less successful if they had not accepted leadership for it. FutureScapes proposals will be implemented at the pace that champions for specific elements of the plan emerge and identify themselves by the energy they expend and the risks they take for the concepts put forth in the FutureScapes proposal.

2. Although the citizens of Pittman Center have been and are conscientious stewards of priceless national treasures—a pure and wild river, spectacular vistas of the highest peaks of the Smokies, an unspoiled and beautiful entrance to the Great Smoky Mountains National Park—the town does not have the resources to exercise that stewardship in the ways that it is willing to do. It bears more than its share of the burden of environmental protection for all of us. A remedy is needed in the form of special assistance for sustainable development planning and plan implementation in places like Pittman Center that are of exceptional environmental significance. It is not reasonable for millions of us who want the pleasure of a scenic drive to the Great Smoky Mountains to put the burden of preserving that pleasure on the few hundred people who live along our route.

3. Small towns are qualitatively different from large towns, not just smaller. As one observer describes the characteristic differences, very small towns have no full-time officials, little or no professional staff, no or few technical and professional services, few training opportunities, severely limited tax bases, disproportionately older populations, fragile economic bases, high infrastructure costs per taxpayer, limited budgets, few or no emergency services, and a weak political position at the state and national level (*Pipeline* 1994). Planners and environmentalists must take those differences into account and find ways to compensate for them by providing loaned staff, stipends for full-time vol-

unteers, or other resources. The stewards of our most fragile environments are the citizens of very small towns and counties. Well-intentioned plans are useful only if local governments have the capacity to carry them out.

4. Pittman Center and other small communities are in a very special position at this moment in history. If our society is indeed redirecting itself toward sustainability, most places will need to spend major resources in the next few decades undoing past mistakes. The Pittman Centers of the world have the opportunity to avoid the mistakes other places have made and are making, the opportunity to avoid the costs of remedial action, and the opportunity to become entirely new kinds of sustainable communities. In the long run they will benefit financially as well as environmentally. States might help small communities reap these benefits and encourage innovation in areas of special environmental significance by establishing regional environmental protection districts in which local governments could exercise exceptional tax and land use incentives for environmental protection.

5. Many sustainable development initiatives entail rethinking and redesigning the political and administrative structures for accomplishing them. For instance, in Pittman Center it appeared that a good way to preserve water quality without incurring the problems and expense of conventional public sewerage would be community ownership and maintenance of individual (or communal) wells and septic tanks. Unfortunately, there are no models for how a community might set up and operate a water and wastewater system made up of individual (or small group) wells and septic tanks. That new institution and many others must be developed along with and in support of physical and financial plans for sustainability.

6. The hardest and saddest lesson is that simple human greed creates most of the barriers to environmental preservation. Pittman Center borders on the country's most visited national park; the major state highway running through the town provides an entrance to the park. The potential profits to be made by developing land for highway strip motels, fast-food restaurants, and amusements are enormous. Pittman Center leaders were determined to find a better way, and FutureScapes helped them describe that way. However, two-thirds of the privately owned land in Pittman Center has changed hands in the past ten years, and most of the land is owned by people who do not live in Pittman Center. As these land speculators push the stakes higher, it will be harder and harder for local politicians to hold the line at reasonable development. Across the country there are twenty-three programs of state and local governments and private foundations to finance purchase of development rights (Williams 1997). Initiation of such a program by the State of Tennessee or private foun-

dations in the state would be one of the few tested strategies that could enable places such as Pittman Center to control land development before speculation drives land prices so high that conventional land use regulations are ineffective.

PITTMAN CENTER AND FUTURESCAPES: A SHORT DESCRIPTION OF THE PROCESS

For FutureScapes or almost any other advocacy effort, putting together the funding to demonstrate a better way to go about community design and planning had to be the first step in the demonstration project. It took the support of eight organizations: Tennessee Valley Authority, Lyndhurst Foundation, National Endowment for the Arts, Americorps Volunteers in Service to America (VISTA), East Tennessee Foundation, Tennessee Arts Commission, University of Tennessee School of Planning, Friends of the Community Design Center, and, of course, the Town of Pittman Center.

The second step probably was almost as important as the funding base to whatever success the planning process may enjoy in the long run. The Community Design Center circulated a description of the FutureScapes concept, what it would offer to and expect from the one community selected, and an invitation to each community in the sixteen surrounding counties. Seven communities responded to the invitation, and the FutureScapes committee visited the four finalists. Pittman Center was selected. The fact that Pittman Center was competitively chosen and treated by the press as a winner was a useful incentive for local participation and a stimulus for regional attention.

While Community Design Center staff and technical assistants organized a work program and began data collection, a recently recruited local VISTA volunteer organized a third successful opening move: the Treasures Campaign. All residents were invited to submit as many as five photographs of the things in Pittman Center that should be preserved, even if everything else changed. Schoolchildren were given special invitations and were allowed to submit drawings if they preferred. Disposable cameras were made available to anyone who needed one to participate.

The exhibition of entries was organized by categories and displayed in City Hall during the Christmas holiday events there and for a month thereafter. Its content ranged from snapshots of families and friends, the kindergarten class, and the two town policemen to spectacular vistas of Mount Le Conte and Greenbrier Pinnacle. The clear winner of the popularity contest, however, was water: eighty-seven photographs of it swirling over rocks, roaring in falls, quiet in a fisher's pool, trickling through a child's fingers. The "Treasures" were reassembled by popular demand for other occasions, including the community's traditional fall festival. They provided a comfortable introduction of FutureScapes to the community, and as part of the planning process they contributed to analysis of the community landscape.

The Treasures Campaign was announced in the first issue of the FutureScapes of Pittman Center newsletter. The monthly newsletter announced upcoming FutureScapes events, reported on past events and local news, and ended with a list of the births and deaths, significant birthdays, and anniversaries of the month. The newsletter continues after FutureScapes with the support of the city and the volunteered services of the VISTA staff who worked on it during the FutureScapes program. It was an important and popular part of the planning process.

After about four months of organizational work, the Treasures Campaign, preliminary data collection, and opening an office in City Hall, the year-long planning process began. It was punctuated by twelve (approximately monthly) community workshops. Four of the workshops brought a wide variety of highly qualified technical people to present, answer questions, and discuss water in all its aspects: supply, disposal, drainage, use, flooding. At least one resident said that he was told more about water than he wanted or needed to know. Another said that the community would be better able to deal with problems "with clarity of mind" because of the workshops. The utility of such intensive community education can be evaluated only by the quality of future community discussion and decisions.

The highlights of the year according to the citizens were two day-long design workshops, called design charrettes, in which community residents and designers and planners worked side by side in small design teams to analyze the community landscape and the opportunities it presents, identify and evaluate development alternatives, and present a schematic plan for overall community development with more detailed plans for the major highway corridor through the town.

The design charrettes were preceded by workshops that identified what should be preserved, what should be built, what should not be built, and, finally, the planning goals that community designs should accomplish. Those goals were to preserve water quality, enhance the natural environment and open space, preserve the community's mountain heritage, build a local economy that promotes the other goals and provides good jobs and good investment returns, and build with an excellence worthy of the environment. A subsequent workshop identified some sixty objectives, or measures by which future accomplishments or lack thereof could be evaluated. The planning commission reviewed proposed goals and specific objectives before they became instructions for the community designers and the community design charrettes.

OUTCOMES

The most immediate outcomes of the year-long planning process were public presentations of the plans. The first was a gala presentation to almost all the participating planners, designers, technical support, and funding organizations at the Knoxville Museum of Art with a two-screen display of slides by the chair of the Pittman Center Planning Commission and workshops led by the major technical consultants. Other presentations were made at Pittman Center community events and more still to a wide variety of interested observers of the process: a session at the national conference of the American Planning Association, the Tennessee conference of the American Society of Landscape Architects, Western North Carolina environmental organizations, the East Tennessee Economic Summit, the Southern Appalachian Man and the Biosphere conference, and others.

The final detailing of all the planning and design appeared in three sets of exquisitely drawn perspective renderings of three key development areas in the community. For each key site one perspective drawing showed the site as it is now; another showed the site as it could be developed under current Pittman Center zoning and in a style seen commonly in adjacent tourist areas (the bad example). Finally, a third perspective drawing showed how the same number of residential or commercial structures could be built on the site in a pattern consistent with Pittman Center goals and objectives (the good example).

These drawings communicated more effectively than any other FutureScapes product both the objectives of the community and the strategies by which they could be accomplished. They were used in both the slide presentation and on large boards in all the presentations. This presentation technique and the principles underlying it were inspired by the imaginative work of Robert Yaro and colleagues for the Connecticut River Valley (Yaro et al. 1993). Elizabeth Brabec, one of Yaro's colleagues, was a FutureScapes consultant. Also important was the writing of the major text of the final report by Jack Neely, one of east Tennessee's most highly respected creative writers. He interviewed most of the major players in the FutureScapes process—people in the community, at the Community Design Center, and in technical support and funding organizations—and wove a story around what he heard from everyone. The Neely story "Pittman Center and FutureScapes" (1995) and the

Yaro-style perspectives rendered by Gerald Klaehn and Michael Ward of the Tennessee Valley Authority were given top billing in the final report. The maps, analysis, planning data, process information, and proposals were given secondary positions, available for those who wanted to study them but not barriers to comfortable and casual reading of the story.

Additional technical information and recommendations were presented in three background papers: "Pittman Center Population and Economic Growth," "Pittman Center Water Quality Issues," and "Regulation of Commercial Development" (East Tennessee Community Design Center 1995).

Some things are happening in Pittman Center that also can be seen as outcomes of FutureScapes. The most interesting of these is the town's acquisition of an option to purchase one of the key development sites. The Planning Commission is developing site plans and financing for final acquisition and development by the town alone, by the town in partnership with a private developer, or by sale to a private developer with deed restrictions that reflect the town's design guidelines.

Implementation of FutureScapes proposals continues to be a major topic on the community agenda. The newsletter continues to be published. A monthly community forum is held for an hour and a half before regular Planning Commission meetings for continued discussion of the FutureScapes proposals to establish a Water and Wastewater Commission, water quality and commercial land use regulations, and other planning and zoning changes. The County Commission has appropriated money for a new school site, and town officials are negotiating with the owners to buy the site recommended in the FutureScapes plan. A graduate student in the University of Tennessee School of Planning has worked with the Mayor and Planning Commission on a strategy to create a Community Development Corporation to develop the site on which the town has an option and to undertake other local economic development projects. The town applied for and received a $125,000 state grant for greenway development proposed in the FutureScapes plan.

SUCCESSES

The overwhelming consensus of all the participants in the FutureScapes process is that its outstanding successes were educational. About twenty residents of Pittman Center's population of 500 probably have a good understanding of the basic principles of planning and sustainable development and have participated in a hands-on way in the design and planning process. At least seventy were involved in the project in some way. Every citizen and property owner in the community received at least fifteen newsletters that put planning and sustainable development in the context of Pittman Center. Many saw and discussed the proposals at the community Fall Festival and other community events. The final report was widely distributed, and the alternative development perspectives still hang in City Hall.

In the professional community of planners and designers, the FutureScapes planning process and practices have had even greater impact in terms of numbers. Thirty planners, designers, and environmental specialists participated in the process directly. At least a hundred more participated in workshops or heard presentations. A Knoxville newspaper feature article, articles in a variety of newsletters, and numerous presentations to organizations of planners, architects, landscape architects, local government officials, and environmentalists spread the word to the wider community.

The quality of presentation documents—the final report, the renderings, and the slide presentation—contributed greatly to the educational impact of FutureScapes. Both community participants and professional designers gave the design charrettes especially high marks for educational and design content.

Other communities in the region want to use the process and practices developed in Pittman Center, and the financial sponsors were adequately convinced of its impact and success to fund its continuation in other communities. The East Tennessee Community Design Center is now replicating the process with appropriate modifications in Loudon, Tennessee, with funding from the town and the National Endowment for the Arts. The Tennessee Valley Authority is funding preparation of a manual for use by other communities.

Another success of the project is reflected in the enduring partnerships it forged, most importantly the partnership between Pittman Center and the National Park Service. Superintendent of the Great Smoky Mountains National Park Karen Wade and her staff were active participants in the planning process. Park staff continue to provide technical assistance to Pittman Center in site planning for the town's potential development project at its key intersection. FutureScapes also helped make friends for Pittman Center in the Tennessee Valley Authority, several important state offices, the University of Tennessee, and other potential sources of continuing support. It also created new potential partners and supporters for the Community Design Center.

Finally, the plan for Pittman Center successfully demonstrates that good planning and good design are essential to resolving the major dilemma in planning for sustainable development: how to achieve a healthy and sustainable environment and a healthy and sustainable economy together for the long haul.

AND FAILURES

FutureScapes planning for Pittman Center was far from a perfect process. In discussing its problems and shortcomings I find it necessary to shift to the first person because as project coordinator I was responsible for most of its failures.

I think that I made the project overly complicated for two reasons. First, I was never clear and therefore was not able to make it clear to others whether FutureScapes in Pittman Center was primarily a discussion and education in sustainable development principles and technologies or a sustainable development planning project. Our initial work plan envisioned a highly participatory but straightforward planning process. As we proceeded, it seemed that everyone, planners and designers as well as community leaders, needed to know more about major issues, a lot more, before intelligent decisions could be made. So at many points in the process, planning was held in abeyance so that everyone could hear together the same information or lack of information and differences of opinion from the technical experts in water quality, waste water disposal, forestry practices, and so on.

I still don't know whether these educational excursions were warranted. In the final independent evaluation of the process, several of the planners and designers who saw FutureScapes as a planning process said that it took much too long, largely because of the workshops. Some community participants said it didn't last long enough, that there wasn't enough time to make decisions. One resident said of the community education, "The deeper I get into it, the more I see it's valuable." And another said, "This way, we'll all evolve with the same objectives."

The difficulty that technical advisors in other agencies had in keeping track of what was going on in Pittman Center was a second major problem. I think the benefits of the partnership of many agencies to the community and to each other outweighed the occasional confusion of people whose other work responsibilities prevented their regular attendance at meetings in Pittman Center. Circulation of a weekly log by all participants would keep everyone informed but at a doubtful benefit in relation to cost. The biggest asset to communication and management would have been one full-time staff person in Pittman Center.

A significant failure, probably the one most often mentioned, was our failure to estimate costs for the alternative development patterns proposed in the three sets of perspective renderings. Lack of cost estimates was not a failure of omission but a decision by the landscape architects responsible for the site plans that meaningful cost estimates would entail field surveys, studies of subsurface conditions, and other information too expensive and time-consuming to be warranted at such a preliminary stage of planning. Without such information, cost estimates are not much more than meaningless guesses. In retrospect, probably it would have been advisable to make those guesses, however inexact, to provide numbers to say the obvious: that savings could be obtained by building less roadway, doing less grading, treating wastewater on site, and pursuing other characteristics of sustainable development site treatment.

Some respondents to the final project evaluation questions felt that more people should have been involved. More involvement was not a major objective of the Pittman Center leaders or of the participating planners because attention was focused on continuity and quality of decision making by the twenty or so people who worked on the plan throughout the year. An affirmative "open door" program and an extensive community information program were put in place, but we recognized that the heavy time commitment needed for active participation would limit numbers of participants. Some FutureScapes participants also felt that the two major outside landowners should have been involved actively in the planning process; local community leaders disagreed, and they prevailed.

If intensive planning were to continue, the next phase of work would focus on program development and adoption of strategies for implementation and should involve larger numbers of citizens to set the course and support the commitment of the champions. The Planning Commission is currently involving one major outside landowner in planning for one key site in the community.

Finally, FutureScapes cost too much to be a realistic demonstration of what a small community can do to plan for sustainable development. Furthermore, the cost of implementing the plan and continuing the planning process does not fit the town budget and is not feasible for its 250 or so taxpayers. No alternative sources of planning and administrative support have been identified. In fact, by 1999 many of the funding sponsors of FutureScapes were suffering from severe federal funding cuts, so they are less likely to be able to support such projects in the future. There are fewer places and smaller amounts of funding for which Pittman Center can apply for assistance in carrying out the FutureScapes plan.

• • •

In summary, the FutureScapes experience in Pittman Center demonstrated that environmental planning in which citizens and professional planners and designers learn and work together can find creative solutions to many of the conflicts between demands for economic wealth and environmental health. It showed also that the key variables in sustaining the environment of southern Appalachia are the human dimensions related to institutional and political change, civic leadership and citizen participation, cultural ties to place, and cultural definitions of private property rights.

FutureScapes highlighted one community in southern Appalachia as a model of community commitment and planning for sustainable development. If it showed that effective planning for sustainable development is possible for an intelligent and committed community, it also showed that more is needed. The task of planning and implementing plans for sustainable development is too expensive for almost any of the very small towns and counties responsible for Appalachia's most fragile and valuable natural areas. Planning for sustainable development requires that all of us invent ways to share the costs and create the government and institutional arrangements that will provide the Pittman Centers of Appalachia the resources they need to act as good stewards of environmental treasures that are the heritage of the whole nation.

References Cited

East Tennessee Community Design Center. 1995. *The FutureScape of Pittman Center* and unpublished background papers. Knoxville: The Center.

Friedmann, John. 1973. *Retracking America*. Garden City, N.Y.: Doubleday.

Neely, Jack. 1995. "Pittman Center and FutureScapes." In *The FutureScape of Pittman Center.* 4–35. Knoxville: East Tennessee Community Design Center.

Pipeline Newsletter. 1994. Washington, D.C.: National Small Flows Clearinghouse, Fall issue.

Williams, Florence. 1997. "Do Fence Me In." *Planning* 63(5): 19.

Yaro, Robert D., Randall G. Arendt, Harry L. Dodson, and Elizabeth A. Brabec. 1993. *Dealing with Change in the Connecticut River Valley: A Design Manual for Conservation and Development.* Amherst: University of Massachusetts Lincoln Institute of Land Policy and the Environmental Law Foundation.

CONTRIBUTORS

ANNETTE ANDERSON is a city planner who has pursued her profession as agency director, researcher, consultant, community volunteer, and teacher. For twenty-three years she directed the program of the East Tennessee Community Design Center, one of the oldest and most highly respected advocacy planning and design organizations in the country. Since 1995 she has been a part-time member of the faculty of the Graduate School of Planning at the University of Tennessee. She is a member of the American Institute of Certified Planners and a graduate of MacMurray College and the University of Missouri at Kansas City.

DAVID BRADY is a former U.S. Navy officer who owns and operates a Christmas tree farm in Giles County, Virginia. Since 1991 he has been involved in protesting a 765,000–volt power line proposed by American Electric Power Company. He worked with Citizens to Preserve Craig County and was a founding member of Preserve Clover Hollow and Plow Screw (two communities in Giles County) and of Citizens Organized to Protect the Environment (COPE). He is a member of the Greater Newport Rural Historic Society and also served on the Giles County Comprehensive Plan revision team.

NANCY KATE GIVENS is a retired teacher of mathematics, a member of the Greater Newport Rural Historic Society, and a founding member of Preserve Clover Hollow and Plow Screw and of Citizens Organized to Protect the Environment (COPE). As a historian of the area that is now Giles County, Virginia, she has collected volumes of information about the founding families of Clover Hollow and Plow Screw and their descendants. Her research was used in preparing nomination of the Greater Newport Rural Historic District to the National Register and Virginia Register of Historic Places.

MICHAEL M. GREGORY is a doctoral candidate in the Department of Anthropology at Arizona State University in Tempe. His historical archaeology dissertation on the economic history of Denmark, Virginia, developed from undergraduate experience in Washington and Lee University's High Hollows Archaeological Project. He became interested in past land use practices while conducting palynological studies as a master's student to document temporal vegetation changes at archaeological sites in the American Southwest. He currently is staff archaeologist with the Center for Archaeological Research at Marquette University, Milwaukee, Wisconsin.

BENITA J. HOWELL holds a Ph.D. in sociocultural anthropology from the University of Kentucky. She is professor of anthropology and chair of the American Studies program at the University of Tennessee. She has been interested in Rugby since conducting a folklife survey for Big South Fork National River and Recreation Area (University of Tennessee, 1981) and recently became a part-time resident and member of the Historic Rugby, Inc. Board of Directors. She has published numerous chapters on cultural heritage conservation, tourism, and local involvement in planning and edited *Cultural Heritage Conservation in the American South* (1990).

MARY HUFFORD is director of the Center for Folklore and Ethnography at the University of Pennsylvania. She holds a doctorate in folklore and folklife from the University of Pennsylvania. Her publications include *Chaseworld: Foxhunting and Storytelling in New Jersey's Pine Barrens* (1992) and an edited collection of essays, *Conserving Culture: A New Discourse on Heritage* (1994). An American memory Web site at the Library of Congress, "Tending the Commons: Folklife and Landscape in Southern West Virginia," is based on her work with communities. With the support of a Guggenheim fellowship, she is completing a book on mountaintop removal and the state of the commons in southern West Virginia.

CLAIRE JANTZ, a native of east Tennessee, holds a master's degree in geography and is pursuing her doctorate in the University of Maryland Department of Geography. Her individualized undergraduate program at the University of Tennessee incorporated biological sciences and ecology, history, and anthropology. A research internship at Great Smoky Mountains National Park led to the senior thesis project on which chapter 3 is based.

DORIS LUCAS LINK is a native of Giles County, Virginia, residing on land owned by her family for nearly 200 years. She is a sixth-generation descendant of pioneer settler Thomas Lucas, the original owner. She is a member of the Greater Newport Rural Historic Society and Citizens Organized to Protect the Environment (COPE).

SUSAN E. NEFF holds a master's degree in landscape architecture from the University of Pennsylvania. She was a planner with the U.S. Army Corps of Engineers, Nashville District, during initial development of Big South Fork National River and

Recreation Area and facilitated Corps of Engineers sponsorship of a Master Plan for Rugby, Tennessee. Her interest in Rugby continued after her retirement. In 1995 she contracted with Historic Rugby, Inc. to prepare a detailed Landscape Master Plan for the town's central historic district.

GERALD F. SCHROEDL is professor of anthropology at the University of Tennessee. He holds a Ph.D. in anthropology from Washington State University. His research focuses on Mississippian cultures in the Southeast and the ethnohistory and archaeology of historic Native Americans, especially the Cherokee. He conducted extensive excavations at the Overhill Cherokee towns on the Little Tennessee River and more recently at the Lower Cherokee town of Chattooga. He is principal author of *Overhill Cherokee Archaeology at Chota-Tanasee* (1986), *Cherokee Ethnohistory and Archaeology from 1540–1838* (2000), and *Cherokee Archaeology Since the 1970s* (2001).

MELINDA BOLLAR WAGNER is a professor of anthropology and associate chair of the Appalachian Studies program at Radford University in Radford, Virginia. She holds a Ph.D. in anthropology from the University of Michigan. She has written about religion in the United States and in the Appalachian region in particular and has recently aided community-based cultural conservation and environmental preservation efforts by directing ethnographic studies of cultural attachment to land in five counties in southwestern Virginia. She has received support and recognition for innovative undergraduate teaching, including student-faculty collaborations in field research, analysis, and writing.

RENEE B. WALKER received her bachelor's degree in anthropology from Indiana University of Pennsylvania in 1990. As a graduate student at the University of Tennessee, she specialized in zooarchaeology, earning her M.A. in 1993 and Ph.D. in 1998. Her research at Dust Cave was conducted between 1994 and 1998 while she served as a summer field school instructor. She is currently a visiting assistant professor at Skidmore College, New York and has drawn archaeology students from Skidmore into the ongoing excavations at Dust Cave.

MICHAEL ANN WILLIAMS is a professor of Folk Studies in the Department of Intercultural Studies at Western Kentucky University. She holds a doctorate in folklore and folklife from the University of Pennsylvania. She has worked as a historic site surveyor and public folklorist in North Carolina and has lectured and written extensively on vernacular architecture and folklife of the Great Smoky Mountains and environs. She is the author of *Homeplace: The Social Use and Meaning of the Folk Dwelling in Southwestern North Carolina* (1991), and *Great Smoky Mountains Folklife* (1995). Her husband, David Carpenter, is a descendant of the Bennett family of Little Cataloochee.

INDEX

The University of Illinois Press
is a founding member of the
Association of American University Presses.

Composed in 9/13 ITC Stone Serif
with Optima display
by Celia Shapland
for the University of Illinois Press
Designed by Paula Newcomb
Manufactured by Thomson-Shore, Inc.

University of Illinois Press
1325 South Oak Street
Champaign, IL 61820-6903
www.press.uillinois.edu